D1125473

Reconstruction
1865–1877

SOURCES IN AMERICAN HISTORY

GENERAL EDITOR: George H. Knoles

Professor of History and Director of the Institute of American History, Stanford University

Reconstruction
1865-1877

EDITED BY

Robert W. Johannsen

THE FREE PRESS, NEW YORK

COLLIER-MACMILLAN LIMITED, LONDON

Copyright © 1970 by The Free Press

A DIVISION OF THE MACMILLAN COMPANY

Printed in the United States of America

Collier-Macmillan Canada, Ltd., Toronto, Ontario

Library of Congress Catalog Card Number: 74–91691

printing number

1 2 3 4 5 6 7 8 9 10

Contents

Preface

THE FREE PRESS sources in American history series reviews the history of the United States from its beginnings in the seventeenth century to the present. Each of the nine volumes consists of from 15 to 35 carefully chosen contemporary documents illustrating the major themes—political, economic, social, and cultural—of American history and civilization. The volume editors, selected for their specialized knowledge of the periods into which the series is divided, have drawn upon the rich resources of the American past for the materials to be included in their respective books. They have ranged over the principal geographical areas of the United States and have exploited a wide variety of genres—governmental and political party documents, descriptive and analytical accounts, theoretical writings, and literary products. History is a seamless web and one learns about himself and his past by exploring the multivarious experiences of his forebears and their reflections upon those experiences.

The editors have kept the student in mind while selecting the items to be reprinted in each volume. They have not only chosen significant documents, but they have respected the intentions of the original writers to the extent that the materials are offered substantially as the authors produced them, with a minimum of cutting and editing. We have, therefore, put together a set of volumes containing a limited number of major documents reproduced *in extenso* rather than a series containing hundreds of snippets which can suggest, at best, only an impressionistic view of history. To promote thoughtful reading and discussion of these materials we have introduced each selection with headnotes containing biographical and bibliographical data. Moreover, we have included in each headnote four or five suggestions indicating what students should look for in reading the documents; these do not tell the reader what is in the material, but they are very useful in directing his attention to the salient points covered. Finally, the editors have added to each note two or three titles of books that might be consulted for further study of the author of the document or of the problem or episode dealt with in the selection.

Each volume contains an extended introductory essay, an interpretive narrative written by the volume editor, which treats the period as a whole and relates the documents to the history under consideration. These essays incorporate both factual and conceptual information obtained from recent historical research; they reflect the new findings of contemporary scholarship.

In the preceding volume of this series, *The Union in Crisis, 1850–1877,* Professor Robert W. Johannsen brought together a collection of documents designed to aid the student in understanding the events of the 1850's that led eventually to the outbreak of a costly civil war that many Americans hoped to avoid and few welcomed. The war itself, as Professor Johannsen concluded, "was a tragedy of mammoth proportion." Reconstruction, too, manifested tragic aspects. An object of the war was the preservation of the Union, but policies adopted in the 1860's and 70's by the victorious North strengthened sectional sentiments in many ways. During the conflict, emancipation of the slaves became a war aim of Union leadership, but reconstruction proved inadequate to the tasks of guaranteeing the full enjoyment of freedom for millions of recently liberated blacks. Fighting began in 1861 amid manifestations of patriotic enthusiasm in support of the participants, but the crusading spirit of the war years flagged and all but petered out during the less dramatic years of reconstruction.

In the present volume Professor Johannsen stresses some of the tragic qualities of the reconstruction period, both in his essay and in the documents themselves. He poses and then treats three major questions that confronted the North following Appomattox: (1) What shall be the status in the Union of the former states of the secession? (2) What shall be the status of the former secessionists? (3) What shall be the status of the newly freed slaves?

Contemporaries gave highest priorities and the most attention to solving the first two problems while neglecting the third. Leadership achieved more or less satisfactory and permanent solutions to the first two problems by 1877. In that year the country, tired of, and perhaps disillusioned with, its efforts at reconstructing the Union, returned to the states of the defeated Confederacy control of their own state governments. Answers to the third question proved more intractable, partly because the victors failed to accord the kind of attention to the problem that it demanded and deserved.

This volume deals primarily, then, with issues arising out of these three questions. The editor has skillfully selected the documents to reveal the principal lineaments of the struggle between the sections following the shooting war. The story is not a happy one; but a careful study of reconstruction helps immeasurably to understand not only the immediate aftermath of the Civil War but also some of the forces at work today that frustrate efforts to achieve a more perfect union in which men and women of all races can live harmoniously together in pursuit of life, liberty, and self-fulfillment.

GEORGE HARMON KNOLES

Stanford University

Introduction

THE END of the Civil War in 1865 found the American people, both North and South, ill-prepared to meet the problems raised by the war. Although some thought had been given to the question of reconstruction during the conflict itself, it had focused principally on the more superficial aspects of government relations, that is, the relationship between the former states of the Confederacy and the United States government. Questions involving the *status* of the seceded states in the new Union seemed uppermost. The restoration of the Union was surely the most important result of the war, yet it was only one of the consequences of that conflict. Of striking significance was the granting of freedom to over four million Negro slaves in the Southern states. Emancipation had been adopted as a Northern war aim but only a few Northerners had anticipated the consequences of this policy and even fewer recognized the obligations which it forced on the nation. The abolition of slavery was, to a degree, adopted as an expedient, born of a wartime situation and justified and defended as a wartime measure. Lincoln's Emancipation Proclamation was based on military considerations, and even the passage of the Thirteenth Amendment was argued on military and political grounds. Whether emancipation actually achieved its military ends and hastened the end of the conflict is questionable. What the policy did do, however, was commit the American people to a cause that would demand their attention and energies for many years to come. It was, unfortunately, a commitment little understood by the Civil War generation; the true dimensions of a policy that brought freedom to millions of people were but dimly seen.

Although most Americans (including many abolitionist leaders) regarded emancipation as an end, it was in fact only a beginning. In the troubled years following the war, it provided the largest and most perplexing problem of reconstruction. Little or nothing had been done to implement emancipation, to make it meaningful, and few of those who would hold the reins of power in the postwar years were aware of the fact that the protection, education, and care of the newly freed Negro had become one of the government's primary responsibilities. Reconstruction, to be effective, would have to be social and economic, as well as political, in its emphasis. In actuality, it was basically a political movement. Its character, as the program unfolded in the decade following the end of hostilities, revealed that to most Northerners the important result of the Civil War, after the restoration of the Union, was a political one—the opportunity to seat national political power permanently in the North and in the Republican party.

Many questions had to be answered by the victorious North at the end of the strife but three were primary: (1) What shall be the status of the seceded states in the Union? (2) What shall be the status in the new political arrangement of those Southern whites who supported the Confederacy? (3) What shall be the status of the ex-slave, the Negro freedman, in Southern (and American) society?

The last was thought by some to be the most important of the questions, but in general the reconstruction generation tended to give prior consideration to the first and second. All three questions were closely interrelated, but it was the first—the relationship between the Southern states and the national government—that received the most attention.

Although there seemed to be consensus on the priorities of reconstruction, the actual policies and actions designed to carry them out were beset with argument and disagreement from the very beginning. The decisions that resulted, and the program that emerged, were frequently little more than compromises between opposing Northern points of view or between Northern and Southern views. Because of this, reconstruction often lacked a principal thrust and coherence, sometimes resembling an awkward, jerry-built construction. Although defeated on the battlefield, Southerners never did wholly concede the sole responsibility of reconstruction to the victors; they maintained that they had a right to a voice in reconstruction and throughout the decade and a half following the war they exercised this belief, sometimes fruitlessly, sometimes with startling effect. Reconstruction was not a monolithic program, devised with unanimity, imposed with effectiveness and received with bland acquiescence. It was a struggle from beginning to end. The struggle among Northern legislators and pressure groups (the phase that has received the most attention from historians) was only part of the reconstruction story; as much or more can be learned of these sometimes puzzling times by looking at the struggles outside of the national capital and especially in the South, where reconstruction policies had to be implemented and given practical application.

The fight over reconstruction began while the war was still being fought, at a time when both President Lincoln and significant numbers of Congressmen began turning their thoughts to the shape of the postwar nation. As the first preliminary plans emerged so did the first signs of disagreement and dissension. Two basic positions were advanced: one grounded on the desirability of a rapid, smooth, and easy transition from wartime conditions to the normal functioning of the new, restored Union; the other looking to guarantees that the perpetrators of the rebellion had learned well the lessons of defeat and that the political gains of the North should not be lost. The former assumed the good faith of the vanquished, an assumption not always justified; the latter was based on distrust. Neither position faced the ultimate racial question raised by the conflict. Policy was directed rather toward Southern whites, their role and their status; even the insistence on abolition was more an attempt to weaken Southern political and economic power than it was a humanitarian effort to uplift Southern Negroes. Corollary to these two basic positions was disagreement over the proper seat of responsibility for reconstruction. One group regarded reconstruction as an executive function, the responsibility of the President and of Presidential policy, whereas another group looked to Congress as the proper authority for defining the character of the postwar Union. The conflict between these broad and sometimes rather ill-defined outlooks would continue for many years following the war; indeed it became a central thread of the reconstruction period.

The first official step toward the formulation of a reconstruction program was taken by President Lincoln in December 1863, when he presented his plan to bring the seceded states back to their normal relationship with the Union as easily and as quickly as the exigencies of the war would allow [Document 1]. Within months, Lincoln's move was answered by his radical Congressional critics with the passage of the Wade-Davis bill, asserting Congress' authority over reconstruction and rejecting the leniency of Lincoln's plan in favor of a more stringent attitude toward the Southern states. When Lincoln pocket-vetoed the Wade-Davis bill, the authors of the legislation penned an angry and blunt denunciation of the President's action. The Wade-Davis manifesto, appearing in the summer of 1864, marked the beginning of a bold (and senseless) confrontation between the executive and legislative branches over the question of reconstruction. It was not an auspicious beginning for a program that was designed to restore order and stability to the war-torn South. From this time on there seemed to be diminishing opportunity for accord, and intragovernment hostility became more and more pronounced. Not only would reconstruction policy have to face a stubborn South, not only would it have to surmount clashing voices in the North, but it would also have to overcome a bitter struggle between President and Congress. These were crippling handicaps for any program.

Yet Lincoln, shrewd and clever when dealing with his opposition, succeeded in quieting his critics; and when the war was over, it was basically his plan (as modified by his successor, Andrew Johnson) that was placed in general operation throughout the South [Document 1]. In the first flushed months following the cessation of hostilities, the mass of Northern opinion seemed to endorse the direction that reconstruction was taking. The end of the war brought a widespread feeling of relief that the bloodshed and agony of the fighting had finally terminated. Soldiers were anxious to return to their homes and civilians were eager to return to a normal existence. The South, beaten and desolated, seemed as eager as the North to let bygones by bygones and, to all appearances, acquiesced in the harsh fact of Northern victory. Lincoln, however, to his credit, had never regarded his proposal as anything but a beginning in the gigantic task of reformation. He alluded to forthcoming elaborations on his policy, possibly dealing with the social and economic problems left by the war, but the assassin's bullet halted his efforts. What Lincoln would have done, of course, no one knows. Andrew Johnson never did provide the missing sequel, and the so-called Presidential plan remained incomplete. Lacking Lincoln's humanitarian impulse, reconstruction was, and continued to be, a truncated program. Some prominent Northern spokesmen recognized this deficiency; others warned against the delusion that the attitudes, hatreds, and problems that had been nurtured by four years of bloody struggle could so easily be wiped away [Document 2].

The actions of the Southern states themselves, as they prepared to re-enter the Union under the aegis of the Presidential plan, gave credence to these warnings. Southerners appeared recalcitrant and did not hesitate to demonstrate their reluctance, in some cases, to accept the conditions imposed upon them. The abolition of slavery, a condition of readmission, was not accepted easily and in good faith, and Southern voters seemed anxious to retain as leaders the same men who had led them out of the Union and guided them in their quest for independence. In the North, such developments were interpreted as deliberate defiance hurled in the teeth of the victors. Most serious of all was the passage by the reconstituted Southern state legislatures of harsh and repressive "black codes," designed to discipline the freed Negroes within the framework of white society. Many of the codes were copied, in some of their provisions, from similar state laws in the North but this fact did not appease the rising anger of Northern opinion (an early example of the double standard that was to prevail during reconstruction). The worst of the black codes was probably that of Mississippi, passed at the end of 1865 and publicized in the North just as Congress was assembling in Washington for its first postwar session [Document 3]. The passage of these codes was, in many Northern minds, nothing more than a blatant effort to re-establish slavery in the South under a different name.

Congress acted swiftly to assert its authority over reconstruction and to answer these Southern gestures of defiance. The timing was right. A Northern mood of impatience with the South was emerging, the end of the war had stripped the Presidential office of the necessity for extraordinary powers, and the incumbent in the White House was a man for whom many members of Congress felt little more than utter contempt. In a sweeping action, the Presidential plan was destroyed when Congress refused to seat the Senators and Representatives elected by the reorganized states. An investigating committee was formed, the Joint Committee on Reconstruction, to determine by various means the prevailing conditions in the South and to recommend appropriate policies for dealing with these conditions. The report of the committee, issued in the spring of 1866, was an important step toward the consolidation of Congressional power over reconstruction [Document 4].

In the meantime, steps were taken to develop a more formal Congressional plan for the reconstruction of the Southern states. It would be a mistake to assume that such steps were dominated by radicals at this time. Their numbers were in fact small in the Congress of 1865–66. The label, usually employed to designate those who urged Negro political and social equality as well as those who demanded a vindictive peace, has been loosely and variously used and recent studies have demonstrated how imprecise it is. The largest group in the legislative branch was of a more moderate persuasion, no less jealous of the powers of Congress over reconstruction but more willing to follow policies that would return the nation rapidly and easily to order and stability. What is significant is that these moderate-thinking men gradually moved toward a more radical position, like much of Northern opinion pushed by the evidences of Southern intransigence and defiance. The passage of the Southern black codes, the resistance of some states to the conditions established in the Presidential plan (as liberal as they were), and the testimony revealed by the Joint Committee on Reconstruction all seemed to point to the development of a new, and as many believed, a more realistic program. A first step, taken early in 1866, was the passage of a civil rights act, a direct response to the black codes. Citizenship was defined in a national sense and equal rights for all citizens were established and guaranteed [Document 5]. The act was vetoed by President Johnson and was just as promptly passed over his veto. With this action, it became crystal clear that the pathways of the President and of Congress were divergent.

Johnson's veto of the Civil Rights Act heightened doubts regarding the constitutionality of the measure and added to an already growing feeling among many Northerners that a constitutional amendment would be necessary to protect the gains of the war from the attacks of both the South and the executive. A constitutional amendment would render Congress' reconstruction program invulnerable. Additionally, Congress faced a dilemma with regard to the representation of Southern states in the lower house. The abolition of slavery had nullified the old three-fifths rule on which Southern representation had been based; all Negroes would now be counted in the population, thus increasing the power of the South in Congress, an uncomfortable prospect to Northern Republicans. Drafting a new amendment was not easy; the final result reflected a compromise between the various groups in Congress, and even some Republicans had misgivings about it. The Fourteenth Amendment was passed by both houses of Congress in June, 1866, and sent out to the states for ratification [Document 5].

The amendment covered much the same ground as the earlier civil rights legislation (indeed, it was designed to make that act constitutional beyond any doubt). In addition, it dealt with the questions of Congressional representation, the requirements for officeholding by Southern whites who had been Confederate leaders, and the Confederate debt. Although the amendment has been subjected to many and diverse interpretations in the years since its adoption, there is little doubt that it sprang from a sincere desire to extend national protection to the Southern Negroes and to define the role of Southern whites in the new nation. It was, in essence, a Congressional plan for reconstruction. When the Amendment was presented to the states, it was with the implication that its ratification by the Southern states would lead to speedy readmission into the Union. In fact, only one Southern state ratified it—Tennessee; all others rejected it.

Where stood Southern reconstruction in the spring of 1866, one year after the end of the war? Actually, very little had been accomplished during that time to meet the many social and economic problems left by the war. The government's main concern had been focused on the more superficial questions relating to the character and composition of the Southern state governments. Some attention had been given to the deeper problems, for example, in the renewal of the Freedmen's Bureau and in the civil rights legislation, but even here political motives were often uppermost. The principal thrust of reconstruction had been weakened by a power struggle in which party politics and rivalry between the executive and legislative branches played a large role. During the year, the battle lines between the President and Congress were indelibly drawn and the pattern of executive-legislative confrontation that had originated with Lincoln continued. There were no signs that the struggle would diminish. Both sides stubbornly refused to budge. Each was guilty of self-centered shortsightedness, placing elements of personal pride, partisanship, spite, and revenge over the main tasks of the time, and reconstruction was the ultimate victim. It was not, however, an equal contest. Johnson's ineptitude, his vulnerability to attack, and his isolated position within the government gave the advantage to Congress.

In one sense, the first year of reconstruction was a period of transition. Congress had expressed its displeasure with the Presidential plan and made a faltering start toward the formulation of its own program. An investigating committee had been formed and was active in amassing evidence to prove that a new direction for reconstruction was both necessary and required. One more hopeful sign had been the extension of the Bureau of Freedmen, Refugees, and Abandoned Lands (commonly known as the Freedmen's Bureau), originally established by Congress in March 1865. This was one clear gesture by the government toward relief and rehabilitation for the Southern Negro. Through its many agents scattered about the South, the Bureau distributed food and medical supplies, established schools and churches, regulated labor contracts, and in some instances administered justice in cases involving freedmen [Document 10]. The results of the Bureau's efforts were mixed, but the intent behind its initial organization was meritorious. As reconstruction policy became more deeply involved in matters of partisan politics, the Bureau became more political in its orientation and less concerned with its original humanitarian purpose.

Political alignments in Congress on the question of reconstruction had not yet become crystallized by the end of the first year. Moderates, standing between the Johnsonian conservatives and the determined, but still small, group of radicals, held the balance of power and were able to exert their influence on legislation. Although the nation was drifting toward a more extreme position on reconstruction, pushed by Southern defiance and Presidential intransigence, Congress did not yet reflect this drift. That would be accomplished by the elections of 1866.

The elections of 1866 provided an opportunity for each side in the reconstruction struggle to test its strength before the people. The President, desperate for a popular endorsement, embarked on an extensive campaign tour designed to support Congressional candidates who were sympathetic to his view of reconstruction. The radicals were equally active, and the elections became charged with emotion. Johnson's effort, in the end, proved disastrous to his cause; ineffective on the stump, he was easily baited by hecklers and drawn into exchanges that he (and his followers) came later to regret. The radicals, on the other hand, emphasized the past sins of the Democratic party in a style of "bloody shirt" oratory that soon became typical of postwar election contests [Document 6]. The results were a repudiation of Johnson and his claim that reconstruction had been completed under the Presidential plan only to be destroyed by a vengeful Congress. The radicals received the mandate they had sought to continue with their own plans for the South. Encouraged by the vote of confidence, Northern spokesmen now urged Congress to embark on new and far-reaching schemes that would restore the Union and secure for the Southern Negro his rightful place in society [Document 7].

The radicals have too often been considered a coherent political group, united by ties of party and by common aims and policies. Actually, no such unity existed. They reflected a variety of motives, sometimes disagreeing strongly among themselves on the proper direction reconstruction ought to take. Many of them were sincere humanitarians, moved by compassion for the Negro and pledged to the uplifting of the race; during the war they were active abolitionists and once emancipation had been achieved they urged complete civil and political equality for the Negro. For some, Negro suffrage was a next and necessary step. These lofty humanitarian impulses were diluted, however, by other less noble motives and desires—the determination to consolidate national power in the legislative branch, the desire to strengthen the Republican party in order to assure its lasting ascendancy, the attempt to preserve the economic power of Northern industrialism against the threat of Southern opposition, and the conviction that Southerners should be punished for the four-year holocaust they had inflicted on the nation. Some radical leaders reflected a bewildering combination of these various motives; for others, the humanitarian aims were clearly secondary to the more partisan and vindictive goals. One of the tragedies of reconstruction was the inability of the radicals to marshal their new strength behind a program that could overcome the desire for immediate political advantage in favor of lasting reform.

Too much emphasis, however, can be placed on the failure of the radicals in Congress to come to grips with the realities of reconstruction. Their attitudes and ideas were but reflective of American (that is, Northern) opinion generally. Few recognized the real needs of reconstruction, and fewer still were willing to follow bold new policies in order to solve these needs. For most Americans, the commitment to the emancipation of Southern Negroes had been shallow and did not carry over into the logical sequel of such a policy. For not only did the Negro need emancipation from slavery but he also required emancipation from the social, economic, and political bondage under which he suffered in the North as well as the postwar South. Racial prejudice ran deep in the North. Whereas some individuals saw the need and the opportunity to extend protection to the Negro throughout the nation, instead of just in the South, the mass of Americans were unwilling to operate on this broader scale. Emancipation had not always been founded on genuine sympathy for the enslaved Negro, and anti-Negro feeling remained undiminished. Indeed, in some ways it was stronger after emancipation than it had been before. For this reason, attempts to secure equality for the Negroes remained confined to the states of the old Confederacy; to an unfortunate degree, these attempts were justified principally as deserved punishment for Southern whites.

When the members of Congress returned to their duties in December 1866, it was with a clear sense of mandate for the formulation of a new program for Southern reconstruction. The precise form this program would take, however, was not so clear. After considerable debate, fruitless maneuvering, and threatened stalemate, a sweeping measure was finally passed early in March 1867, the first of several Reconstruction Acts [Document 8]. The law gave the final deathblow to the existing state governments in the South (set up under the Presidential plan) and replaced them with military rule, virtually reducing them to the status of "conquered provinces" called for by Thaddeus Stevens shortly after the end of the war. The commanders of the five military districts into which the South (except for Tennessee) was divided were charged with overseeing the steps by which the states could regain their places in the Union. Ratification of the Fourteenth Amendment was required and Negro suffrage was established. Additional Reconstruction Acts followed, designed to implement the provisions of the first and to clarify some of its ambiguities [Document 8].

With the passage of the Reconstruction Acts, Southern reconstruction entered a new stage. Although the military rule was not as evident or as repressive as many supposed, the very fact of its existence proved galling to Southern whites. Instead of winning their cooperation to a mutually advantageous program, the radical policy drove them to heightened bitterness and resistance. Southern leaders lashed out at the program with ill-disguised shock and anger [Document 9], especially because they found themselves effectively excluded from participation in the new governments. Before they could vote, they were required to take an oath that automatically ruled out any who had previously been disfranchised for participation in civil war, who had rendered "aid, countenance, counsel or encouragement" to persons engaged in armed hostility against the government or who had "yielded a voluntary support to any pretended government" hostile to the United States. There were few Southerners who could, in good conscience, subscribe to such an oath. The result was the domination of the new radical-inspired state governments by Northern carpetbaggers who had gone South either to serve the Union or themselves, by Southern "scalawags" who had resisted the authority of the Confederacy during the war, and by the newly enfranchised Negroes.

The Southern protests fell on deaf ears. Finding the normal

legal channels for redress blocked, many Southerners turned to extralegal, and illegal, means. Acts of terror and intimidation, particularly against the Negroes, increased. Organizations such as the Ku Klux Klan, devoted to violence against the radical state governments and their supporters, brought fear and tension to the Southern countryside. New acts of Federal Legislation designed to suppress the lawlessness were passed. In 1870 and 1871, Congress enlarged the responsibility of the central government in the new states as a hedge against fraud and intimidation in elections, and in the most comprehensive of the measures, gave the government sweeping powers to deal with unlawful combinations whose activities bordered on open rebellion. The intervention of the Federal government eventually discouraged the continuation of the Southern campaign of violence but not until after it had left its legacy of fear and terror deeply impressed on the Southern Negro mind.

What did the Southern whites want? Simply stated, they wanted the control of their own governmental institutions, free from the hated influence of the radical North. They resented the new political power that had been thrust into the hands of the Negroes and sought, with increasing success, to counteract it. The fate of the freedman must be decided, they argued, not by a lawmaking agency far removed from the scene but by Southerners who best appreciated the problems faced by their section [Document 11]. But in spite of the protestations, the progress of reconstruction under the radical plan was not stayed. One by one, the Southern states were reorganized with new radical governments and were granted readmission into the Union under the watchful eye of Congress.

Having provided a new reconstruction program, Congress in 1867 turned its attention to another area of concern—the relationship between the executive and legislative branches of the government. President Johnson had been persistent in his efforts to frustrate radical strategy. Virtually every bill passed by Congress relating to reconstruction received his veto, only to be re-enacted over his objections by easy and resounding margins. In order to meet the threat that the hostile President would neglect to execute the Reconstruction Acts and, through his executive power, otherwise negate the radical program, Congress passed a series of laws that were clearly designed to limit the power of the Presidency and to increase that of Congress. The action led to the final confrontation between the adversaries.

President Johnson had been threatened with impeachment ever since he first made known his opposition to the course of radical reconstruction, but it was not until 1868 that charges were actually levied against him. As with so much else that emanated from the radicals, the charges were hastily drawn, originating more in emotion than in careful thought. Johnson was charged with willfully defying the Tenure of Office Act, Congress' measure restricting the power of the President to dismiss his own Cabinet officers. This was the most concrete objection Congress could bring against the President, and it was one that Johnson readily conceded, since he had deliberately ignored the legislation on the ground that it was unconstitutional. To some radicals, this defiance amounted to "high crimes and misdemeanors" and justified impeachment proceedings. Other charges, equally serious, were brought forth, including the accusation that President Johnson had cast Congress into "disgrace, ridicule, hatred, contempt and reproach." In spite of the self-confidence with which the radicals launched their attack, they were unable to secure a conviction, but only by the hairbreadth margin of one vote. The impeachment trial was a side show to the main event of reconstruction and reflected little credit on its instigators. Johnson, in any case, had only a few more months to serve as chief executive. Just short of six months after the President's acquittal, the nation turned to its war hero, Ulysses S. Grant, as the man best qualified to lead the nation through its postwar travail. With Grant, the radicals had little fear that their program would meet executive opposition.

By election day 1868 most of the Southern states had been readmitted to the Union, and by 1870 the movement was complete. With the establishment and subsequent recognition of these new state governments, reconstruction entered yet another stage. This period of radical rule in the South has traditionally been labeled "Black Reconstruction," a misnomer on at least two counts. The degree to which Negroes dominated the new governments, or even served in them, has been greatly exaggerated; the governments were by no means "black." Secondly, Southern whites regarded this stage as a dismal period of turbulence and disorder, a sort of "dark ages" through which they had to pass before their final redemption. Actually, the radical state governments exhibited a more enlightened attitude than Southerners had witnessed for decades and were responsible for reforms that were long overdue in the South. Nonetheless, most Southerners grumbled and lived only for the day when radical rule could be overturned. Stories of corruption, fraud, and maladministration on a vast and unimaginable scale were concocted in an effort to discredit the governments in the eyes of all Americans. There was just enough truth in the assertions to lend credence to the exaggerations. Inexperienced in public life, officeholders, both white and black, abused their offices, squandered public funds, and brought disrepute down upon their heads [Document 13]. In this, Southern officeholders were little different from those in other states and in the national government. The years of Grant's two administrations were not renowned for displays of exemplary honesty and ethical behavior; the instances of corruption in the radical Southern governments were but part of a national way of life during the late 60's and 70's. To dwell on the examples of bad government is to obscure the many advances that the reconstructed states accomplished. The new constitutions and legislation passed under their aegis extended the limits of democracy by making more state offices elective and by enlarging the franchise, improved the tax systems, reformed penal codes, established public education, and encouraged reforms in agricultural and commercial life. It was the so-called "black reconstruction" governments, according to one authority, that "were instrumental in putting the Southern states in line with the progressive spirit of the nineteenth century."

The radical Southern governments, however, were unable to withstand the combination of forces that stood against them and weakened them: the attacks of conservative Southern whites, the terroristic activities of the Ku Klux Klan, the dissensions within the governments themselves, and the adverse publicity stemming from their corruption and mismanagement. But the most important weakening influence lay outside the South altogether —the gradual loss of interest in the North in matters relating to reconstruction. By the early 70's, Americans were simply growing tired of reconstruction. Their commitment had, in any case, never been deep; they now found it easy to be distracted before the task had been completed. The periodic reminders of Democratic and Southern evil by Republican "bloody shirt" orators had a diminishing effect in the face of the shocking developments in the Grant administrations. The public wearied of the reports of violence in the South and of the appeals of Southern radicals for aid and support. The ardor with which many Americans had undertaken the difficult task of reconstruction rapidly cooled as the dimensions of the difficulty were revealed. A concomitant factor was the appearance of new issues to hold their attention. Northern industrialism was burgeoning, railroads were being extended, and the West was being conquered by farmers, miners, and cattlemen. Next to the exciting prospects of great economic and material advances, the troublesome problems of reconstruction seemed insignificant.

This loss of interest in the North was further reflected by an effort within the Republican party to defeat President Grant's bid for a second term. Many Republicans had become disenchanted with Grant, and as revelations of graft and corruption in high places were made they expressed increased shock and disbelief. One answer to the problem was found in the demand for civil service reform, an attempt to bring honesty into government by reducing the Presidential patronage, and it was on this issue that some Republicans hoped to unseat Grant in 1872. By concentrating on this issue, the Liberal Republicans, as they were called, necessarily reduced reconstruction to a secondary role. In fact, many Liberal Republicans were convinced that reconstruction had gone far enough; it was time for the government to turn to other tasks. The results of reconstruction had proved disappointing, and even many of the leading supporters of radical reconstruction now joined the Liberal movement. Although they stressed the need for reform in the structure of the government, they also urged the withdrawal of troops from the South and universal amnesty for Southern whites—in other words, a speedy termination of reconstruction [Document 12]. In a great gesture of weakness and political error, the erratic Horace Greeley was nominated to lead the campaign and Democratic support was received. The movement proved no match for the regular Republican organization; Grant was renominated and re-elected with little difficulty. But the effort of the Liberal Republicans was symptomatic of the changing attitude toward reconstruction. Without Northern and government support, the Southern radical state governments could not hope to exist, at least not yet. As that support was gradually withdrawn, reconstruction came closer to its ultimate failure. Five years before reconstruction ended (taking 1877 as the terminal date) the nation was turning its back on the problems of the South.

With few exceptions, these last five years were devoid of any real advances in reconstruction. Many radicals still cherished their former dream of racial equality in the United States but found it difficult to translate this dream into positive enactment. In 1870, the last of the great Civil War era amendments, the Fifteenth, was ratified, providing suffrage to the Negroes. Too many agreed with the Northern editor who rejoiced that with the ratification of the Fifteenth Amendment the agitation over slavery had been brought to a triumphant conclusion. There was still much to be done, but few recognized the fact. Charles Sumner was still one of the few. Concerned with the protection of the freedman in his social relations, he sought new legislation that would eliminate racial segregation in the South and guarantee to the Negro his social equality. In 1875, a new Civil Rights Act was passed (after Sumner's death) dealing with the problem in a limited fashion [Document 14]. But passing laws was one thing, enforcing them in these latter days of reconstruction was quite another. The Fifteenth Amendment was honored in the breach by Southerners bent on restoring conservative white rule to the South, and the new Civil Rights Act, never effective, was declared unconstitutional eight years after its passage.

In general, the early 1870's were years of declining interest and gradual withdrawal, while in the South efforts were made to return that section to as near the *status quo ante bellum* as the changed circumstances of the intervening years would allow. In 1874, the Democrats secured control of the lower house of Congress for the first time since before the war and gained considerable strength in the Senate. Two years later, Democratic strength proved more than a match for the Republicans in the Presidential election. The resurgence of the Democratic party, however, was as much the result of the loosening of reconstruction policy as it was indicative of waning interest. Some Congressional leaders, observing the shaky foundations of the Southern radical governments, concluded that the old conservative leadership in the South was after all the best guarantee of stability and order. In early 1872, partly as a result of pressures from the Liberal Republicans, Congress passed a general amnesty act, removing political disabilities from Southern whites and allowing them to participate fully in the political life of their states.

With the passage of the amnesty act, the days of the radical governments in the South (those that were left) were clearly numbered. Their power was now effectively challenged at the polls by the conservatives, who were dubbed "Redeemers" by those who sought to rid the South of the hated radical influences. One by one, the Southern states overthrew their radical leaders and were returned to conservative control. In some states, the Redeemers were aided by bitter and often violent power struggles among the Republicans themselves. By the end of 1874, only four states of the original eleven still remained in the hands of Republican radical governments. Within the next three years, these fell before the growing "Redemption" movement and the increasing indifference of the North.

To speed their effort, some Southerners adopted a finely developed and well-organized program of harassment, intimidation, and violence designed to prevent their opponents (chiefly Negroes and carpetbaggers) from exercising their political rights. This program had its most effective expression in the state of Mississippi, where it was employed in the elections of 1875. So successful did it prove that it became known as the "Mississippi Plan," to be emulated by other Southern states [Document 15]. Appeals for Federal intervention to protect the targets of Southern intimidation and to maintain order fell on deaf ears in Washington.

By the mid-1870's, then, only a tattered remnant of reconstruction remained. Radical governments persisted in but three states, Florida, Louisiana, and South Carolina, where they were still supported by the spirit if not the reality of military rule. Even in these three, the downfall of the radicals seemed imminent. Groups of armed men roamed the Southern countryside, especially at election time, spreading terror among the Negroes and their allies and discouraging (in their own fashion) resistance to the dominant white conservative element. Legislation passed by Congress to prevent violence and to guarantee the free and fair exercise of the ballot was not enforced by a government that no longer cared. The Northern people, never deeply committed to reconstruction, were withdrawn, their backs turned to the plight of the freedmen. New issues captured the popular interest and new political voices were being heard. There was simply no place for reconstruction, and its continuing obligations, in the new scheme of things. Travelers to the South merely reinforced the popular image of the Southern conditions: Republican rule in the South had failed, with the triumph of conservative rule came order and stability, the South was developing economically, the fate of the Negro was best left in the capable hands of Southern whites [Document 16].

It was little wonder that the end of reconstruction was welcomed. When the Democratic candidate for President in 1876, New York's governor Samuel J. Tilden, won the popular vote and tied the Republican contender, Rutherford B. Hayes, in the electoral college, with several electoral votes in dispute, the occasion for a new North-South compromise seemed at hand. Hayes was awarded the disputed votes and was declared President but at the price, among other things, of reconstruction. The last troops were withdrawn from the South and the last radical governments fell. The South had finally been "redeemed." In the North, the termination of a program that had kept national politics in turmoil since the end of the war was greeted with relief. Some Northerners deluded themselves into thinking that all the problems had in fact been solved [Document 17].

Reconstruction, like the Civil War, was a great tragedy. It was a tragedy because it never received the deep and abiding commitment it deserved, because its measures became entangled with partisan politics in the worst sense, because its social and humanitarian purposes (if indeed they ever really existed) were soon discarded, because the tasks that were undertaken remained unfinished. It has been fashionable at times in the study of the coming of the Civil War to speak of a "blundering generation." Whatever its applicability before the war, this phrase might with some justification be applied to the men who led the nation during the reconstruction years. The final element in the tragedy is that the American people did not become aware of the full meaning of their "blundering" until almost a century later.

Some Suggestions for Further Reading

Beale, Howard K., *The Critical Year: A Study of Andrew Johnson and Reconstruction* (New York, 1930).

Brock, W. R., *An American Crisis: Congress and Reconstruction, 1865–1867* (New York, 1963).

Brodie, Fawn M., *Thaddeus Stevens: Scourge of the South* (New York, 1959).

Buck, Paul H., *The Road to Reunion, 1865–1890* (Boston, 1937).

Coulter, E. Merton, *The South During Reconstruction, 1865–1877* (Baton Rouge, 1947).

Cox, John H., and LaWanda Cox, *Politics, Principle, and Prejudice, 1865–1866* (New York, 1963).

Donald, David, *The Politics of Reconstruction, 1863–1867* (Baton Rouge, 1965).

Franklin, John Hope, *Reconstruction After the Civil War* (Chicago, 1961).

Hyman, Harold M., *The Radical Republicans and Reconstruction, 1861–1870* (Indianapolis, 1967).

McKitrick, Eric L., *Andrew Johnson and Reconstruction* (Chicago, 1960).

Patrick, Rembert W., *The Reconstruction of the Nation* (New York, 1967).

Sharkey, Robert P., *Money, Class and Party: An Economic Study of Civil War and Reconstruction* (Baltimore, 1959).

Stampp, Kenneth M., *The Era of Reconstruction* (New York, 1965).

Thomas, Benjamin P., and Harold M. Hyman, *Stanton: Life and Times of Lincoln's Secretary of War* (New York, 1962).

1

Presidential Reconstruction

Proclamations of Abraham Lincoln and Andrew Johnson

On December 8, 1863, President Abraham Lincoln (1809–1865) made his first official pronouncement on reconstruction. The movement of Union troops into the South and the occupation of large areas of some Southern states necessitated the formulation of terms by which these states might be restored to the nation. In his "Proclamation of Amnesty and Reconstruction" Lincoln presented his plan, admittedly tentative because he conceded at the same time that future changes might be made in the terms he suggested. It was, however, the only plan Lincoln formally announced. Following Lincoln's assassination in April 1865, Andrew Johnson (1808–1875) picked up where his predecessor had left off. Although Johnson's approach to reconstruction differed from Lincoln's, he followed the general outline that had already been established. In two proclamations, both issued on May 29, 1865, he defined the terms for granting amnesty to Southerners, expanding on those that Lincoln had proposed, and described the steps by which a Southern state could regain its former position in the Union. To the provisional governors whom he appointed for each state, he further emphasized that no Southern state would receive executive recognition that did not ratify the Thirteenth Amendment, abrogate its ordinance of secession, and repudiate the debt that it had incurred during the Confederate period. For discussions of Presidential reconstruction, see Charles H. McCarthy, *Lincoln's Plan of Reconstruction* (New York, 1901), old but still useful, and the more recent study by William B. Hesseltine, *Lincoln's Plan of Reconstruction* (Tuscaloosa, Alabama, 1960). In the documents that follow, note (1) the nature of the oath of allegiance required for pardon; (2) the exemptions from pardon enumerated by each President; (3) the steps prescribed by which a state government might be re-established; (4) Lincoln's suggestion concerning the "freed people" of each state; and (5) the manner in which Johnson's plan differed from Lincoln's.

Roy P. Basler *et al.,* eds., *The Collected Works of Abraham Lincoln* (9 vols., New Brunswick, N.J.: Rutgers University Press, 1953), VII, 53–56; James D. Richardson, comp., *A Compilation of the Messages and Papers of the Presidents* (10 vols., Washington, D.C.: Government Printing Office, 1897), VI, 310–14.

PROCLAMATION OF AMNESTY AND
RECONSTRUCTION
BY THE PRESIDENT OF THE UNITED STATES

A Proclamation

December 8, 1863

WHEREAS, in and by the Constitution of the
United States, it is provided that the President
"shall have power to grant reprieves and pardons for offences
against the United States, except in cases of impeachment;" and

Whereas a rebellion now exists whereby the loyal State governments of several States have for a long time been subverted, and many persons have committed and are now guilty of treason against the United States; and

Whereas, with reference to said rebellion and treason, laws have been enacted by Congress declaring forfeitures and confiscation of property and liberation of slaves, all upon terms and conditions therein stated, and also declaring that the President was thereby authorized at any time thereafter, by proclamation, to extend to persons who may have participated in the existing rebellion, in any State or part thereof, pardon and amnesty, with such exceptions and at such times and on such conditions as he may deem expedient for the public welfare; and

Whereas the congressional declaration for limited and conditional pardon accords with well-established judicial exposition of the pardoning power; and

Whereas, with reference to said rebellion, the President of the United States has issued several proclamations, with provisions in regard to the liberation of slaves; and

Whereas it is now desired by some persons heretofore engaged in said rebellion to resume their allegiance to the United States, and to reinaugurate loyal State governments within and for their respective States; therefore,

I, Abraham Lincoln, President of the United States, do proclaim, declare, and make known to all persons who have, directly or by implication, participated in the existing rebellion, except as hereinafter excepted, that a full pardon is hereby granted to them and each of them, with restoration of all rights of property, except as to slaves, and in property cases where rights of third parties shall have intervened, and upon the condition that every such person shall take and subscribe an oath, and thenceforward keep and maintain said oath inviolate; and which oath shall be registered for permanent preservation, and shall be of the tenor and effect following, to wit:

"I,————, do solemnly swear, in presence of Almighty God, that I will henceforth faithfully support, protect and defend the Constitution of the United States, and the union of the States thereunder; and that I will, in like manner, abide by and faithfully support all acts of Congress passed during the existing rebellion with reference to slaves, so long and so far as not repealed, modified or held void by Congress, or by decision of the Supreme Court; and that I will, in like manner, abide by and faithfully support all proclamations of the President made during the existing rebellion having reference to slaves, so long and so far as not modified or declared void by decision of the Supreme Court. So help me God."

The persons excepted from the benefits of the foregoing provisions are all who are, or shall have been, civil or diplomatic officers or agents of the so-called confederate government; all who have left judicial stations under the United States to aid the rebellion; all who are, or shall have been, military or naval officers of said so-called confederate government above the rank of colonel in the army, or of lieutenant in the navy; all who left seats in the United States Congress to aid the rebellion; all who resigned commissions in the army or navy of the United States, and afterwards aided the rebellion; and all who have engaged in any way in treating colored persons or white persons, in charge of such, otherwise than lawfully as prisoners of war, and which persons may have been found in the United States service, as soldiers, seamen, or in any other capacity.

And I do further proclaim, declare, and make known, that whenever, in any of the States of

Arkansas, Texas, Louisiana, Mississippi, Tennessee, Alabama, Georgia, Florida, South Carolina, and North Carolina, a number of persons, not less than one-tenth in number of the votes cast in such State at the Presidential election of the year of our Lord one thousand eight hundred and sixty, each having taken the oath aforesaid and not having since violated it, and being a qualified voter by the election law of the State existing immediately before the so-called act of secession, and excluding all others, shall re-establish a State government which shall be republican, and in no wise contravening said oath, such shall be recognized as the true government of the State, and the State shall receive thereunder the benefits of the constitutional provision which declares that "The United States shall guaranty to every State in this union a republican form of government, and shall protect each of them against invasion; and, on application of the legislature, or the executive, (when the legislature cannot be convened,) against domestic violence."

And I do further proclaim, declare, and make known that any provision which may be adopted by such State government in relation to the freed people of such State, which shall recognize and declare their permanent freedom, provide for their education, and which may yet be consistent, as a temporary arrangement, with their present condition as a laboring, landless, and homeless class, will not be objected to by the national Executive. And it is suggested as not improper, that, in constructing a loyal State government in any State, the name of the State, the boundary, the subdivisions, the constitution, and the general code of laws, as before the rebellion, be maintained, subject only to the modifications made necessary by the conditions hereinbefore stated, and such others, if any, not contravening said conditions, and which may be deemed expedient by those framing the new State government.

To avoid misunderstanding, it may be proper to say that this proclamation, so far as it relates to State governments, has no reference to States wherein loyal State governments have all the while been maintained. And for the same reason, it may be proper to further say that whether members sent to Congress from any State shall be admitted to seats, constitutionally rests exclusively with the respective Houses, and not to any extent with the Executive. And still further, that this proclamation is intended to present the people of the States wherein the national authority has been suspended, and loyal State governments have been subverted, a mode in and by which the national authority and loyal State governments may be re-established within said States, or in any of them; and, while the mode presented is the best the Executive can suggest, with his present impressions, it must not be understood that no other possible mode would be acceptable.

Given under my hand at the city, of Washington, the 8th. day of December, A.D. one thousand eight hundred and sixty-three, and of the independence of the United States of America the eighty-eighth.

ABRAHAM LINCOLN

By the President:

WILLIAM H. SEWARD,
Secretary of State.

BY THE PRESIDENT OF THE UNITED STATES OF AMERICA

A PROCLAMATION

WHEREAS the President of the United States, on the 8th day of December, A.D. 1863, and on the 26th day of March, A.D. 1864, did, with the object to suppress the existing rebellion, to induce all persons to return to their loyalty, and to restore the authority of the United States, issue proclamations offering amnesty and pardon to certain persons who had, directly or by implication, participated in the said rebellion; and

Whereas many persons who had so engaged in said rebellion have, since the issuance of said proclamations, failed or neglected to take the benefits offered thereby; and

Whereas many persons who have been justly deprived of all claim to amnesty and pardon thereunder by reason of their participation, directly or by implication, in said rebellion and continued hostility to the Government of the United States since the date of said proclamations now desire to apply for and obtain amnesty and pardon.

To the end, therefore, that the authority of the Government of the United States may be restored and that peace, order, and freedom may be established, I, Andrew Johnson, President of the

United States, do proclaim and declare that I hereby grant to all persons who have, directly or indirectly, participated in the existing rebellion, except as hereinafter excepted, amnesty and pardon, with restoration of all rights of property, except as to slaves and except in cases where legal proceedings under the laws of the United States providing for the confiscation of property of persons engaged in rebellion have been instituted; but upon the condition, nevertheless, that every such person shall take and subscribe the following oath (or affirmation) and thenceforward keep and maintain said oath inviolate, and which oath shall be registered for permanent preservation and shall be of the tenor and effect following, to wit:

I,—— ——, do solemnly swear (or affirm), in presence of Almighty God, that I will henceforth faithfully support, protect, and defend the Constitution of the United States and the Union of the States thereunder, and that I will in like manner abide by and faithfully support all laws and proclamations which have been made during the existing rebellion with reference to the emancipation of slaves. So help me God.

The following classes of persons are excepted from the benefits of this proclamation:

FIRST. All who are or shall have been pretended civil or diplomatic officers or otherwise domestic or foreign agents of the pretended Confederate government.

SECOND. All who left judicial stations under the United States to aid the rebellion.

THIRD. All who shall have been military or naval officers of said pretended Confederate government above the rank of colonel in the army or lieutenant in the navy.

FOURTH. All who left seats in the Congress of the United States to aid the rebellion.

FIFTH. All who resigned or tendered resignations of their commissions in the Army or Navy of the United States to evade duty in resisting the rebellion.

SIXTH. All who have engaged in any way in treating otherwise than lawfully as prisoners of war persons found in the United

States service as officers, soldiers, seamen, or in other capacities.

SEVENTH. All persons who have been or are absentees from the United States for the purpose of aiding the rebellion.

EIGHTH. All military and naval officers in the rebel service who were educated by the Government in the Military Academy at West Point or the United States Naval Academy.

NINTH. All persons who held the pretended offices of governors of States in insurrection against the United States.

TENTH. All persons who left their homes within the jurisdiction and protection of the United States and passed beyond the Federal military lines into the pretended Confederate States for the purpose of aiding the rebellion.

ELEVENTH. All persons who have been engaged in the destruction of the commerce of the United States upon the high seas and all persons who have made raids into the United States from Canada or been engaged in destroying the commerce of the United States upon the lakes and rivers that separate the British Provinces from the United States.

TWELFTH. All persons who, at the time when they seek to obtain the benefits hereof by taking the oath herein prescribed, are in military, naval, or civil confinement or custody, or under bonds of the civil, military, or naval authorities or agents of the United States as prisoners of war, or persons detained for offenses of any kind, either before or after conviction.

THIRTEENTH. All persons who have voluntarily participated in said rebellion and the estimated value of whose taxable property is over $20,000.

FOURTEENTH. All persons who have taken the oath of amnesty as prescribed in the President's proclamation of December 8, A.D. 1863, or an oath of allegiance to the Government of the United States since the date of said proclamation and who have not thenceforward kept and maintained the same inviolate.

Provided, That special application may be made to the President for pardon by any person belonging to the excepted classes, and such clemency will be liberally extended as may be consistent with the facts of the case and the peace and dignity of the United States.

The Secretary of State will establish rules and regulations for administering and recording the said amnesty oath, so as to insure its benefit to the people and guard the Government against fraud.

In testimony whereof I have hereunto set my hand and caused the seal of the United States to be affixed.

Done at the city of Washington, the 29th day of May, A.D. *1865, and of the Independence of the United States the eighty-ninth.*

ANDREW JOHNSON

By the President:

WILLIAM H. SEWARD,
Secretary of State.

BY THE PRESIDENT OF THE UNITED STATES OF AMERICA

A PROCLAMATION

WHEREAS the fourth section of the fourth article of the Constitution of the United States declares that the United States shall guarantee to every State in the Union a republican form of government and shall protect each of them against invasion and domestic violence; and

Whereas the President of the United States is by the Constitution made Commander in Chief of the Army and Navy, as well as chief civil executive officer of the United States, and is bound by solemn oath faithfully to execute the office of President of the United States and to take care that the laws be faithfully executed; and

Whereas the rebellion which has been waged by a portion of the people of the United States against the properly constituted authorities of the Government thereof in the most violent and revolting form, but whose organized and armed forces have now been almost entirely overcome, has in its revolutionary progress deprived the people of the State of North Carolina of all civil government; and

Whereas it becomes necessary and proper to carry out and enforce the obligations of the United States to the people of North Carolina in securing them in the enjoyment of a republican form of government:

Now, therefore, in obedience to the high and solemn duties imposed upon me by the Constitution of the United States and for the purpose of enabling the loyal people of said State to organize a State government whereby justice may be established, domestic tranquillity insured, and loyal citizens protected in all their rights of life, liberty, and property, I, Andrew Johnson, President of the United States and Commander in Chief of the Army and Navy of the United States, do hereby appoint William W. Holden provisional governor of the State of North Carolina, whose duty it shall be, at the earliest practicable period, to prescribe such rules and regulations as may be necessary and proper for convening a convention composed of delegates to be chosen by that portion of the people of said State who are loyal to the United States, and no others, for the purpose of altering or amending the constitution thereof, and with authority to exercise within the limits of said State all the powers necessary and proper to enable such loyal people of the State of North Carolina to restore said State to its constitutional relations to the Federal Government and to present such a republican form of State government as will entitle the State to the guaranty of the United States therefor and its people to protection by the United States against invasion, insurrection, and domestic violence: *Provided,* That in any election that may be hereafter held for choosing delegates to any State convention as aforesaid no person shall be qualified as an elector or shall be eligible as a member of such convention unless he shall have previously taken and subscribed the oath of amnesty as set forth in the President's proclamation of May 29, A.D. 1865, and is a voter qualified as prescribed by the constitution and laws of the State of North Carolina in force immediately before the 20th day of May, A.D. 1861, the date of the so-called ordinance of secession; and the said convention, when convened, or the legislature that may be thereafter assembled, will prescribe the qualification of electors and the eligibility of persons to hold office under the constitution and laws of the State—a power the people of the several States composing the Federal Union have rightfully exercised from the origin of the Government to the present time.

And I do hereby direct—

FIRST. That the military commander of the department and all officers and persons in the military and naval service aid and assist the said provisional governor in carrying into effect this proclamation; and they are enjoined to abstain from in any way hindering, impeding, or discouraging the loyal people from the organization of a State government as herein authorized.

SECOND. That the Secretary of State proceed to put in force all laws of the United States the administration whereof belongs to the State Department applicable to the geographical limits aforesaid.

THIRD. That the Secretary of the Treasury proceed to nominate for appointment assessors of taxes and collectors of customs and internal revenue and such other officers of the Treasury Department as are authorized by law and put in execution the revenue laws of the United States within the geographical limits aforesaid. In making appointments the preference shall be given to qualified loyal persons residing within the districts where their respective duties are to be performed; but if suitable residents of the districts shall not be found, then persons residing in other States or districts shall be appointed.

FOURTH. That the Postmaster-General proceed to establish post-offices and post routes and put into execution the postal laws of the United States within the said State, giving to loyal residents the preference of appointment; but if suitable residents are not found, then to appoint agents, etc., from other States.

FIFTH. That the district judge for the judicial district in which North Carolina is included proceed to hold courts within said State in accordance with the provisions of the act of Congress. The Attorney-General will instruct the proper officers to libel and bring to judgment, confiscation, and sale property subject to confiscation and enforce the administration of justice within said State in all matters within the cognizance and jurisdiction of the Federal courts.

SIXTH. That the Secretary of the Navy take possession of all public property belonging to the Navy Department within said geographical limits and put in operation all acts of Congress in relation to naval affairs having application to the said State.

SEVENTH. That the Secretary of the Interior put in force the laws relating to the Interior Department applicable to the geographical limits aforesaid.

In testimony whereof I have hereunto set my hand and caused the seal of the United States to be affixed.

Done at the City of Washington, this 29th day of May, A.D. *1865, and of the Independence of the United States the eighty-ninth.*

ANDREW JOHNSON

By the President

WILLIAM H. SEWARD

Secretary of State.

2

"Southern Policy"

The Nation Warns Against a Hasty Settlement, 1865

The months following the end of the war witnessed a widespread feeling of relief in both the North and the South. The killing was over and only the problems of restoring the Union (the real complexity of which had not yet become fully apparent) remained. Southern leaders wisely counseled acquiescence in the results of the conflict and an acceptance of the North's terms. Travelers through the South invariably reported the willingness of most Southerners to concede Northern victory, with its major consequence, the abolition of Negro slavery. As President Johnson initiated his reconstruction program, many Americans felt that the wounds of four years of bloody fighting would soon be healed. Some in the North, however, were not so prepared to credit Southern acquiescence with sincerity and good faith. Long years of suspicion and distrust of Southern motives and a memory of how tenaciously the South had clung to its institutions aroused a latent distrust of the South now that the war was over. Edwin Lawrence Godkin (1831–1902), editor of the newly established magazine *The Nation,* feared that the North would be lulled by these signs into a "hasty and premature settlement" that could only have disastrous consequences for the future. For additional information on this immediate postwar period, see the appropriate chapters in the general histories of reconstruction by Coulter, Patrick, and Stampp. In the document that follows, note (1) the attitude toward President Johnson and his reconstruction program; (2) the effect on the North of Southern acquiescence; (3) the predicted consequences of a too hasty settlement; and (4) the comments on the role and fate of the freedmen in the South.

[E. L. Godkin], "Southern Policy," *The Nation,* I (Oct. 26, 1865), 516–17.

WE PUBLISH in another column some very striking and suggestive letters from the commercial correspondent sent down to the South by some Massachusetts manufacturers. His opinions, as we have remarked before, are entitled to all the greater weight from the fact that he is looking at things from a purely business point of view, and his conclusions, we may add, are those which any intelligent person might fairly draw from the interesting mass of observations forwarded to us every week by our special correspondent. They are, more-over, conclusions at which any intelligent reader of the history of the last twenty years might have arrived *a priori,* without ever seeing a Southern newspaper or hearing a word of news from the rebellious States. The stories which the "Conservative" press tell us of the hearty acquiescence of the Southern people in the new order of things, and of their sudden determination to forget the past and become in feeling as in fact citizens of the United States, would, if true, contradict all the teachings of history and all our experience of human nature. So many wonderful things have lately happened, however, that many people doubtless con-sider knowledge of history and of human nature of very little value; we are, therefore, glad to have these reasons confirmed by deductions from actual observations of the facts.

In commenting a few weeks ago upon the course which the South is pursuing, we spoke of it as "a display of consummate political ability" and so we still consider it. At no time in its history have its leading men given stronger proofs of proficiency in the political art than during the last six months. A stupid, inexperienced, or clumsy-minded people would, after such a con-flict as they have just gone through, have done what their admir-ers in England expected them to do—kept up an irregular warfare, or displayed their passion and mortification in sullen, passive resistance to Federal authority. But Lee had hardly laid down his arms when their leaders seemed to take the whole situation in at a glance, and decide upon their course with that swiftness, precision, and unanimity which won them so many Congressional victories in by-gone days, and are, in our opinion, destined to win them many more. Northern fury was at once disarmed by loud protestations of submission and resignation. No pride, or sentiment, was allowed for one moment to stand in the way of any declarations which appeared to be necessary to appease the conqueror. And what has been more remarkable— and it furnishes a striking illustration of the extraordinary polit-ical discipline which is still maintained amongst the Southern population—whatever the leading men of each State decided upon was unhesitatingly supported by the whole people, without any preliminary agitation or discussion, without even meetings or newspapers. Every sacrifice which the fortune of war made necessary—such as the abolition of slavery, the repudiation of the rebel debt—or which would facilitate reconstruction, has been made with a cheerfulness which took from it all appearance of sacrifice, and has actually cheated half the North into the belief that it was no sacrifice at all, but a free-will offering. We venture to say that there is not in history a more brilliant example of power of adaptation to circumstances.

And no piece of policy, hopeless as it must have seemed at the outset to many of the Southerners themselves, hopeless as it did seem last June to all the world beside, was ever more successful. It completely disarmed Mr. Johnson in a few weeks. When he took office he was breathing nothing but threatening and slaughter against traitors—and the whole South was traitorous. He incorporated, while in his first state of mind, a clause in his amnesty proclamation intended to strike down what was left of the aristocracy at a blow, a regular declaration of "war to the châteaux." But he had hardly been two months in power, and had had a few interviews with prominent "pardon-seekers" when he roared as gently as any sucking dove. Rarey never performed more tricks with "Cruiser"* than the Southern president-tamers now perform on the terrible Tennesseean Democrat [President Johnson]. They sit on him, turn him over, tie up his hands, put their heads in his mouth, make him shed as many tears and make as many "conciliatory speeches" as they please. And they took all the sting out of the "$20,000 clause" by getting him to establish a pardoning machine, which works day and night, and into which the vilest traitor may step at any moment in the full assurance that, after a little formal tossing about inside, he will be turned out in a week or two a clean, white-robed "citizen," without a speck or stain of guilt upon him.

The effect on the country has been not less remarkable. The wrath of the North appears to have almost entirely evaporated. There seems little doubt that by New Year's Day even Jefferson Davis himself might be dismissed to his home, with the acquiescence or approval of the great majority of the community. The indignation excited by the horrors of the rebel prison-pens has

---

*EDITOR'S NOTE. John Solomon Rarey (1827–1866) was a noted American trainer of horses.

apparently concentrated itself upon one wretched underling, whose brutality, be it ever so great, is after all a more "damned spot" on the hands of those who appointed and kept him in office than on his. The real chiefs of the rebellion, the real authors of all its woes and horrors, are one by one dropping off to their homes, amidst much hand-shaking, dining, and "paying of respects." The newspapers are filled with eulogies on the Southern temper, and glowing pictures of the peace, prosperity, and, above all, of the harmony in store for us in the future. The country is tired of agitation and of strife, and is not disposed to look too narrowly into the proofs the South offers of its sincerity. Trade, too, is reviving, and Southern trade, as we all know, has always been the great anodyne of Northern politicians. In neither the Republican nor Democratic platform is there a single proposition or proviso to which the assent of the South is not already secured; so that we do not, for our parts, anticipate the exaction, next December, from the States lately in revolt of a single condition of their formal reinstalment in the Union to which they are not already fully reconciled. Their concessions to what they consider the negro-mania of the North are great. It is sheer absurdity to tell us that the abolition of slavery is nothing, the legalization of marriage and of education is nothing. They are the very foundations of civil society; but though much, they are still little. As long as the whites retain the exclusive power of legislation, the spirit of caste and the political power of the South remain unbroken, and "that unconquerable hate and study of revenge" which the correspondent whose letters we quote describes as still existing, will find a thousand means of display and gratification.

What, then, are we to look for as the result of the hasty and premature settlement which we now fear? Not, certainly, the triumph of Southern ideas, or the utter and final defeat of Northern policy; but, as we believe, a prolongation of the agitation which has torn the country for the last forty years; a renewal in the press and in Congress of the old conflict, in which the North, rich, prosperous, unwieldy, and divided, will labor under the old disadvantages in watching and foiling its adroit, astute, and compact adversary. That the South will ever be allowed to retain the negroes in its hands as political outcasts, and embody its prejudices about them in legislation, without vigorous resistance and final defeat, scarcely anybody can believe. The North is burdened with a conscience of which Southern dexterity has never been able to rob it, and the existence of a body of freemen deprived of civil rights in the midst of a democratic republic, is so great a scandal, and so revolting to the democratic feeling, that there is no chance of the country ever finally submitting to it or forgetting it. Negro disabilities will have eventually to disappear; though at what cost, or by what process, the political emancipation of the race will have to be secured, if it be not secured or provided for now, he would be a shrewd man who could conjecture.

If our fears should be realized, of course a greater portion than ever of the burden of their own deliverance will fall upon the blacks. They will have to support the exertions of their allies at the North by a constantly increasing display of energy, industry, and moral worth, for the great argument for their confirmed degradation will unquestionably be always drawn, as it is now drawn, from their ignorance or idleness. And if this view of the case be correct, the responsibility resting on all charitable persons at the North becomes greatly increased. The political importance of the work of negro education, during the next few years, becomes immense, greater far than could be ever claimed before for any similar undertaking.

3
The Mississippi Black Code
Governor Humphreys' Message, 1865

From the Southern point of view, one of the first needs following the cessation of hostilities was for legislation that would control the vast number of freed Negroes in the South. The rigorous discipline of slavery had suddenly been lifted; roughly four million Negroes, heretofore held in bondage, now found themselves free. Fearful that this large population, lacking training and for the most part unprepared to assume new roles in Southern society, would engage in disorder and lawlessness, and concerned lest they become a burden on an already prostrated social order, Southerners sought new legal codes that could fill the void left by emancipation and, at the same time, preserve white domination. The passage of these codes, known as "black codes," was given first priority by the new state governments. One of the most severe was that passed by the Mississippi legislature at the end of 1865 and urged by Mississippi's Governor Benjamin Grubb Humphreys (1808–1882). A native of Mississippi, Humphreys, following his dismissal from West Point in 1826, had studied law, served in the state legislature and engaged in planting. Although he opposed secession, he had served as an officer in the Confederate Army. Following the war, he was elected Governor of Mississippi and President Johnson granted him pardon so that he could serve. Humphreys remained in office until 1868, when he was ejected by the military government established under Congressional reconstruction. For a brief survey of the Southern black codes, see Theodore Brantner Wilson, *The Black Codes of the South* (University, Alabama, 1965); for Mississippi during reconstruction, see James W. Garner, *Reconstruction in Mississippi* (New York, 1901) and William C. Harris, *Presidential Reconstruction in Mississippi* (Baton Rouge, 1967). In the message that follows, note (1) Humphreys' attitude toward emancipation and the freed Negro; (2) the importance of allowing Negro testimony in the courts; and (3) his justification for action by the legislature.

The New York Times, Dec. 3, 1865.

EXECUTIVE OFFICE,

Jackson, Miss., Nov. 20, 1865.

> *GENTLEMEN of the Senate and House of Representatives:*

In view of your resolution to take, at an early day, a recess until after the holidays, I deem it proper to call your attention to a few subjects of vital importance to the welfare of the State.

By the sudden emancipation of over 300,000 slaves, Mississippi has imposed upon her a problem of vast magnitude, upon the proper solution of which depend the hopes and future prosperity of ourselves and our children.

Under the pressure of Federal bayonets, urged on by the misdirected sympathies of the world, in behalf of the enslaved African, the people of Mississippi have abolished the institution of slavery, and have solemnly declared in their State Constitution that "the Legislature should provide by law for the protection and security of the persons and property of the freedmen of the State against evils that may arise from their sudden emancipation." How this important provision and requirement of the constitution is to be carried into effect is the question now presented for our solution. We must now meet the question as it is, and not as we would like to have it. The rule must be justice. The negro is free, whether we like it or not; we must realize that fact now and forever. To be free, however, does not make him a citizen, or entitle him to political or social equality with the white man. But the constitution and justice do entitle him to protection and security in his person and property, both real and personal.

In my humble judgment, no man, bond or free, under any form of government, can be assured of protection or security, either in person or property, except through an independent and enlightened judiciary. The courts, then, should be open to the negro. But of what avail is it to open the courts, and invite the negro "to sue and be sued," if he is not permitted to testify himself and introduce such testimony as he or his attorney may deem essential to establish the truth and justice of his case? Whether the witness be white or black, it is the denial of the most common privilege of freedom, an unmeaning delusion, the merest mockery.

As a measure of domestic policy, whether for the protection of the person or property of the freedman, or for the protection of society, the negro should be allowed and required to testify for or against the white and black, according to the truth. There are few men living in the South who have not known many white criminals to go "unwhipped of justice" because negro testimony was not permitted in the courts. And now that the negro is no longer under the restraint or care of his master, he will become the dupe and "cats-paw" of the vile and vicious white man who seeks his association, and will plunder our land with entire security from punishment, unless he can be reached through negro testimony. It is an insult to the intelligence and virtue of our courts, and juries of white men, to say or suspect that they cannot or will not protect the innocent, whether white or black, against the falsehood and perjury of black witnesses.

The question of admitting negro testimony for the protection of their persons and property sinks into insignificance by the side of the other great question of *guarding them and the State* against the evils that may arise from their sudden emancipation. What are the evils that have already arisen against which we are to guard the negro and the State? The answer is patent to all— vagrancy and pauperism, and their inevitable concomitant crime and misery, hang like a dark pall over a once prosperous and happy, but now desolated land.

To the guardian care of the Freedmen's Bureau has been intrusted the emancipated slaves. The civil law, and the white man outside of the bureau, has been deprived of all jurisdiction over them. Look around you and see the result. Idleness and vagrancy has been the rule. Our rich and productive fields have been deserted for the filthy garrets and sickly cellars of our towns and cities. From producers they are converted into consumers, and as Winter approaches their only salvation from starvation and want is Federal rations, plunder and pillage. Four years of cruel war, conducted upon principles of vandalism disgraceful to the civilization of the age was scarcely more blighting and destructive to the homes of the white man, and impoverishing and degrading to the negro, than has resulted in the last six or eight months from the administration of this black incubus. Many of the officers connected with that bureau are gentlemen of honor and integrity, but they seem incapable of protecting the rights and property of the white man against the villainies of the vile and villains with whom they are associated.

How long this hideous course, permitted of Heaven, is to be allowed to rule and ruin our happy people, I regret it is not in my power to give any assurance further than can be gathered from the public and private declarations of President Johnson that "the troops will be withdrawn from Mississippi, when in the opinion of the government the peace and order and civil authority has been restored and can be maintained without them." In this uncertainty as to what will satisfy the government of our loyalty and ability to maintain order and peace and civil government, our duty under the constitution to guard the negro and the State from the evils arising from sudden emancipation, must not be neglected. Our duty to the State and to the freedmen seems to me to be clear, and I respectfully recommend—

FIRST. That negro testimony should be admitted to our courts, not only for the protection of the person and property of the freedmen, but for the protection of society against the crimes of both races.

SECOND. That the freedman be encouraged at once to enter in some pursuit of industry for the support of his family and the education of his children, by laws assuring him of friendship and protection. Tax the freedman for the support of the indigent and helpless freedmen, and then, with an iron will and the strong hand of power, take hold of the idler and the vagrant and force him to some profitable employment.

THIRD. Pass a militia law that will enable the militia to protect our people against insurrection, or any possible combination of vicious white men and negroes.

I deem the passage of these measures, before you take a recess, of vital importance. By them we may secure the withdrawal of the Federal troops, and thus again inspire our people with hope and confidence in the future, and encourage them to engage again in agricultural pursuits, upon which our all depends. If we fail to pass them, the future is all uncertainty, gloom and despondency.

BENJAMIN HUMPHREYS,
Governor of Mississippi.

4
"The Condition of the Confederate States"

Report of the Joint Committee on Reconstruction, 1866

Shortly after the convening of Congress in December 1865, Thaddeus Stevens, Representative from Pennsylvania, proposed the appointment of a Joint Committee on Reconstruction, to inquire into the condition of the states that had formed the Confederate States of America and to report whether any of these states were entitled to representation in Congress. The committee contained fifteen members, only three of whom were Democrats. The radicals had an edge over the moderates on the Republican side, but their influence was not a controlling one. During the following months, the committee heard testimony regarding conditions in the South and compiled a voluminous report. Its appointment was notice to President Johnson that his reconstruction plan was not accepted by the legislative branch and its subsequent activities clearly revealed the conviction of members of Congress that responsibility over reconstruction was essentially theirs. Meanwhile, Republicans in Congress were given valuable time to formulate a reconstruction plan of their own. In June 1866 the committee report, written by the chairman, William P. Fessenden (1806–1869), was presented; in substance, it denied Johnson's claim that new loyal governments had been established in the South, repudiated the Presidential plan of reconstruction, and asserted the responsibility of the legislative branch to enact measures to restore the former disloyal states to the Union. See Benjamin B. Kendrick, ed., *The Journal of the Joint Committee of Fifteen on Reconstruction* (New York, 1914). In the following report, note (1) the attitude toward Johnson's reconstruction plan; (2) the reaction to the claim that the Southern states should be represented in Congress; (3) the description of Southern attitudes toward the North and Northern victory; and (4) the conclusions of the committee.

"Report of the Joint Committee on Reconstruction, June 8, 1866," *Senate Reports,* No. 112 (39th Congress, 1st Session).

The Joint Committee of the two houses of Congress appointed under the concurrent resolution of December 13, 1865, with direction "to inquire into the condition of the States which formed the so-called Confederate States

*of America, and report whether they or any of them are entitled
to be represented in either house of Congress, with leave to report by bill or otherwise," ask leave to report:*

That they have attended to the duty assigned them as assiduously as other duties would permit, and now submit to Congress,
as the result of their deliberations, a resolution proposing
amendments to the Constitution, and two bills, of which they
recommend the adoption.

Before proceeding to set forth in detail their reasons for the
conclusion to which, after great deliberation, your committee
have arrived, they beg leave to advert, briefly, to the course of
proceedings they found it necessary to adopt, and to explain the
reasons therefor.

The resolution under which your committee was appointed
directed them to inquire into the condition of the Confederate
States, and report whether they were entitled to representation
in Congress. It is obvious that such an investigation, covering so
large an extent of territory and involving so many important
considerations, must necessarily require no trifling labor, and
consume a very considerable amount of time. It must embrace
the condition in which those States were left at the close of the
war; the measures which have been taken towards the reorganization of civil government, and the disposition of the people towards the United States; in a word, their fitness to take an active
part in the administration of national affairs.

As to their condition at the close of the rebellion, the evidence
is open to all and admits of no dispute. They were in a state of
utter exhaustion. Having protracted their struggle against federal authority until all hope of successful resistance had ceased,
and laid down their arms only because there was no longer any
power to use them, the people of those States were left bankrupt
in their public finances, and shorn of the private wealth which
had before given them power and influence. They were also
necessarily in a state of complete anarchy, without governments
and without the power to frame governments except by the permission of those who had been successful in the war. The President of the United States, in the proclamations under which he
appointed provisional governors, and in his various communica-

tions to them, has, in exact terms, recognized the fact that the people of those States were, when the rebellion was crushed, "deprived of all civil government," and must proceed to organize anew. . . . Finding the southern States in this condition, and Congress having failed to provide for the contingency, his duty was obvious. As President of the United States, he had no power, except to execute the laws of the land as Chief Magistrate. These laws gave him no authority over the subject of reorganization, but by the Constitution he was commander-in-chief of the army and navy of the United States. These Confederate States embraced a portion of the people of the Union who had been in a state of revolt, but had been reduced to obedience by force of arms. They were in an abnormal condition, without civil government, without commercial connexions, without national or international relations, and subject only to martial law. By withdrawing their representatives in Congress, by renouncing the privilege of representation, by organizing a separate government, and by levying war against the United States, they destroyed their State constitutions in respect to the vital principle which connected their respective States with the Union and secured their federal relations; and nothing of those constitutions was left of which the United States were bound to take notice. For four years they had a *de facto* government, but it was usurped and illegal. They chose the tribunal of arms wherein to decide whether or not it should be legalized, and they were defeated. At the close of the rebellion, therefore, the people of the rebellious States were found as the President expresses it, "deprived of all civil government."

Under this state of affairs it was plainly the duty of the President to enforce existing national laws, and to establish, as far as he could, such a system of government as might be provided for by existing national statutes. As commander-in-chief of a victorious army, it was his duty, under the law of nations and the army regulations, to restore order, to preserve property, and to protect the people against violence from any quarter until provision should be made by law for their government. He might, as President, assemble Congress and submit the whole matter to the law-making power; or he might continue military supervision and control until Congress should assemble on its regular appointed day. Selecting the latter alternative, he proceeded, by virtue of his power as commander-in-chief, to appoint provisional governors over the revolted States. These were regularly commissioned, and their compensation was paid, as the Secretary of War states, "from the appropriation for army contingencies, because the duties performed by the parties were regarded as of a temporary character; ancillary to the withdrawal of military force, the disbandment of armies, and reduction of military expenditure; by provisional organizations for the protection of civil rights, the preservation of peace, and to take the place of armed force in the respective States." It cannot, we think, be contended that these governors possessed, or could exercise, any but military authority. They had no power to organize civil governments, nor to exercise any authority except that which inhered in their own persons under their commissions. Neither had the President, as commander-in-chief, any other than military power. But he was in exclusive possession of the military authority. It was for him to decide how far he would exercise it, how far he would relax it, when and on what terms he would withdraw it. He might properly permit the people to assemble, and to initiate local governments, and to execute such local laws as they might choose to frame not inconsistent with, nor in opposition to, the laws of the United States. And, if satisfied that they might safely be left to themselves, he might withdraw the military forces altogether, and leave the people of any or all of these States to govern themselves without his interference. . . . All this was within his own discretion, as military commander. But it was not for him to decide upon the nature or effect of any system of government which the people of these States might see fit to adopt. This power is lodged by the Constitution in the Congress of the United States, that branch of the government in which is vested the authority to fix the political relations of the States to the Union, whose duty it is to guarantee to each State a republican form of government, and to protect each and all of them against foreign or domestic violence, and against each other. We cannot, therefore, regard the various acts of the President in relation to the formation of local governments in the insurrectionary States, and the conditions imposed by him upon their action, in any other light than as intimation to the people that, as commander-in-chief of the army, he would consent to withdraw military rule just in proportion as they should, by their acts, manifest a disposition to preserve order among themselves, establish governments denoting loyalty to the Union, and exhibit a settled determination to return to their allegiance, leaving with the law-making power to fix the terms of their final restoration to all their rights and privileges as States of the Union. That this was the view of his power taken by the President is evident from expressions to that effect in the communications of the Secretary of State to the various provisional governors, and the repeated declarations of the President himself. Any other supposition inconsistent with this would impute to the President designs of encroachment upon a co-ordinate branch of the government, which should not be lightly attributed to the Chief Magistrate of the nation.

When Congress assembled in December last the people of most of the States lately in rebellion had, under the advice of the President, organized local governments, and some of them had acceded to the terms proposed by him. In his annual message he stated, in general terms, what had been done, but he did not see fit to communicate the details for the information of Congress. While in this and in a subsequent message the President urged the speedy restoration of these States, and expressed the opinion that their condition was such as to justify their restoration, yet it is quite obvious that Congress must either have acted blindly on that opinion of the President, or proceeded to obtain the information requisite for intelligent action on the subject. The impropriety of proceeding wholly on the judgment of any one man, however exalted his station, in a matter involving the welfare of the republic in all future time, or of adopting any plan, coming from any source, without fully understanding all its bearings and comprehending its full effect, was apparent. The first step, therefore, was to obtain the required information. A call was accordingly made on the President for the information in his possession as to what had been done, in order that Congress might judge for itself as to the grounds of the belief expressed by him in the fitness of States recently in rebellion to participate fully in the conduct of national affairs. This information was not immediately communicated. When the response was finally made, some six weeks after your committee had been in actual session, it was found that the evidence upon which the President seemed to have based his suggestions was incomplete and unsatisfactory. . . .

Failing to obtain the desired information, and left to grope for light wherever it might be found, your committee did not deem it either advisable or safe to adopt, without further examination, the suggestions of the President, more especially as he had not deemed it expedient to remove the military force, to suspend martial law, or to restore the writ of *habeas corpus,* but still thought it necessary to exercise over the people of the rebellious States his military power and jurisdiction. This conclusion derived still greater force from the fact, undisputed, that in all these States, except Tennessee and perhaps Arkansas, the elections which were held for State officers and members of Congress had resulted, almost universally, in the defeat of candidates who had been true to the Union, and in the election of notorious and unpardoned rebels, men who could not take the prescribed oath of office, and who made no secret of their hostility to the government and the people of the United States. Under these circumstances, anything like hasty action would have been as dangerous as it was obviously unwise. It appeared to your committee that but one course remained, viz: to investigate carefully and thoroughly the state of feeling and opinion existing among the people of these States; to ascertain how far their pretended loyalty could be relied upon, and thence to infer whether it would be safe to admit them at once to a full participation in the government they had fought for four years to destroy. It was an equally important inquiry whether their restoration to their former relations with the United States should only be granted upon certain conditions and guarantees which would effectually secure the nation against a recurrence of evils so disastrous as those from which it had escaped at so enormous a sacrifice. . . .

A claim for the immediate admission of senators and representatives from the so-called Confederate States has been urged, which seems to your committee not to be founded either in reason or in law, and which cannot be passed without comment. Stated in a few words, it amounts to this: That inasmuch as the lately insurgent States had no legal right to separate themselves from the Union, they still retain their positions as States, and consequently the people thereof have a right to immediate representation in Congress without the imposition of any conditions whatever; and further, that until such admission Congress has no right to tax them for the support of the government. It has even been contended that until such admission all legislation affecting their interests is, if not unconstitutional, at least unjustifiable and oppressive.

It is believed by your committee that all these propositions are not only wholly untenable, but, if admitted, would tend to the destruction of the government.

It must not be forgotten that the people of these States, without justification or excuse, rose in insurrection against the United States. They deliberately abolished their State governments so far as the same connected them politically with the Union as members thereof under the Constitution. They deliberately renounced their allegiance to the federal government, and proceeded to establish an independent government for themselves. In the prosecution of this enterprise they seized the national forts, arsenals, dock-yards, and other public property within their borders, drove out from among them those who remained true to the Union, and heaped every imaginable insult and injury upon the United States and its citizens. Finally, they opened hostilities, and levied war against the government. They continued this war for four years with the most determined and malignant spirit, killing in battle, and otherwise, large numbers of loyal people, destroying the property of loyal citizens on the sea and on the land, and entailing on the government an enormous debt, incurred to sustain its rightful authority. Whether legally and constitutionally or not, they did, in fact, withdraw from the Union and made themselves subjects of another government of their own creation. And they only yielded when, after a long, bloody, and wasting war, they were compelled by utter exhaustion to lay down their arms; and this they did, not willingly, but declaring that they yielded because they could no longer resist, affording no evidence whatever of repentance for their crime, and expressing no regret, except that they had no longer the power to continue the desperate struggle.

It cannot, we think, be denied by any one, having a tolerable acquaintance with public law, that the war thus waged was a civil war of the greatest magnitude. The people waging it were necessarily subject to all the rules which, by the law of nations, control a contest of that character, and to all the legitimate consequences following it. One of those consequences was that, within the limits prescribed by humanity, the conquered rebels were at the mercy of the conquerors. That a government thus outraged had a most perfect right to exact indemnity for the injuries done, and security against the recurrence of such outrages in the future, would seem too clear for dispute. What the nature of that security should be, what proof should be required of a return to allegiance, what time should elapse before a people thus demoralized should be restored in full to the enjoyment of political rights and privileges, are questions for the law-making power to decide, and that decision must depend on grave considerations of the public safety and the general welfare.

It is moreover contended, and with apparent gravity, that, from the peculiar nature and character of our government, no such right on the part of the conqueror can exist; that from the moment when rebellion lays down its arms and actual hostilities cease, all political rights of rebellious communities are at once restored; that, because the people of a State of the Union were once an organized community within the Union, they necessarily so remain, and their right to be represented in Congress at any and all times, and to participate in the government of the country under all circumstances, admits of neither question nor dispute. If this is indeed true, then is the government of the United States powerless for its own protection, and flagrant rebellion, carried to the extreme of civil war, is a pastime which any State may play at, not only certain that it can lose nothing in any event, but may even be the gainer by defeat. If rebellion succeeds, it accomplishes its purpose and destroys the government. If it fails, the war has been barren of results, and the battle may be still fought out in the legislative halls of the country. Treason, defeated in the field, has only to take possession of Congress and the cabinet.

Your committee does not deem it either necessary or proper to discuss the question whether the late Confederate States are still States of this Union, or can even be otherwise. Granting this profitless abstraction about which so many words have been wasted, it by no means follows that the people of those States may not place themselves in a condition to abrogate the powers and privileges incident to a State of the Union, and deprive themselves of all pretence of right to exercise those powers and enjoy those privileges. A State within the Union has obligations to discharge as a member of the Union. It must submit to federal laws and uphold federal authority. It must have a government republican in form, under and by which it is connected with the general government, and through which it can discharge its obligations. It is more than idle, it is a mockery, to contend that a people who have thrown off their allegiance, destroyed the local government which bound their States to the Union as members thereof, defied its authority, refused to execute its laws, and abrogated every provision which gave them political rights within the Union, still retain, through all, the perfect and entire right to resume, at their own will and pleasure, all their privileges within the Union, and especially to participate in its government, and to control the conduct of its affairs. To admit such a principle for one moment would be to declare that treason is always master and loyalty a blunder. Such a principle is void by its very nature and essence, because inconsistent with the theory of government and fatal to its very existence.

On the contrary, we assert that no portion of the people of this country, whether in State or Territory, have the right, while remaining on its soil, to withdraw from or reject the authority of the United States. They must obey its laws as paramount, and acknowledge its jurisdiction. They have no right to secede; and while they can destroy their State governments, and place themselves beyond the pale of the Union, so far as the exercise of State privileges is concerned, they cannot escape the obligations imposed upon them by the Constitution and the laws, nor impair the exercise of national authority. The Constitution, it will be observed, does not act upon States, as such, but upon the people; while, therefore, the people cannot escape its authority, the States may, through the act of their people, cease to exist in an organized form, and thus dissolve their political relations with the United States. . . .

While thus exposing fallacies which, as your committee believe, are resorted to for the purpose of misleading the people and distracting their attention from the questions at issue, we freely admit that such a condition of things should be brought, if possible, to a speedy termination. It is most desirable that the Union of all the States should become perfect at the earliest moment consistent with the peace and welfare of the nation; that all these States should become fully represented in the national councils, and take their share in the legislation of the country. The possession and exercise of more than its just share of power by any section is injurious, as well to that section as to all others. Its tendency is distracting and demoralizing, and such a state of affairs is only to be tolerated on the ground of a necessary regard to the public safety. As soon as that safety is secured it should terminate.

Your committee came to the consideration of the subject referred to them with the most anxious desire to ascertain what was the condition of the people of the States recently in insurrection, and what, if anything, was necessary to be done before restoring them to the full enjoyment of all their original privileges. It was undeniable that the war into which they had plunged the country had materially changed their relations to the people of the loyal States. Slavery had been abolished by constitutional amendment. A large proportion of the population had become, instead of mere chattels, free men and citizens. Through all the past struggle these had remained true and loyal, and had, in large numbers, fought on the side of the Union. It was impossible to abandon them without securing them their rights as free men and citizens. The whole civilized world would have cried out against such base ingratitude, and the bare idea is offensive to all right-thinking men. Hence it became important to inquire what could be done to secure their rights, civil and political. It was evident to your committee that adequate security could only be found in appropriate constitutional provisions. By an original provision of the Constitution, representation is based on the whole number of free persons in each State, and three-fifths of all other persons. When all become free, representation for all necessarily follows. As a consequence the inevitable effect of the rebellion would be to increase the political power of the insurrectionary States, whenever they should be allowed to resume their positions as States of the Union. As representation is by the Constitution based upon population, your committee did not think it advisable to recommend a change of that basis. The increase of representation necessarily resulting from the abolition of slavery, was considered the most important element in the questions arising out of the changed condition of affairs, and the necessity for some fundamental action in this regard seemed imperative. It appeared to your committee that the rights of these persons by whom the basis of representation had been thus increased should be recognized by the general government. While slaves they were not considered as having any rights, civil or political. It did not seem just or proper that all the political advantages derived from their becoming free should be confined to their former masters, who had fought against the Union, and withheld from themselves, who had always been loyal. Slavery, by building up a ruling and dominant class, had produced a spirit of oligarchy adverse to republican institutions, which finally inaugurated civil war. The tendency of continuing the domination of such a class, by leaving it in the exclusive possession of political power, would be to encourage the same spirit, and lead to a similar result. Doubts were entertained whether Congress had power, even under the amended Constitution, to prescribe the qualifications of voters in a State, or could act directly on the subject. It was doubtful, in the opinion of your committee, whether the States would consent to surrender a power they had always exercised, and to which they were attached. As the best if not the only method of surmounting the difficulty, and as eminently just and proper in itself, your committee came to the conclusion that political power should be possessed in all the States exactly in proportion as the right of suffrage should be granted, without distinction of color or race. This it was thought would leave the whole question with the people of each State, holding out to all the advantage of increased political power as an inducement to allow all to participate in its exercise. Such a provision would be in its nature gentle and persuasive, and would lead, it was hoped, at no distant day, to an equal participation of all without distinction, in all the rights and privileges of citizenship, thus affording a full and adequate protection to all classes of citizens, since all would have, through the ballot-box, the power of self-protection.

Holding these views, your committee prepared an amendment

to the Constitution to carry out this idea, and submitted the same to Congress. Unfortunately, as we think, it did not receive the necessary constitutional support in the Senate, and therefore could not be proposed for adoption by the States. The principle involved in that amendment is, however, believed to be sound, and your committee have again proposed it in another form, hoping that it may receive the approbation of Congress. Your committee have been unable to find, in the evidence submitted to Congress by the President, under date of March 6, 1866, in compliance with the resolutions of January 5 and February 27, 1866, any satisfactory proof that either of the insurrectionary States, except, perhaps, the State of Tennessee, has placed itself in a condition to resume its political relations to the Union. The first step towards that end would necessarily be the establishment of a republican form of government by the people. It has been before remarked that the provisional governors, appointed by the President in the exercise of his military authority, could do nothing by virtue of the power thus conferred towards the establishment of a State government. They were acting under the War Department and paid out of its funds. They were simply bridging over the chasm between rebellion and restoration. And yet we find them calling conventions and convening legislatures. Not only this, but we find the conventions and legislatures thus convened acting under executive direction as to the provisions required to be adopted in their constitutions and ordinances as conditions precedent to their recognition by the President. The inducement held out by the President for compliance with the conditions imposed was, directly in one instance, and presumably, therefore, in others, the immediate admission of senators and representatives to Congress. The character of the conventions and legislatures thus assembled was not such as to inspire confidence in the good faith of their members. Governor Perry, of South Carolina, dissolved the convention assembled in that State before the suggestion had reached Columbia from Washington that the rebel war debt should be repudiated, and gave as his reason that it was a "revolutionary body." There is no evidence of the loyalty or disloyalty of the members of those conventions and legislatures except the fact of pardons being asked for on their account. Some of these States now claiming representation refused to adopt the conditions imposed. No reliable information is found in these papers as to the constitutional provisions of several of these States, while in not one of them is there the slightest evidence to show that these "amended constitutions," as they are called, have ever been submitted to the people for their adoption. In North Carolina alone an ordinance was passed to that effect, but it does not appear to have been acted on. Not one of them, therefore, has been ratified. Whether, with President Johnson, we adopt the theory that the old constitutions were abrogated and destroyed, and the people "deprived of all civil government," or whether we adopt the alternative doctrine that they were only suspended and were revived by tne suppression of the rebellion, the new provisions must be considered as equally destitute of validity before adoption by the people. If the conventions were called for the sole purpose of putting the State government into operation, they had no power either to adopt a new constitution or to amend an old one without the consent of the people. Nor could either a convention or a legislature change the fundamental law without power previously conferred. In the view of your committee, it follows, therefore, that the people of a State where the constitution has been thus amended might feel themselves justified in repudiating altogether all such unauthorized assumptions of power, and might be expected to do so at pleasure.

So far as the disposition of the people of the insurrectionary States, and the probability of their adopting measures conforming to the changed condition of affairs, can be inferred from the papers submitted by the President as the basis of his action, the prospects are far from encouraging. It appears quite clear that the anti-slavery amendments, both to the State and federal constitutions, were adopted with reluctance by the bodies which did adopt them, while in some States they have been either passed by in silence or rejected. The language of all the provisions and ordinances of these States on the subject amounts to nothing more than an unwilling admission of an unwelcome truth. As to the ordinance of secession, it is, in some cases, declared "null and void," and in others simply "repealed;" and in no instance is a refutation of this deadly heresy considered worthy of a place in the new constitution. . . .

It is quite evident from all these facts, and indeed from the whole mass of testimony submitted by the President of the Senate, that in no instance was regard paid to any other consideration than obtaining immediate admission to Congress, under the barren form of an election in which no precautions were taken to secure regularity of proceedings, or the assent of the people. No constitution has been legally adopted except, perhaps, in the State of Tennessee, and such elections as have been held were without authority of law. Your committee are accordingly forced to the conclusion that the States referred to have not placed themselves in a condition to claim representation in Congress, unless all the rules which have, since the foundation of the government, been deemed essential in such cases, should be disregarded.

It would undoubtedly be competent for Congress to waive all formalities and to admit these Confederate States to representation at once, trusting that time and experience would set all things right. Whether it would be advisable to do so, however, must depend upon other considerations of which it remains to treat. But it may well be observed, that the inducements to such a step should be of the very highest character. It seems to your committee not unreasonable to require satisfactory evidence that the ordinances and constitutional provisions which the President deemed essential in the first instance will be permanently adhered to by the people of the States seeking restoration, after being admitted to full participation in the government, and will not be repudiated when that object shall have been accomplished. And here the burden of proof rests upon the late insurgents who are seeking restoration to the rights and privileges which they willingly abandoned, and not upon the people of the United States who have never undertaken, directly or indirectly, to deprive them thereof. It should appear affirmatively that they are prepared and disposed in good faith to accept the results of the war, to abandon their hostility to the government, and to live in peace and and amity with the people of the loyal States, extending to all classes of of citizens equal rights and privileges, and conforming to the republican idea of liberty and equality. They should exhibit in their acts something more than an unwilling submission to an unavoidable necessity—a feeling, if not cheerful, certainly not offensive and defiant. And they should evince an entire repudiation of all hostility to the general government, by an acceptance of such just and reasonable conditions as that government snould think the public safety demands. Has this been done? Let us look at the facts shown by the evidence taken by the committee.

Hardly is the war closed before the people of these insurrectionary States come forward and haughtily claim, as a right, the privilege of participating at once in that government which they had for four years been fighting to overthrow. Allowed and encouraged by the Executive to organize State governments, they at once place in power leading rebels, unrepentant and unpardoned, excluding with contempt those who had manifested an attachment to the Union, and preferring, in many instances, those who had rendered themselves the most obnoxious. In the face of the law requiring an oath which would necessarily exclude all such men from federal offices, they elect, with very few exceptions, as senators and representatives in Congress men who had actively participated in the rebellion, insultingly denouncing the law as unconstitutional. It is only necessary to instance the election to the Senate of the late vice-president of the confederacy, a man who, against his own declared convictions, had lent all the weight of his acknowledged ability and his influence as a most prominent public man to the cause of the rebellion, and who, unpardoned rebel as he is, with that oath staring him in the face, had the assurance to lay his credentials on the table of the Senate. Other rebels of scarcely less note or notoriety were selected from other quarters. Professing no repentance, glorying apparently in the crime they had committed, avowing still, as the uncontradicted testimony of Mr. Stephens and many others proves, an adherence to the pernicious doctrine of secession, and declaring that they yielded only to necessity, they insist, with unanimous voice, upon their rights as States, and proclaim that they will submit to no conditions whatever as preliminary to their resumption of power under that Constitution which they still claim the right to repudiate.

Examining the evidence taken by your committee still further, in connexion with facts too notorious to be disputed, it appears that the southern press, with few exceptions, and those mostly of newspapers recently established by northern men, abounds with weekly and daily abuse of the institutions and people of the loyal States; defends the men who led, and the principles which incited, the rebellion; denounces and reviles southern men who adhered to the Union; and strives, constantly and unscrupulously, by every means in its power, to keep alive the fire of hate and discord between the sections; calling upon the President to violate his oath of office, overturn the government by force of arms, and drive the representatives of the people from their seats in Congress. The national banner is openly insulted, and the national airs scoffed at, not only by an ignorant populace, but at public meetings, and once, among other notable instances, at a dinner given in honor of a notorious rebel who had violated his oath and abandoned his flag. The same individual is elected to an important office in the leading city of his State, although an unpardoned rebel, and so offensive that the President refuses to allow him to enter upon his official duties. In another State the leading general of the rebel armies is openly nominated for governor by the speaker of the house of delegates, and the nomination is hailed by the people with shouts of satisfaction.

Looking still further at the evidence taken by your committee, it is found to be clearly shown by witnesses of the highest character and having the best means of observation, that the Freedmen's Bureau, instituted for the relief and protection of freedmen and refugees, is almost universally opposed by the mass of the population, and exists in an efficient condition only under military protection, while the Union men of the south are earnest in its defence, declaring with one voice that without its protection the colored people would not be permitted to labor at fair prices and could hardly live in safety. They also testify that without the protection of United States troops, Union men, whether of northern or southern origin, would be obliged to abandon their homes. The feeling in many portions of the country towards emancipated slaves, especially among the uneducated and ignorant, is one of vindictive and malicious hatred. This deep-seated prejudice against color is assiduously cultivated by the public journals, and leads to acts of cruelty, oppression, and murder, which the local authorities are at no pains to prevent or punish. There is no general disposition to place the colored race, constituting at least two-fifths of the population, upon terms even of civil equality. While many instances may be found where large planters and men of the better class accept the situation, and honestly strive to bring about a better order of things, by employing the freedmen at fair wages and treating them kindly, the general feeling and disposition among all classes are yet totally averse to the toleration of any class of people friendly to the Union, be they white or black; and this aversion is not unfrequently manifested in an insulting and offensive manner.

The witnesses examined as to the willingness of the people of the south to contribute, under existing laws, to the payment of the national debt, prove that the taxes levied by the United States will be paid only on compulsion and with great reluctance, while there prevails, to a considerable extent, an expectation that compensation will be made for slaves emancipated and property destroyed during the war. The testimony on this point comes from officers of the Union army, officers of the late rebel army, Union men of the southern States, and avowed secessionists, almost all of whom state that, in their opinion, the people of the rebellious States would, if they should see a prospect of success, repudiate the national debt.

While there is scarcely any hope or desire among leading men :o renew the attempt at secession at any future time, there is still, according to a large number of witnesses, including A. H. Stephens, who may be regarded as good authority on that point, a generally prevailing opinion which defends the legal right of secession, and upholds the doctrine that the first allegiance of the people is due to the States, and not to the United States. This belief evidently prevails among leading and prominent men as well as among the masses everywhere, except in some of the northern counties of Alabama and the eastern counties of Tennessee.

The evidence of an intense hostility to the federal Union, and an equally intense love of the late confederacy, nurtured by the war, is decisive. While it appears that nearly all are willing to submit, at least for the time being, to the federal authority, it is equally clear that the ruling motive is a desire to obtain the advantages which will be derived from a representation in Congress. Officers of the Union army on duty, and northern men who go south to engage in business, are generally detested and pro-scribed. Southern men who adhered to the Union are bitterly hated and relentlessly persecuted. In some localities prosecutions have been instituted in State courts against Union officers for acts done in the line of official duty, and similar prosecutions are threatened elsewhere as soon as the United States troops are removed. All such demonstrations show a state of feeling against which it is unmistakably necessary to guard.

The testimony is conclusive that after the collapse of the confederacy the feeling of the people of the rebellious States was that of abject submission. Having appealed to the tribunal of arms, they had no hope except that by the magnanimity of their conquerors their lives, and possibly their property, might be pre-served. Unfortunately, the general issue of pardons to persons who had been prominent in the rebellion, and the feeling of kindliness and conciliation manifested by the Executive, and very generally indicated through the northern press, had the effect to render whole communities forgetful of the crime they had committed, defiant towards the federal government, and re-gardless of their duties as citizens. The conciliatory measures of the government do not seem to have been met even half way. The bitterness and defiance exhibited toward the United States under such circumstances is without parallel in the history of the world. In return for our leniency we receive only an insulting denial of our authority. In return for our kind desire for the resumption of fraternal relations we receive only an insolent assumption of rights and privileges long since forfeited. The crime we have punished is paraded as a virtue, and the principles of republican government which we have vindicated at so terri-ble a cost are denounced as unjust and oppressive.

If we add to this evidence the fact that, although peace has been declared by the President, he has not, to this day, deemed it safe to restore the writ of *habeas corpus,* to relieve the insur-rectionary States of martial law, nor to withdraw the troops from many localities, and that the commanding general deems an increase of the army indispensable to the preservation of order and the protection of loyal and well-disposed people in the south, the proof of a condition of feeling hostile to the Union and dan-gerous to the government throughout the insurrectionary States would seem to be overwhelming.

With such evidence before them, it is the opinion of your committee—

I. That the States lately in rebellion were, at the close of the war, disorganized communities, without civil government, and without constitutions or other forms, by virtue of which political relations could legally exist between them and the federal government.

II. That Congress cannot be expected to recognize as valid the election of representatives from disorganized communities, which, from the very nature of the case, were unable to present their claim to representation under those established and recognized rules, the observance of which has been hitherto required.

III. That Congress would not be justified in admitting such communities to a participation in the government of the country without first providing such constitutional or other guarantees as will tend to secure the civil rights of all citizens of the republic; a just equality of representation; protection against claims founded in rebellion and crime; a temporary restoration of the right of suffrage to those who have not actively participated in the efforts to destroy the Union and overthrow the government, and the exclusion from positions of public trust of, at least, a portion of those whose crimes have proved them to be enemies to the Union, and unworthy of public confidence.

Your committee will, perhaps, hardly be deemed excusable for extending this report further; but inasmuch as immediate and unconditional representation of the States lately in rebellion is demanded as a matter of right, and delay and even hesitation is denounced as grossly oppressive and unjust, as well as unwise and impolitic, it may not be amiss again to call attention to a few undisputed and notorious facts, and the principles of public law applicable thereto, in order that the propriety of that claim may be fully considered and well understood. . . .

To ascertain whether any of the so-called Confederate States "are entitled to be represented in either house of Congress," the essential inquiry is, whether there is, in any one of them, a constituency qualified to be represented in Congress. The question how far persons claiming seats in either house possesses the credentials necessary to enable them to represent a duly qualified constituency is one for the consideration of each house separately, after the preliminary question shall have been finally determined.

We now propose to re-state, as briefly as possible, the general facts and principles applicable to all the States recently in rebellion:

FIRST. The seats of the senators and representatives from the so-called Confederate States became vacant in the year 1861, during the second session of the thirty-sixth Congress, by the voluntary withdrawal of their incumbents, with the sanction and by direction of the legislatures or conventions of their respective States. This was done as a hostile act against the Constitution and government of the United States, with a declared intent to overthrow the same by forming a southern confederation. This act of declared hostility was speedily followed by an organization of the same States into a confederacy, which levied and waged war, by sea and land, against the United States. This war continued more than four years, within which period the rebel armies besieged the national capital, invaded the loyal States, burned their towns and cities, robbed their citizens, destroyed more than 250,000 loyal soldiers, and imposed an increased national burden of not less than $3,500,000,000, of which seven or eight hundred millions have already been met and paid. From the time these confederated States thus withdrew their representation in Congress and levied war against the United States, the great mass of their people became and were insurgents, rebels, traitors, and all of them assumed and occupied the political, legal, and practical relation of enemies of the United States. This position is established by acts of Congress and judicial decisions, and is recognized repeatedly by the President in public proclamations, documents, and speeches.

SECOND. The States thus confederated prosecuted their war against the United States to final arbitrament, and did not cease until all their armies were captured, their military power destroyed, their civil officers, State and confederate, taken prisoners or put to flight, every vestige of State and confederate government obliterated, their territory overrun and occupied by the federal armies, and their people reduced to the condition of enemies conquered in war, entitled only by public law to such rights, privileges, and conditions as might be vouchsafed by the conqueror. This position is also established by judicial decisions, and is recognized by the President in public proclamations, documents, and speeches.

THIRD. Having voluntarily deprived themselves of representation in Congress for the criminal purpose of destroying the federal Union, and having reduced themselves, by the act of levying war, to the condition of public enemies, they have no right to complain of temporary exclusion from Congress; but, on the contrary, having voluntarily renounced the right to representation, and disqualified themselves by crime from participating in the government, the burden now rests upon them, before claiming to be reinstated in their former condition, to show that they are qualified to resume federal relations. In order to do this, they must prove that they have established, with the consent of the people, republican forms of government in harmony with the Constitution and laws of the United States, that all hostile purposes have ceased, and should give adequate guarantees against future treason and rebellion—guarantees which shall prove satisfactory to the government against which they rebelled, and by whose arms they were subdued.

FOURTH. Having, by this treasonable withdrawal from Congress, and by flagrant rebellion and war, forfeited all civil and political rights and privileges under the federal Constitution, they can only be restored thereto by the permission and authority of that constitutional power against which they rebelled and by which they were subdued.

FIFTH. These rebellious enemies were conquered by the people of the United States, acting through all the co-ordinate branches of the government, and not by the executive department alone. The powers of conqueror are not so vested in the President that he can fix and regulate the terms of settlement and confer congressional representation on conquered rebels and traitors. Nor can he, in any way, qualify enemies of the government to exercise its law-making power. The authority to restore rebels to political power in the federal government can be exercised only with the concurrence of all the departments in which political power is vested; and hence the several proclamations of the President to the people of the Confederate States cannot be considered as extending beyond the purposes declared, and can only be regarded as provisional permission by the commander-in-chief of the army to do certain acts, the effect and validity whereof is to be determined by the constitutional government, and not solely by the executive power.

SIXTH. The question before Congress is, then, whether conquered enemies have the right, and shall be permitted at their own pleasure and on their own terms, to participate in making laws for their conquerors; whether conquered rebels may change their theatre of operations from the battle-field, where they were defeated and overthrown, to the halls of Congress, and, through their representatives, seize upon the government which they fought to destroy; whether the national treasury, the army of the nation, its navy, its forts and arsenals, its whole civil administration, its credit, its pensioners, the widows and orphans of those who perished in the war, the public honor, peace and safety, shall all be turned over to the keeping of its recent enemies without delay, and without imposing such conditions as, in the opinion of Congress, the security of the country and its institutions may demand.

SEVENTH. The history of mankind exhibits no example of such madness and folly. The instinct of self-preservation protests against it. The surrender by Grant to Lee, and by Sherman to Johnston, would have been disasters of less magnitude, for new armies could have been raised, new battles fought, and the government saved. The anti-coercive policy, which, under pretext of avoiding bloodshed, allowed the rebellion to take form and gather force, would be surpassed in infamy by the matchless wickedness that would now surrender the halls of Congress to those so recently in rebellion until proper precautions shall have been taken to secure the national faith and the national safety.

EIGHTH. As has been shown in this report, and in the evidence submitted, no proof has been afforded to Congress of a constituency in any one of the so called Confederate States, unless we except the State of Tennessee, qualified to elect senators and representatives in Congress. No State constitution, or amendment to a State constitution, has had the sanction of the people. All the so-called legislation of State conventions and legislatures has been had under military dictation. If the President may, at his will, and under his own authority, whether as military commander or chief executive, qualify persons to appoint senators and elect representatives, and empower others to appoint and elect them, he thereby practically controls the organization of the legislative department. The constitutional form of government is thereby practically destroyed, and its powers absorbed in the Executive. And while your committee do not for a moment impute to the President any such design, but cheerfully concede to him the most patriotic motives, they cannot but look with alarm upon a precedent so fraught with danger to the republic.

NINTH. The necessity of providing adequate safeguards for the future, before restoring the insurrectionary States to a participation in the direction of public affairs, is apparent from the bitter hostility to the government and people of the United States yet existing throughout the conquered territory, as proved incontestably by the testimony of many witnesses and by undisputed facts.

TENTH. The conclusion of your committee therefore is, that the so-called Confederate States are not, at present, entitled to representation in the Congress of the United States; that, before allowing such representation, adequate security for future peace and safety should be required; that this can only be found in such changes of the organic law as shall determine the civil rights and privileges of all citizens in all parts of the republic, shall place representation on an equitable basis, shall fix a stigma upon treason, and protect the loyal people against future claims for the expenses incurred in support of rebellion and for manumitted slaves, together with an express grant of power in Congress to enforce those provisions. To this end they offer a joint resolution for amending the Constitution of the United States, and the two several bills designed to carry the same into effect, before referred to. . . .

5

Civil Rights for Freedmen

Civil Rights Act, 1866, and Fourteenth Amendment, 1866

One of the first tasks to which the Congress addressed itself was the question of civil rights for the Southern freedmen. Civil rights legislation that would provide national protection to the newly freed Negro was rendered all the more urgent by the passage in the South of the black codes. Early in the year, Illinois Senator Lyman Trumbull (1813–1896) introduced the first civil rights law of the reconstruction period. It passed quickly and by decisive margins. President Johnson vetoed the measure on the ground that it was both unconstitutional and unnecessary, but Congress was able to muster enough strength to override the veto. Johnson's arguments, however, produced some qualms in Congress and the necessity for a new Constitutional amendment was soon realized. The Fourteenth Amendment was formulated later in the spring of 1866 and by June had been passed and submitted to the states. The amendment included the substance of the Civil Rights Act, in an effort to protect that legislation from an adverse ruling by the Supreme Court, but it also represented an initial effort of the Republican majority to develop a Congressional program for reconstruction. The amendment was not finally ratified by the requisite number of states until 1868. For the story of the amendment's development and passage, see Joseph B. James, *The Framing of the Fourteenth Amendment* (Urbana, 1956). In the selections that follow, note (1) the citizenship provisions of both the Civil Rights Act and the Fourteenth Amendment; (2) the penalties established in the Act for the deprivation of civil rights; and (3) the "reconstruction" provisions of the amendment.

United States Statutes at Large, XIV (39th Congress, 1st–2nd Sessions, 1865–67), 27–29, 358–59.

CIVIL RIGHTS ACT OF 1866

An Act to protect all Persons in the United States in their Civil Rights, and furnish the Means of their Vindication.

Be it enacted by the Senate and House of Representatives of the United States of America in Congress assembled, That all persons born in the United States and not subject to any foreign power, excluding Indians not taxed, are hereby declared to be citizens of the United States; and such citizens, of every race and color, without regard to any previous condition of slavery or involuntary servitude, except as a punishment for crime whereof the party shall have been duly convicted, shall have the same right, in every State and Territory in the United States, to make and enforce contracts, to sue, be parties, and give evidence, to inherit, purchase, lease, sell, hold, and convey real and personal property, and to full and equal benefit of all laws and proceedings for the security of person and property, as is enjoyed by white citizens, and shall be subject to like punishment, pains, and penalties, and to none other, any law, statute, ordinance, regulation, or custom, to the contrary notwithstanding.

SECTION 2. *And be it further enacted,* That any person who, under color of any law, statute, ordinance, regulation, or custom, shall subject, or cause to be subjected, any inhabitant of any State or Territory to the deprivation of any right secured or protected by this act, or to different punishment, pains, or penalties on account of such person having at any time been held in a condition of slavery or involuntary servitude, except as a punishment for crime whereof the party shall have been duly convicted, or by reason of his color or race, than is prescribed for the punishment of white persons, shall be deemed guilty of a misdemeanor, and, on conviction, shall be punished by fine not exceeding one thousand dollars, or imprisonment not exceeding one year, or both, in the discretion of the court.

SECTION 3. *And be it further enacted,* That the district courts of the United States, within their respective districts, shall have, exclusively of the courts of the several States, cognizance of all crimes and offences committed against the provisions of this act, and also, concurrently with the circuit courts of the United States, of all causes, civil and criminal, affecting persons who are denied or cannot enforce in the courts or judicial tribunals of the State or locality where they may be any of the rights secured to them by the first section of this act; and if any suit or prosecution, civil or criminal, has been or shall be commenced in any State court, against any such person, for any cause whatsoever, or against any officer civil or military, or other person, for any arrest or imprisonment, trespasses, or wrongs done or committed by virtue or under color of authority derived from this act or the act establishing a Bureau for the relief of Freedmen and Refugees, and all acts amendatory thereof, or for refusing to do any act upon the ground that it would be inconsistent with this act, such defendant shall have the right to remove such cause for trial to the proper district or circuit court in the manner prescribed by the "Act relating to habeas corpus and regulating judicial proceedings in certain cases," approved March three, eighteen hundred and sixty-three, and all acts amendatory thereof. The jurisdiction in civil and criminal matters hereby conferred on the district and circuit courts of the United States shall be exercised and enforced in conformity with the laws of the United States, so far as such laws are suitable to carry the same into effect; but in all cases where such laws are not adapted to the object, or are deficient in the provisions necessary to furnish suitable remedies and punish offences against law, the common law, as modified and changed by the constitution and statutes of the State wherein the court having jurisdiction of the cause, civil or criminal, is held, so far as the same is not inconsistent with the Constitution and laws of the United States, shall be extended to and govern said courts in the trial and disposition of such cause, and, if of a criminal nature, in the infliction of punishment on the party found guilty.

SECTION 4. *And be it further enacted,* That the district attorneys, marshals, and deputy marshals of the United States, the commissioners appointed by the circuit and territorial courts of the United States, with powers of arresting, imprisoning, or bailing offenders against the laws of the United States, the officers and agents of the Freedmen's Bureau, and every other officer who may be specially empowered by the President of the United States, shall be, and they are hereby, specially authorized and required, at the expense of the United States, to institute proceedings against all and every person who shall violate the provisions of this act, and cause him or them to be arrested and imprisoned, or bailed, as the case may be, for trial before such court of the United States or territorial court as by this act has cognizance of the offence. And with a view to affording reasonable protection to all persons in their constitutional rights of equality before the law, without distinction of race or color, or previous condition of slavery or involuntary servitude, except as a punishment for crime, whereof the party shall have been duly convicted, and to the prompt discharge of the duties of this act, it shall be the duty of the circuit courts of the United States and the superior courts of the Territories of the United States, from time to time, to increase the number of commissioners, so as to afford a speedy and convenient means for the arrest and examination of persons charged with a violation of this act; and such commissioners are hereby authorized and required to exercise and discharge all the powers and duties conferred on them by this act, and the same duties with regard to offences created by this act, as they are authorized by law to exercise with regard to other offences against the laws of the United States.

SECTION 5. *And be it further enacted,* That it shall be the duty of all marshals and deputy marshals to obey and execute all warrants and precepts issued under the provisions of this act, when to them directed; and should any marshal or deputy marshal refuse to receive such warrant or other process when tendered, or to use all proper means diligently to execute the same, he shall, on conviction thereof, be fined in the sum of one thousand dollars, to the use of the person upon whom the accused is alleged to have committed the offence. And the better to enable the said commissioners to execute their duties faithfully and efficiently, in conformity with the Constitution of the United States and the requirements of this act, they are hereby authorized and empowered, within their counties respectively, to appoint, in writing, under their hands, any one or more suitable persons, from time to time, to execute all such warrants and other process as may be issued by them in the lawful performance of their respective duties; and the persons so appointed to execute any warrant or process as aforesaid shall have authority to summon and call to their aid the bystanders or posse comitatus of the proper county, or such portion of the land or naval forces of the United States, or of the militia, as may be necessary to the performance of the duty with which they are charged, and to insure a faithful observance of the clause of the Constitution which prohibits slavery, in conformity with the provisions of this act; and said warrants shall run and be executed by said officers anywhere in the State or Territory within which they are issued.

SECTION 6. *And be it further enacted,* That any person who shall knowingly and wilfully obstruct, hinder, or prevent any officer, or other person charged with the execution of any warrant or process issued under the provisions of this act, or any person or persons lawfully assisting him or them, from arresting any person for whose apprehension such warrant or process may have been issued, or shall rescue or attempt to rescue such person from the custody of the officer, other person or persons, or those lawfully assisting as aforesaid, when so arrested pursuant to the authority herein given and declared, or shall aid, abet, or assist any person so arrested as aforesaid, directly or indirectly, to escape from the custody of the officer or other person legally authorized as aforesaid, or shall harbor or conceal any person for whose arrest a warrant or process shall have been issued as aforesaid, so as to prevent his discovery and arrest after notice or knowledge of the fact that a warrant has been issued for the apprehension of such person, shall, for either of said offences, be subject to a fine not exceeding one thousand dollars, and imprisonment not exceeding six months, by indictment and conviction before the district court of the United States for the district in which said offence may have been committed, or before the proper court of criminal jurisdiction, if committed within any one of the organized Territories of the United States.

SECTION 7. *And be it further enacted,* That the district attorneys, the marshals, their deputies, and the clerks of the said district and territorial courts shall be paid for their services the like fees as may be allowed to them for similar services in other cases; and in all cases where the proceedings are before a commissioner, he shall be entitled to a fee of ten dollars in full for his services in each case, inclusive of all services incident to such arrest and examination. The person or persons authorized to execute the process to be issued by such commissioners for the arrest of offenders against the provisions of this act shall be entitled to a fee of five dollars for each person he or they may arrest and take before any such commissioner as aforesaid, with such other fees as may be deemed reasonable by such commissioner for such other additional services as may be necessarily performed by him or them, such as attending at the examination, keeping the prisoner in custody, and providing him with food and lodging during his detention, and until the final determination of such commissioner, and in general for performing such other duties as may be required in the premises; such fees to be made up in conformity with the fees usually charged by the officers of the courts of justice within the proper district or county, as near as may be practicable, and paid out of the Treasury of the United States on the certificate of the judge of the district within which the arrest is made, and to be recoverable from the defendant as part of the judgment in case of conviction.

SECTION 8. *And be it further enacted,* That whenever the President of the United States shall have reason to believe that offences have been or are likely to be committed against the provisions of this act within any judicial district, it shall be lawful for him, in his discretion, to direct the judge, marshal, and district attorney of such district to attend at such place within the district, and for such time as he may designate, for the purpose of the more speedy arrest and trial of persons charged with a violation of this act; and it shall be the duty of every judge or other officer, when any such requisition shall be received by him, to attend at the place and for the time therein designated.

SECTION 9. *And be it further enacted,* That it shall be lawful for the President of the United States, or such person as he may empower for that purpose, to employ such part of the land or naval forces of the United States, or of the militia, as shall be necessary to prevent the violation and enforce the due execution of this act.

SECTION 10. *And be it further enacted,* That upon all questions of law arising in any cause under the provisions of this act a final appeal may be taken to the Supreme Court of the United States.

THE FOURTEENTH AMENDMENT

Joint Resolution proposing an Amendment to the Constitution of the United States.

*Be it resolved by the Senate and House of Representatives of
the United States of America in Congress assembled,* (two thirds
of both Houses concurring.) That the following article be proposed to the legislatures of the several States as an amendment
to the Constitution of the United States, which, when ratified by
three fourths of said legislatures, shall be valid as part of the
Constitution, namely:—

ARTICLE XIV.

SECTION 1. All persons born or naturalized in the United States,
and subject to the jurisdiction thereof, are citizens of the United
States and of the State wherein they reside. No State shall make
or enforce any law which shall abridge the privileges or immunities of citizens of the United States; nor shall any State deprive
any person of life, liberty, or property, without due process of
law, nor deny to any person within its jurisdiction the equal
protection of the laws.

SECTION 2. Representatives shall be apportioned among the
several States according to their respective numbers, counting
the whole number of persons in each State, excluding Indians not
taxed. But when the right to vote at any election for the choice
of electors for President and Vice-President of the United States,
representatives in Congress, the executive and judicial officers
of a State, or the members of the legislature thereof, is denied to
any of the male inhabitants of such State, being twenty-one years
of age, and citizens of the United States, or in any way abridged,
except for participation in rebellion or other crime, the basis of
representation therein shall be reduced in the proportion which
the number of such male citizens shall bear to the whole number
of male citizens twenty-one years of age in such State.

SECTION 3. No person shall be a senator, or representative in
Congress, or elector of President and Vice-President, or hold any
office, civil or military under the United States, or under any
State, who having previously taken an oath, as a member of
Congress, or as an officer of the United States, or as a member of
any State legislature, or as an executive or judicial officer of any
State, to support the Constitution of the United States, shall have
engaged in insurrection or rebellion against the same, or given

aid or comfort to the enemies thereof. But Congress may by a vote of two thirds of each house remove such disability.

SECTION 4. The validity of the public debt of the United States, authorized by law, including debts incurred for payment of pensions and bounties for services in suppressing insurrection or rebellion, shall not be questioned. But neither the United States nor any State shall assume or pay any debt or obligation incurred in aid of insurrection or rebellion against the United States, or any claim for the loss or emancipation of any slave; but all such debts, obligations, and claims shall be held illegal and void.

SECTION 5. The Congress shall have power to enforce, by appropriate legislation, the provisions of this article.

6

Waving the Bloody Shirt

Oliver P. Morton Speaks at Indianapolis, 1866

The Congressional elections provided the first opportunity to take the issues of reconstruction directly to the people. President Johnson, anxious to secure support for his resistance to the Congressional program, embarked on a strenuous campaign tour on behalf of moderate and conservative candidates—the famous "swing around the circle." The Republicans themselves were far from idle. Victory for the party in the Congressional elections would bring a popular mandate for the more stringent and extreme program of reconstruction that many of the radicals had in mind. The stakes were considered high and the excitement of the campaign reflected its importance. Oliver Perry Morton (1823–1877), Indiana's wartime governor and an intense and bitter partisan, had taken a moderate position in the issues of reconstruction, hoping at one point to effect a compromise between Johnson and Congress. By the summer of 1866, he had begun to move to a more radical position. In his campaign speech in Indianapolis on June 20, Morton indulged in oratory that was to become characteristic of future Republican campaigns. Known as "waving the bloody shirt," this style of speaking sought to avoid the issues of reconstruction in favor of those of the war, and by keeping the war constantly before the people, persuade the voters to support the Republican party, the party of loyalty and Union. For further information on the relations between Johnson and Congress and on the elections of 1866, see LaWanda and John H. Cox, *Politics, Principle, and Prejudice, 1865–1866* (New York, 1963) and Howard K. Beale, *The Critical Year: A Study of Andrew Johnson and Reconstruction* (New York, 1930). In the following speech, note (1) the wartime role ascribed to Democrats; and (2) the nature of the invective used by the speaker.

William Dudley Foulke, *Life of Oliver P. Morton, Including His Important Speeches* (2 vols.; Indianapolis, 1899), I, 470–76.

"*The WAR* is over, the rebellion has been suppressed, the victory has been won, and now the question is presented to us at the coming election, whether the fruits of victory shall be preserved or lost.

It is beyond doubt that the temper of the Democratic party is not changed or improved since the termination of the war, but, on the contrary, it seems to have been greatly embittered by defeat in the field and at the ballot-box. Its sympathy with those who were lately in arms against the government is more boldly avowed than ever, and it becomes argumentative and enthusiastic in behalf of the right of secession and the righteousness of the rebellion. The true spirit of the Democratic party in Indiana has recently received a remarkable illustration that should command the solemn consideration of the people.

Some four or five weeks ago a convention was held in the city of Louisville, composed in large part of men who had been engaged in the rebel armies. These men, assembled in convention, proclaimed themselves members of the national Democratic party, and declared their unfaltering devotion to its time-honored principles. They vindicated the righteousness of the rebellion and declared their stern purpose to maintain at the ballot-box the sacred principles for which they had taken up arms. Prominent Indiana Democrats met with them in convention, mingled their tears with the tears of those who wept over Southern heroes; uttered glowing eulogies upon the memory of Stonewall Jackson and John Morgan, and reiterated the most treasonable doctrines, and to show the complete identity between this assembly of traitors and the Democratic party of Indiana, the Indianapolis *Herald,* the organ of the party, in the broadest and most unqualified manner, earnestly and enthusiastically indorsed these proceedings. . . .

The leaders, who are now managing the Democratic party in this state, are the men who, at the regular session of the legislature in 1861, declared that if an army went from Indiana to assist in putting down the then approaching rebellion it must first pass over their dead bodies.

They are the men who, in speeches and resolutions, proclaimed that "Southern defeats gave them no joy, and Northern disasters no sorrow." They are the men who exerted their influence to prevent their Democratic friends from going into the army, and who, by their incessant and venomous slanders against the government, checked the spirit of volunteering, and made drafting a necessity. And when the draft had thus been forced upon the country, their wretched subordinates, inspired by their devilish teachings, endeavored in many places by force of arms and the murder of enrolling officers, to prevent its execution.

They are the men who corresponded with the rebel leaders in the South, giving them full information of our condition, and assuring them that a revolution in public opinion was at hand, and that they had but to persevere a few months longer and the national government would fall to pieces of its own weight.

They are the men who, in the legislature of 1863, attempted to overturn the state government and establish a legislative revolution by seizing the military power of the state and transferring it to the hands of four state officers, three of whom were members of the treasonable society known as the "Sons of Liberty."

They are the men, who, having failed to overturn the state government by seizing the military power, determined to defeat its operations and bring about anarchy, by locking up the public treasure and thus withholding the money necessary to carry on the government.

They are the men who, for the purpose of private speculation, and of discrediting the state before the world, conspired to prevent the payment of the interest on the public debt by withholding, through a fraudulent lawsuit, the money received from taxes, paid for that very purpose. This lawsuit was smuggled through the circuit court and lodged in the Supreme Court before the minutes of the case had been read and signed by the circuit judge, or he had been made acquainted with its character, and it was hastily decided by the Supreme Court against the credit of the state.

They are the men who introduced and organized in this state that dangerous and wide-spread conspiracy first known as the "Knights of the Golden Circle," and afterwards as the "Sons of Liberty," which had for its purpose the overthrow of the state and national governments. Not all of them, it is true, belonged formally to this infamous order, but such as stood on the outside had knowledge of its existence, purposes and plans, and carefully concealing their knowledge, were ready to accept its work. To accomplish the hellish schemes of this conspiracy, military officers were appointed, military organizations created, arms and ammunition purchased in immense quantities and smug-

gled into the state, correspondence opened with rebel commanders and military combinations agreed upon, rebel officers and
agents introduced into the capital and concealed in hotels and
boardinghouses, and it was deliberately planned and agreed that,
upon a day fixed, they would suddenly rise and murder the executive, seize the arsenal with its arms and ammunition, and releas-
ing nine thousand rebel prisoners in Camp Morton, put arms into
their hands, and with their combined forces effect a military and
bloody revolution in the state. This dreadful scheme necessarily
involved murder, conflagration, robbery, and the commission of
every crime which makes black the chronicles of civil war, and
yet its authors and abettors, with the proofs of their guilt piled
mountain high, are again struggling for power and asking the
people to put into their guilty hands the government and prosperity of the state. Some of these men who are high in favor and
authority in their party, and are largely intrusted with its management, have heretofore occupied offices of great trust and responsibility in which they proved to be recreant and corrupt.

They are the men who, in the legislature of Indiana, bitterly
opposed and denounced every effort to confer the right of suffrage upon soldiers in the field who could not come home to vote.

They are the men who labored with devilish zeal to destroy the
ability of the government to carry on the war by depreciating its
financial credit. They assured the people that "greenbacks"
would die on their hands, and warned them solemnly against
government bonds, as a wicked device to rob them of their
money.

They are the men who refused to contribute to the Sanitary
Commission for the relief of sick and wounded soldiers, upon the
lying and hypocritical pretense that the contributions were consumed by the officers of the army.

They are the men who excused themselves from contributing
for the relief of soldiers' families at home by the infamous slan-
der that they were living better than they had ever done, and by
foul imputations on the chastity of soldiers' wives.

They are the men who declared in speeches and resolutions,
and by their votes in Congress, that not another man nor another
dollar should be voted to carry on a cruel war against their Southern brethren.

They are the men who, in the midst of the last great campaign of 1864—at the time when Sherman was fighting his way, step by step, from Chattanooga to Atlanta, and Grant was forcing Lee back into the defenses of Richmond in desperate and bloody battles from day to day; when the fate of the nation hung in the balance, and the world watched with breathless interest the gigantic struggle which was to settle the question of republican government—assembled in convention in Chicago and resolved that the war was a failure; that our cause was unjust, and that we ought to lay down our arms and sue for peace. It was a bold and desperate interference in behalf of the rebellion, at the very crisis of the fight. It was an insult to the loyal armies of the nation, so vast, malignant and deadly that language can convey no adequate idea of its wickedness. And in future times the historian will record the fact with astonishment that the government, at the most critical moment of its life, when a few hours, or a few days at the farthest, must determine whether it should live or die, could permit a large body of its enemies to meet upon its soil in peace and security and publish a flagrant manifesto in behalf of the rebellion.

Now, I do not mean to say that all the Democratic leaders have done all these things, but what I do say is this: that the men who have done these things are combined together, and constitute the real leaders of the Democratic party. The few moderate men of the party have been stripped of all power and influence, and are carried along merely for numbers and policy, while the living and aggressive element which controls it are the "Sons of Liberty" and those who acted in sympathy and concert with them.

They are the men who have perverted the word Democracy from its once honorable meaning to be a shield and cover for rebellion and for every crime that attaches to a causeless and atrocious civil war.

Every unregenerate rebel lately in arms against his government calls himself a Democrat.

Every bounty jumper, every deserter, every sneak who ran away from the draft calls himself a Democrat. Bowles, Milligan, Walker, Dodd, Horsey and Humphreys call themselves Democrats. Every "Son of Liberty" who conspired to murder, burn, rob arsenals and release rebel prisoners calls himself a Democrat.

John Morgan, Champ Ferguson, Wirtz, Payne and Booth proclaimed themselves Democrats. Every man who labored for the rebellion in the field, who murdered Union prisoners by cruelty and starvation, who conspired to bring about civil war in the loyal states, who invented dangerous compounds to burn steamboats and Northern cities, who contrived hellish schemes to introduce into Northern cities the wasting pestilence of yellow fever, calls himself a Democrat. Every dishonest contractor who has been convicted of defrauding the government, every dishonest paymaster or disbursing officer who has been convicted of squandering the public money at the gaming table or in gold gambling operations, every officer in the army who was dismissed for cowardice or disloyalty, calls himself a Democrat. Every wolf in sheep's clothing, who pretends to preach the gospel but proclaims the righteousness of man-selling and slavery; every one who shoots down negroes in the streets, burns negro school-houses and meeting-houses, and murders women and children by the light of their own flaming dwellings, calls himself a Democrat; every New York rioter in 1863 who burned up little children in colored asylums, who robbed, ravished and murdered indiscriminately in the midst of a blazing city for three days and nights, called himself a Democrat. In short, the Democratic party may be described as a common sewer and loathsome receptacle, into which is emptied every element of treason North and South, and every element of inhumanity and barbarism which has dishonored the age.

And this party, composed of the men and elements I have described, in defiance of truth and decency asserts that it is the special champion of the constitution and the Union, which but a short sixteen months ago it was in arms to destroy, and proclaims to an astonished world that the only effect of vanquishing armed rebels in the field is to return them to seats in Congress, and to restore them to political power. Having failed to destroy the constitution by force, they seek to do it by construction, and assume to have made the remarkable discovery that the rebels who fought to destroy the constitution were its true friends, and that the men who shed their blood and gave their substance to preserve it were its only enemies. . . .

Beware how you connect your fortunes with a decayed and

dishonored party, indelibly stained with treason, upon whose tombstone the historian will write, "false to liberty, false to its country, and false to the age in which it lived." The Democratic party has committed a crime for which history has no pardon, and the memories of men no forgetfulness; whose colors grow darker from age to age, and for which the execrations of mankind become more bitter from generation to generation. It committed treason against liberty in behalf of slavery; against civilization in behalf of barbarism, and its chronicles will be written in the volume which records the deeds of the most dangerous and malignant factions that have ever afficted government and retarded the progress of mankind. . . .

7

"No Chinese Wall Can Now Be Tolerated"

Frederick Douglass on Reconstruction, 1866

The decisive victories of Republican candidates in the fall of 1866 fore-shadowed a new and clear direction for reconstruction policies. President Johnson's appeals had failed to persuade the electorate that reconstruction had been accomplished under Presidential auspices and that the Southern states were now prepared to assume their rightful, and equal, places in the American Union. Radical Republicans, on the other hand, were jubilant, interpreting the election results as a repudiation of the President and a vigorous mandate for Congressional leadership. The second or "lame duck" session of the Thirty-ninth Congress assembled in December 1866; Johnson, ignoring the election returns, unwisely continued to defy Congressional leaders, and the session gave every indication of becoming a battleground between the Executive and Congress. As the nation's lawmakers gathered in Washington, Frederick Douglass (1817–1895), an ex-slave and the nation's most prominent Negro leader, urged swift and unequivocal action on Congress, in keeping with the demonstration of support received at the polls. The work of the previous session, he insisted, must be brought to fruition; the role of the Negro freedman in society must be made secure and the South "opened to the light of law and liberty." One way to achieve this was to give the Negro the vote. This, for Douglass, was the "central theme" of reconstruction. For a discussion of Douglass' activities during reconstruction, with a collection of his statements, see Philip S. Foner, *The Life and Writings of Frederick Douglass*, VI: "Reconstruction and After" (New York, 1955). A good biography of Douglass is Benjamin Quarles, *Frederick Douglass* (Washington, 1948). In the following article, note (1) Douglass' view of the importance of the Negro to a solution of the nation's troubles; (2) his argument for the enfranchisement of the Negro; and (3) his attitude toward President Johnson.

Frederick Douglass, "Reconstruction," *Atlantic Monthly,* XVIII (December 1866), 761–65.

THE ASSEMBLING of the Second Session of the Thirty-ninth Congress may very properly be made the occasion of a few earnest words on the already much-worn topic of reconstruction. Seldom has any legislative body been the subject of a solicitude more intense, or of aspirations more sincere and ardent. There are the best of reasons for this profound interest. Questions of vast moment, left undecided by the last session of Congress, must be manfully grappled with by this. No political skirmishing will avail. The occasion demands statesmanship.

Whether the tremendous war so heroically fought and so victoriously ended shall pass into history a miserable failure, barren of permanent results,—a scandalous and shocking waste of blood and treasure,—a strife for empire, as Earl Russell characterized it, of no value to liberty or civilization—an attempt to re-establish a Union by force, which must be the merest mockery of a Union,—an effort to bring under Federal authority States into which no loyal man from the North may safely enter, and to bring men into the national councils who deliberate with daggers and vote with revolvers, and who do not even conceal their deadly hate of the country that conquered them; or whether, on the other hand, we shall, as the rightful reward of victory over treason, have a solid nation, entirely delivered from all contradictions and social antagonisms, based upon loyalty, liberty, and equality, must be determined one way or the other by the present session of Congress. The last session really did nothing which can be considered final as to these questions. The Civil Rights Bill and the Freedmen's Bureau Bill and the proposed constitutional amendments, with the amendment already adopted and recognized as the law of the land, do not reach the difficulty, and cannot, unless the whole structure of the government is changed from a government by States to something like a despotic central government, with power to control even the municipal regulations of States, and to make them conform to its own despotic will. While there remains such an idea as the right of each State to control its own local affairs,—an idea, by the way, more deeply rooted in the minds of men of all sections of the country than perhaps any one other political idea,—no general assertion of human rights can be of any practical value. To change the character of the government at this point is neither possible nor desirable. All that is necessary to be done is to make the government consistent with itself, and render the rights of the States compatible with the sacred rights of human nature.

The arm of the Federal government is long, but it is far too short to protect the rights of individuals in the interior of distant States. They must have the power to protect themselves, or they will go unprotected, spite of all the laws the Federal government can put upon the national statute-book.

Slavery, like all other great systems of wrong, founded in the depths of human selfishness, and existing for ages, has not neglected its own conservation. It has steadily exerted an influence upon all around it favorable to its own continuance. And to-day it is so strong that it could exist, not only without law, but even against law. Custom, manners, morals, religion, are all on its side everywhere in the South; and when you add the ignorance and servility of the ex-slave to the intelligence and accustomed authority of the master, you have the conditions, not out of which slavery will again grow, but under which it is impossible for the Federal government to wholly destroy it, unless the Federal government be armed with despotic power, to blot out State authority, and to station a Federal officer at every cross-road. This, of course, cannot be done, and ought not even if it could. The true way and the easiest way is to make our government entirely consistent with itself, and give to every loyal citizen the elective franchise,—a right and power which will be ever present, and will form a wall of fire for his protection.

One of the invaluable compensations of the late Rebellion is the highly instructive disclosure it made of the true source of danger to republican government. Whatever may be tolerated in monarchical and despotic governments, no republic is safe that tolerates a privileged class, or denies to any of its citizens equal rights and equal means to maintain them. What was theory before the war has been made fact by the war.

There is cause to be thankful even for rebellion. It is an impressive teacher, though a stern and terrible one. In both characters it has come to us, and it was perhaps needed in both. It is an instructor never a day before its time, for it comes only when all other means of progress and enlightenment have failed. Whether the oppressed and despairing bondman, no longer able to repress his deep yearnings for manhood, or the tyrant, in his pride and impatience, takes the initiative, and strikes the blow for a firmer hold and a longer lease of oppression, the result is the same,—society is instructed, or may be.

Such are the limitations of the common mind, and so thoroughly engrossing are the cares of common life, that only the few among men can discern through the glitter and dazzle of present prosperity the dark outlines of approaching disasters, even though they may have come up to our very gates, and are already within striking distance. The yawning seam and corroded bolt conceal their defects from the mariner until the storm calls all hands to the pumps. Prophets, indeed, were abundant before the war; but who cares for prophets while their predictions remain unfulfilled, and the calamities of which they tell are masked behind a blinding blaze of national prosperity?

It is asked, said Henry Clay, on a memorable occasion, Will slavery never come to an end? That question, said he, was asked fifty years ago, and it has been answered by fifty years of unprecedented prosperity. Spite of the eloquence of the earnest Abolitionists,—poured out against slavery during thirty years,—even they must confess, that, in all the probabilities of the case, that system of barbarism would have continued its horrors far beyond the limits of the nineteenth century but for the Rebellion, and perhaps only have disappeared at last in a fiery conflict, even more fierce and bloody than that which has now been suppressed.

It is no disparagement to truth, that it can only prevail where reason prevails. War begins where reason ends. The thing worse than rebellion is the thing that causes rebellion. What that thing is, we have been taught to our cost. It remains now to be seen whether we have the needed courage to have that cause entirely removed from the Republic. At any rate, to this grand work of national regeneration and entire purification Congress must now address itself, with full purpose that the work shall this time be thoroughly done. The deadly upas, root and branch, leaf and fibre, body and sap, must be utterly destroyed. The country is evidently not in a condition to listen patiently to pleas for postponement, however plausible, nor will it permit the responsibility to be shifted to other shoulders. Authority and power are here commensurate with the duty imposed. There are no cloud-flung shadows to obscure the way. Truth shines with brighter light and intenser heat at every moment, and a country torn and rent and bleeding implores relief from its distress and agony.

If time was at first needed, Congress has now had time. All the requisite materials from which to form an intelligent judgment are now before it. Whether its members look at the origin, the progress, the termination of the war, or at the mockery of a peace now existing, they will find only one unbroken chain of argument in favor of a radical policy of reconstruction. For the omissions of the last session, some excuses may be allowed. A treacherous President stood in the way; and it can be easily seen how reluctant good men might be to admit an apostasy which involved so much of baseness and ingratitude. It was natural that they should seek to save him by bending to him even when he leaned to the side of error. But all is changed now. Congress knows now that it must go on without his aid, and even against his machinations. The advantage of the present session over the last is immense. Where that investigated, this has the facts. Where that walked by faith, this may walk by sight. Where that halted, this must go forward, and where that failed, this must succeed, giving the country whole measures where that gave us half-measures, merely as a means of saving the elections in a few doubtful districts. That Congress saw what was right, but distrusted the enlightenment of the loyal masses; but what was forborne in distrust of the people must now be done with a full knowledge that the people expect and require it. The members go to Washington fresh from the inspiring presence of the people. In every considerable public meeting, and in almost every conceivable way, whether at court-house, school-house, or cross-roads, in doors and out, the subject has been discussed, and the people have emphatically pronounced in favor of a radical policy. Listening to the doctrines of expediency and compromise with pity, impatience, and disgust, they have everywhere broken into demonstrations of the wildest enthusiasm when a brave word has been spoken in favor of equal rights and impartial suffrage. Radicalism, so far from being odious, is now the popular passport to power. The men most bitterly charged with it go to Congress with the largest majorities, while the timid and doubtful are sent by lean majorities, or else left at home. The strange controversy between the President and Congress, at one time so threatening, is disposed of by the people. The high reconstructive powers which he so confidently, ostentatiously, and haughtily claimed, have been disallowed, denounced, and utterly repudiated; while those claimed by Congress have been confirmed.

Of the spirit and magnitude of the canvass nothing need be said. The appeal was to the people, and the verdict was worthy of the tribunal. Upon an occasion of his own selection, with the advice and approval of his astute Secretary, soon after the members of Congress had returned to their constituents, the President quitted the executive mansion, sandwiched himself between two recognized heroes,—men whom the whole country delighted to honor,—and, with all the advantage which such company could give him, stumped the country from the Atlantic to the Mississippi, advocating everywhere his policy as against that of Congress. It was a strange sight, and perhaps the most disgraceful exhibition ever made by any President; but, as no evil is entirely unmixed, good has come of this, as from many others. Ambitious, unscrupulous, energetic, indefatigable, voluble, and plausible,— a political gladiator, ready for a "set-to" in any crowd,—he is beaten in his own chosen field, and stands to-day before the country as a convicted usurper, a political criminal, guilty of a bold and persistent attempt to possess himself of the legislative powers solemnly secured to Congress by the Constitution. No vindication could be more complete, no condemnation could be more absolute and humiliating. Unless reopened by the sword, as recklessly threatened in some circles, this question is now closed for all time.

Without attempting to settle here the metaphysical and somewhat theological question (about which so much has already been said and written), whether once in the Union means always in the Union,—agreeably to the formula, Once in grace always in grace,—it is obvious to common sense that the rebellious States stand to-day, in point of law, precisely where they stood when, exhausted, beaten, conquered, they fell powerless at the feet of Federal authority. Their State governments were overthrown, and the lives and property of the leaders of the Rebellion were forfeited. In reconstructing the institutions of these shattered and overthrown States, Congress should begin with a clean slate, and make clean work of it. Let there be no hesitation. It would be a cowardly deference to a defeated and treacherous President, if any account were made of the illegitimate, one-sided, sham governments hurried into existence for a malign purpose in the absence of Congress. These pretended governments, which were never submitted to the people, and from participation in which four millions of the loyal people were excluded by Presidential order, should now be treated according to their true character, as shams and impositions, and supplanted by true and legitimate governments, in the formation of which loyal men, black and white, shall participate.

It is not, however, within the scope of this paper to point out the precise steps to be taken, and the means to be employed. The people are less concerned about these than the grand end to be attained. They demand such a reconstruction as shall put an end to the present anarchical state of things in the late rebellious States,—where frightful murders and wholesale massacres are perpetrated in the very presence of Federal soldiers. This horrible business they require shall cease. They want a reconstruction such as will protect loyal men, black and white, in their persons and property; such a one as will cause Northern industry, Northern capital, and Northern civilization to flow into the South, and make a man from New England as much at home in Carolina as elsewhere in the Republic. No Chinese wall can now be tolerated. The South must be opened to the light of law and liberty, and this session of Congress is relied upon to accomplish this important work.

The plain, common-sense way of doing this work, as intimated at the beginning, is simply to establish in the South one law, one government, one administration of justice, one condition to the exercise of the elective franchise, for men of all races and colors alike. This great measure is sought as earnestly by loyal white men as by loyal blacks, and is needed alike by both. Let sound political prescience but take the place of an unreasoning prejudice, and this will be done.

Men denounce the negro for his prominence in this discussion; but it is no fault of his that in peace as in war, that in conquering Rebel armies as in reconstructing the rebellious States, the right of the negro is the true solution of our national troubles. The stern logic of events, which goes directly to the point, disdaining all concern for the color or features of men, has determined the interests of the country as identical with and inseparable from those of the negro.

The policy that emancipated and armed the negro—now seen to have been wise and proper by the dullest—was not certainly more sternly demanded than is now the policy of enfranchisement. If with the negro was success in war, and without him failure, so in peace it will be found that the nation must fall or flourish with the negro.

Fortunately, the Constitution of the United States knows no distinction between citizens on account of color. Neither does it know any difference between a citizen of a State and a citizen of the United States. Citizenship evidently includes all the rights of citizens, whether State or national. If the Constitution knows none, it is clearly no part of the duty of a Republican Congress now to institute one. The mistake of the last session was the attempt to do this very thing, by a renunciation of its power to secure political rights to any class of citizens, with the obvious purpose to allow the rebellious States to disfranchise, if they should see fit, their colored citizens. This unfortunate blunder must now be retrieved, and the emasculated citizenship given to the negro supplanted by that contemplated in the Constitution of the United States, which declares that the citizens of each State shall enjoy all the rights and immunities of citizens of the several States,—so that a legal voter in any State shall be a legal voter in all the States.

8

Congressional Reconstruction

The Reconstruction Acts of 1867–1868

When Congress met in December 1866, Republican leaders sought to translate the recent election returns into positive policy. The first order of business was to replace the Presidential program for reconstruction with one that reflected the views of the majority in Congress. Unlike the Presidential plan, Congressional reconstruction did not emerge as a single, coherent program but was rather embodied in a series of laws and amendments, some of them hurriedly and loosely drawn, the result of an evolutionary development that had been going on since the first confrontations between Congress and the President during the preceding session. Congressional reconstruction also reflected a compromise between the severe proposals of some Radical Republicans and the less stringent suggestions of the moderates in the party; Democrats, weak and few in numbers, consistently opposed the acts. The first Reconstruction Act, passed on March 2, 1867, over the President's veto, declared that no legal governments existed in the South (the final death blow to the Presidential plan) and divided the South into ten military districts, each to be commanded by a general officer in the Army. The commander of each district was charged with overseeing the steps by which each Southern state could return to the Union. Three weeks later, a supplementary act was passed, again over Johnson's veto, providing additional details for the readmission of Southern states. The third and fourth Reconstruction Acts were later passed to clarify the provisions of the first two. These four pieces of legislation, in their aggregate, formed the basis for Congress' program; many other laws dealing with various aspects of Southern reconstruction were passed but the essential characteristics of Congressional attitudes were reflected in these four initial efforts. In the acts that follow, note (1) the extent of the powers of the military commanders; (2) the steps by which a state could be readmitted to the Union; (3) the provision for Negro suffrage ; and (4) the treatment of former Confederates.

United States Statutes at Large, XIV, 428–29; XV, 2–4, 14–16, 41.

FIRST RECONSTRUCTION ACT,

March 2, 1867
An Act to provide for the more efficient Government of the Rebel States.

WHEREAS no legal State governments or adequate protection for life or property now exists in the rebel States of Virginia, North Carolina, South Carolina, Georgia, Mississippi, Alabama, Louisiana, Florida, Texas, and Arkansas; and whereas it is necessary that peace and good order should be enforced in said States until loyal and republican State governments can be legally established: Therefore,

Be it enacted . . ., That said rebel States shall be divided into military districts and made subject to the military authority of the United States as hereinafter prescribed, and for that purpose Virginia shall constitute the first district; North Carolina and South Carolina the second district; Georgia, Alabama, and Florida the third district; Mississippi and Arkansas the fourth district; and Louisiana and Texas the fifth district.

SECTION 2. *And be it further enacted,* That it shall be the duty of the President to assign to the command of each of said districts an officer of the army, not below the rank of brigadier-general, and to detail a sufficient military force to enable such officer to perform his duties and enforce his authority within the district to which he is assigned.

SECTION 3. *And be it further enacted,* That it shall be the duty of each officer assigned as aforesaid, to protect all persons in their rights of person and property, to suppress insurrection, disorder, and violence, and to punish, or cause to be punished, all disturbers of the public peace and criminals; and to this end he may allow local civil tribunals to take jurisdiction of and to try offenders, or, when in his judgment it may be necessary for the trial of offenders, he shall have power to organize military commissions or tribunals for that purpose, and all interference under color of State authority with the exercise of military authority under this act, shall be null and void.

SECTION 4. *And be it further enacted,* That all persons put under military arrest by virtue of this act shall be tried without unnecessary delay, and no cruel or unusual punishment shall be inflicted, and no sentence of any military commission or tribunal hereby authorized, affecting the life or liberty of any person, shall be executed until it is approved by the officer in command of the district, and the laws and regulations for the government of the army shall not be affected by this act, except in so far as they conflict with its provisions: *Provided,* That no sentence of death under the provisions of this act shall be carried into effect without the approval of the President.

SECTION 5. *And be it further enacted,* That when the people of any one of said rebel States shall have formed a constitution of government in conformity with the Constitution of the United States in all respects, framed by a convention of delegates elected by the male citizens of said State, twenty-one years old and upward, of whatever race, color, or previous condition, who have been resident in said State for one year previous to the day of such election, except such as may be disfranchised for participation in the rebellion or for felony at common law, and when such constitution shall provide that the elective franchise shall be enjoyed by all such persons as have the qualifications herein stated for electors of delegates, and when such constitution shall be ratified by a majority of the persons voting on the question of ratification who are qualified as electors for delegates, and when such constitution shall have been submitted to Congress for examination and approval, and Congress shall have approved the same, and when said State, by a vote of its legislature elected under said constitution, shall have adopted the amendment to the Constitution of the United States, proposed by the Thirty-ninth Congress, and known as article fourteen and when said article shall have become a part of the Constitution of the United States said State shall be declared entitled to representation in Congress, and senators and representatives shall be admitted therefrom on their taking the oath prescribed by law, and then and thereafter the preceding sections of this act shall be inoperative in said State: *Provided,* That no person excluded from the privilege of holding office by said proposed amendment to the Constitution of the United States, shall be eligible to election as a member of the convention to frame a constitution for any of said rebel States, nor shall any such person vote for members of such convention.

SECTION 6. *And be it further enacted,* That, until the people of said rebel States shall be by law admitted to representation in the Congress of the United States, any civil governments which may exist there in shall be deemed provisional only, and in all respects subject to the paramount authority of the United States at any time to abolish, modify, control, or supersede the same; and in all elections to any office under such provisional governments all persons shall be entitled to vote, and none others, who are entitled to vote, under the provisions of the fifth section of this act; and no persons shall be eligible to any office under any such provisional governments who would be disqualified from holding office under the provisions of the third article of said constitutional amendment.

SECOND RECONSTRUCTION ACT,

March 23, 1867

An Act supplementary to an Act entitled "An Act to provide for the more efficient Government of the Rebel States," passed March second, eighteen hundred and sixty-seven, and to facilitate Restoration.

Be it enacted . . ., That the first day of September, eighteen hundred and sixty-seven, the commanding general in each district defined by an act entitled "An act to provide for the more efficient government of the rebel States," passed March second, eighteen hundred and sixty-seven, shall cause a registration to be made of the male citizens of the United States, twenty-one years of age and upwards, resident in each county or parish in the State or States included in his district, which registration shall include only those persons who are qualified to vote for delegates by the act aforesaid, and who shall have taken and subscribed the following oath or affirmation: "I, —— ——, do solemnly swear (or affirm), in the presence of Almighty God, that I am a citizen of the State of ——; that I have resided in said State for ——months next preceding this day, and now reside in the county of——, or the parish of——, In said State (as the case may be); that I am twenty-one years old; that I have not been disfranchised for participation in any rebellion or civil war against the United States, or for felony committed against the laws of any State or of the United States; that I have never been a member of any State legislature, nor held any executive or judicial office in any State, and afterwards engaged in insurrection or rebellion against the United States, or given aid or comfort to the enemies thereof; that I have never taken an oath as a member of Congress of the United States, or as an officer of the United States, or as a member of any State legislature, or as an executive or judicial officer of any State, to support the Constitution of the United States, and afterwards engaged in insurrection or rebellion against the United States, or given aid or comfort to the enemies thereof; that I will faithfully support the Constitution and obey the laws of the United States, and will, to the best of my ability, encourage others so to do, so help me God"; which oath or affirmation may be administered by any registering officer.

SECTION 2. *And be it further enacted,* That after the completion of the registration hereby provided for in any State, at such time and places therein as the commanding general shall appoint and direct, of which at least thirty days' public notice shall be given, an election shall be held of delegates to a convention for the purpose of establishing a constitution and civil government for such State loyal to the Union, said convention in each State, except Virginia, to consist of the same number of members as the most numerous branch of the State legislature of such State in the year eighteen hundred and sixty, to be apportioned among the several districts, counties, or parishes of such State by the commanding general, giving to each representation in the ratio of voters registered as aforesaid as nearly as may be. The convention in Virginia shall consist of the same number of members as represented the territory now constituting Virginia in the most numerous branch of the legislature of said State in the year eighteen hundred and sixty, to be apportioned as aforesaid.

SECTION 3. *And be it further enacted,* That at said election the registered voters of each State shall vote for or against a convention to form a constitution therefor under this act. . . . Those voting in favor of such a convention shall have written or printed on the ballots by which they vote for delegates, as aforesaid, the words "For a convention," and those voting against such a convention shall have written or printed on such ballots the words

"Against a convention." The persons appointed to superintend said election, and to make return of the votes given thereat, as herein provided, shall count and make return of the votes given for and against a convention; and the commanding general to whom the same shall have been returned shall ascertain and declare the total vote in each State for and against a convention. If a majority of the votes given on that question shall be for a convention, then such a convention shall be held as hereinafter provided; but if a majority of said votes shall be against a convention, then no such convention shall be held under this act: *Provided,* That such convention shall not be held unless a majority of all such registered voters shall have voted on the question of holding such convention.

SECTION 4. *And be it further enacted,* That the commanding general of each district shall appoint as many boards of registration as may be necessary, consisting of three loyal officers or persons, to make and complete the registration, superintend the election, and make return to him of the votes, lists of voters, and of the persons elected as delegates by a plurality of the votes cast at said election; and upon receiving said returns he shall open the same, ascertain the persons elected as delegates, according to the returns of the officers who conducted said election, and make proclamation thereof; and if a majority of the votes given on that question shall be for a convention, the commanding general, within sixty days from the date of election, shall notify the delegates to assemble in convention, at a time and place to be mentioned in the notification, and said convention, when organized, shall proceed to frame a constitution and civil government according to the provisions of this act, and the act to which it is supplementary; and when the same shall have been framed, said constitution shall be submitted by the convention for ratification to the persons registered under the provisions of this act at an election to be conducted by the officers or persons appointed or to be appointed by the commanding general, as hereinbefore provided, and to be held after the expiration of thirty days from the date of notice thereof, to be given by said convention; and the returns thereof shall be made to the commanding general of the district.

SECTION 5. *And be it further enacted,* That if, according to said returns, the constitution shall be ratified by a majority of the votes of the registered electors qualified as herein specified, cast at said election, at least one half of all the registered voters voting upon the question of such ratification, the president of the convention shall transmit a copy of the same, duly certified, to the President of the United States, who shall forthwith transmit the same to Congress, if then in session, and if not in session, then immediately upon its next assembling; and if it shall moreover appear to Congress that the election was one at which all the registered and qualified electors in the State had an opportunity to vote freely and without restraint, fear, or the influence of fraud, and if the Congress shall be satisfied that such constitution meets the approval of a majority of all the qualified electors in the State, and if the said constitution shall be declared by Congress to be in conformity with the provisions of the act to which this is supplementary, and the other provisions of said act shall have been complied with, and the said constitution shall be approved by Congress, the State shall be declared entitled to representation, and senators and representatives shall be admitted therefrom as therein provided.

SECTION 6. *And be it further enacted,* That all elections in the States mentioned in the said "Act to provided for the more efficient government of the rebel States," shall, during the operation of said act, be by ballot; and all officers making the said registration of voters and conducting said elections shall, before entering upon the discharge of their duties, take and subscribe the oath prescribed by the act approved July second, eighteen hundred and sixty-two, entitled "An act to prescribe an oath of office": *Provided,* That if any person shall knowingly and falsely take and subscribe any oath in this act prescribed, such person so offending and being thereof duly convicted shall be subject to the pains, penalties, and disabilities which by law are provided for the punishment of the crime of wilful and corrupt perjury.

SECTION 7. *And be it further enacted,* That all expenses incurred by the several commanding generals, or by virtue of any orders issued, or appointments made, by them, under or by virtue of this act, shall be paid out of any moneys in the treasury not otherwise appropriated.

SECTION 8. *And be it further enacted,* That the convention for each State shall prescribe the fees, salary, and compensation to be paid to all delegates and other officers and agents herein authorized or necessary to carry into effect the purposes of this act not herein otherwise provided for, and shall provide for the levy and collection of such taxes on the property in such State as may be necessary to pay the same.

SECTION 9. *And be it further enacted,* That the word "article," in the sixth section of the act to which this is supplementary, shall be construed to mean "section."

THIRD RECONSTRUCTION ACT,

July 19, 1867

An Act supplementary to an Act entitled "An Act to provide for the more efficient Government of the Rebel States," passed the second day of March, eighteen hundred and sixty-seven, and the Act supplementary thereto, passed on the twenty-third day of March, eighteen hundred and sixty-seven.

Be it enacted . . ., That it is hereby declared to have been the true intent and meaning . . . [of the acts of March 2 and March 23, 1867] . . . , that the governments then existing in the rebel States of Virginia, North Carolina, South Carolina, Georgia, Mississippi, Alabama, Louisiana, Florida, Texas, and Arkansas were not legal State governments; and that thereafter said governments, if continued, were to be continued subject in all respects to the military commanders of the respective districts, and to the paramount authority of Congress.

SECTION 2. *And be it further enacted,* That the commander of any district named in said act shall have power, subject to the disapproval of the General of the army of the United States, and to have effect till disapproved, whenever in the opinion of such commander the proper administration of said act shall require it, to suspend or remove from office, or from the performance of official duties and the exercise of official powers, any officer or person holding or exercising, or professing to hold or exercise, any military office or duty in such district under any power, election, appointment or authority derived from, or granted by, or claimed under, any so-called State or the government thereof, or any municipal or other division thereof, and upon such suspension or removal such commander, subject to the disapproval of the General as aforesaid, shall have power to provide from time to time for the performance of the said duties of such officer or person so suspended or removed, by the detail of some competent officer or soldier of the army, or by the appointment of some other person, to perform the same, and to fill vacancies occasioned by death, resignation, or otherwise.

SECTION 3. *And be it further enacted,* That the General of the army of the United States shall be invested with all the powers of suspension, removal, appointment, and detail granted in the preceding section to district commanders.

SECTION 4. *And be it further enacted,* That the acts of the officers of the army already done in removing in said districts persons exercising the functions of civil officers, and appointing others in their stead, are hereby confirmed: *Provided,* That any person heretofore or hereafter appointed by any district commander to exercise the functions of any civil office, may be removed either by the military officer in command of the district, or by the General of the army. And it shall be the duty of such commander to remove from office as aforesaid all persons who are disloyal to the government of the United States, or who use their official influence in any manner to hinder, delay, prevent, or obstruct the due and proper administration of this act and the acts to which it is supplementary.

SECTION 5. *And be it further enacted,* That the boards of registration provided for in the act . . . [of March 23, 1867] . . . , shall have power, and it shall be their duty before allowing the registration of any person, to ascertain, upon such facts or information as they can obtain, whether such person is entitled to be registered under said act, and the oath required by said act shall not be conclusive on such question, and no person shall be registered unless such board shall decide that he is entitled thereto; and such board shall also have power to examine, under oath, (to be administered by any member of such board,) any one touching the qualification of any person claiming registration; but in every case of refusal by the board to register an applicant, and in every case of striking his name from the list as hereinafter provided, the board shall make a note or memorandum, which shall

be returned with the registration list to the commanding general
of the district, setting forth the grounds of such refusal or such
striking from the list: *Provided,* That no person shall be disqualified as member of any board of registration by reason of
race or color.

Section 6. *And be it further enacted,* That the true intent and
meaning of the oath prescribed in said supplementary act is,
(among other things,) that no person who has been a member of
the legislature of any State, or who has held any executive or
judicial office in any State, whether he has taken an oath to
support the Constitution of the United States or not, and whether
he was holding such office at the commencement of the rebellion,
or had held it before, and who has afterwards engaged in insurrection or rebellion against the United States, or given aid or
comfort to the enemies thereof, is entitled to be registered or to
vote; and the words "executive or judicial office in any State" in
said oath mentioned shall be construed to include all civil offices
created by law for the administration of any general law of a
State, or for the administration of justice.

Section 7. *And be it further enacted,* That the time for comp-
leting the original registration provided for in said act may, in
the discretion of the commander of any district, be extended to
the first day of October, eighteen hundred and sixty-seven; and
the boards of registration shall have power, and it shall be their
duty, commencing fourteen days prior to any election under said
act, and upon reasonable public notice of the time and place
thereof, to revise, for a period of five days, the registration lists,
and upon being satisfied that any person not entitled thereto has
been registered, to strike the name of such person from the list,
and such person shall not be allowed to vote. And such board
shall also, during the same period, add to such registry the names
of all persons who at that time possess the qualifications required by said act who have not been already registered; and no
person shall, at any time, be entitled to be registered or to vote
by reason of any executive pardon or amnesty for any act or
thing which, without such pardon or amnesty, would disqualify
him from registration or voting.

Section 8. *And be it further enacted,* That section four of said
last-named act shall be construed to authorize the commanding

general named herein, whenever he shall deem it needful, to remove any member of a board of registration and to appoint another in his stead, and to fill any vacancy in such board.

SECTION 9. *And be it further enacted,* That all members of said boards of registration and all persons hereafter elected or appointed to office in said military districts, under any so-called State or municipal authority, or by detail or appointment of the district commanders, shall be required to take and to subscribe the oath of office prescribed by law for officers of the United States.

SECTION 10. *And be it further enacted,* That no district commander or member of the board of registration, or any of the officers or appointees acting under them, shall be bound in his action by any opinion of any civil officer of the United States.

SECTION 11. *And be it further enacted,* That all the provisions of this act and of the acts to which this is supplementary shall be construed liberally, to the end that all the intents thereof may be fully and perfectly carried out.

FOURTH RECONSTRUCTION ACT,

March 11, 1868

An Act to amend the Act passed March twenty-third, eighteen hundred and sixty-seven, entitled "An Act supplementary to An Act to provide for the more efficient government of the rebel States; passed March second, eighteen hundred and sixty-seven, and to facilitate their Restoration."

Be it enacted . . . , That hereafter any election authorized by the act [of March 23, 1867] . . . , shall be decided by a majority of the votes actually cast; and at the election in which the question of the adoption or rejection of any constitution is submitted, any person duly registered in the State may vote in the election district where he offers to vote when he has resided therein for ten days next preceding such election, upon presentation of his certificate of registration, his affidavit, or other satisfactory evidence, under such regulations as the district commanders may prescribe.

SECTION 2. *And be it further enacted,* That the constitutional convention of any of the States mentioned in the acts to which this is amendatory may provide that at the time of voting upon the ratification of the constitution the registered voters may vote also for members of the House of Representatives of the United States, and for all elective officers provided for by the said constitution; and the same election officers who shall make the return of the votes cast on the ratification or rejection of the constitution, shall enumerate and certify the votes cast for members of Congress.

9

A Southern Reply to Congressional Reconstruction

Benjamin H. Hill's Speech in Atlanta, 1867

The passage of the Reconstruction Acts, the elimination of the Presidential reconstruction governments, and the imposition of military rule on the South deeply shocked the Southern people. Misled in part by President Johnson's unrealistic appraisals of the situation and his constant assurance, they had been confident that the day was close at hand when the Southern states would resume their former places in the Union. When Congress passed the Reconstruction Acts, Southern bitterness against the radicals became widespread and intense. Many Southerners, declaring that their armies had surrendered in 1865 on the basis of Lincoln's reconstruction plans, charged the North with perfidy and betrayal. Probably the most outspoken and influential critic of Congressional reconstruction was Georgia's Benjamin Harvey Hill (1823–1882). Hill, a strong Unionist and opponent of secession before the war, had nevertheless served in the Confederate States Senate throughout the conflict, earning the reputation of a champion and defender of the Jefferson Davis administration. After a brief incarceration after the war, he was paroled by President Johnson and returned to private life in Georgia, but the Reconstruction Acts thrust him once more into political life. The speech that follows, delivered in Atlanta on July 16, 1867, signaled his return to politics and formed the basis for Hill's aggressive opposition to radical reconstruction during the following years. In 1875 he was elected to the lower house of Congress, and two years later became one of Georgia's United States senators. For a sound biographical study of Hill, see Haywood J. Pierce, *Benjamin H. Hill, Secession and Reconstruction* (Chicago, 1928). In the speech that follows, note (1) the grounds of Hill's objections to the Reconstruction Acts; (2) why he thinks Congressional reconstruction will fail; (3) the action he advises Georgians to take and (4) his advice to the Negroes.

Benjamin H. Hill, Jr., *Senator Benjamin H. Hill of Georgia: His Life, Speeches and Writings* (Atlanta: H. C. Hudgins & Co., 1891), 294–307.

> *LADIES and Fellow-citizens:* Human governments, like everything else human, naturally tend to decay. They can only be preserved by constant watchfulness,

77648

courage, and adherence to correct principles. These remarks apply with unusual force to free governments, which are the most difficult of all to maintain. If we, the people of the United States, were the first in history who had attempted the experiment of living under a democratic or republican form of government, we might be excused if we failed to discover the symptoms of approaching death, and to apply the remedies to preserve our liberty and the blessings we have heretofore enjoyed. But we are not the first who have made this experiment. Other peoples and nations, for thousands of years, have had commonwealths, republics, and democracies, which have risen and fallen times almost without number. I but assert a great truth—one which finds no contradiction or exception in all history—when I say that the great leading and substantial causes of the decay of freedom in all countries, have ever been the same. How inexcusable must we be if we fail to discover the symptoms, and how cowardly and recreant if we fail to apply the proper remedy to prevent so foul a death!

No people ever commenced to build up a free government under such favorable auspices as we. What a climate, soil, variety of productions, and material resources do we possess; and what an ancestry and what a common struggle for liberty did our fathers pass through! Did any people ever before commence with such advantages? Rome commenced as a small city, and was despised by the barbarians around it. She extended her power by her arms and increased till at last she became mistress of the world. We commenced with such a people, country, and productions as no people ever had before, and we had fewer dissensions and elements of discord than any people ever suffered from; and Providence, as if to separate us from the crimes and corrupting influences of the old world, spread out this great continent before us, with the wide sea to separate us from them, with no influence of monarchy and oppressive systems to threaten or make war upon us. If we fail, it will be by our own folly. What excuse can we render to our posterity and to the world if we, in this day, with the lessons of history before us, allow free institutions to perish on this continent? And our race will have been the soonest run. We have not yet lived a century. It is but seventy-eight years since the Constitution was framed, and but ninety-one years since independence was declared by our fathers, while the commonwealth of Rome lived four hundred years before the measures which produced her decay were proposed. What a spectacle! The best people, the richest soil, the most valuable productions, established as if by the Providence of God, as a new era in the history of the world—and bidding fair to be the shortest lived of any free government in the history of nations!

There is no difficulty whatever—and I assert it without fear of contradiction—in discovering when and how a nation is dying. I cannot now go into an analysis of all the symptoms of national decay and death. It is only important to present the leading one, which controls all others—which existing, produces all others, and which, being remedied, cures all others. Then hear it: the great symptom of the decay and death of a government is the disregard of the fundamental law of the government. Whenever a people come to treat lightly their own fundamental law, they have arrived at the most dangerous point that is possible short of entire destruction. Republics above all other kind of governments are maintained by respect for law. If the people of the United States fail to have a sacred regard for their own law—which is not, like that of other nations, to be ascertained by argument, by decisions, or by searching, but is a plain and wisely written Constitution—they will deserve that awful fate that awaits them; and he who disregards its plain language has no excuse to shield himself from the infamy of a traitor. Old as it is—trampled upon, torn, and tattered as it is, it is still the Constitution of our country and the law of our country. I charge before Heaven and the American people this day, that every evil by which we have been afflicted is attributable directly to the violation of the Constitution. Tinkers may work, quacks may prescribe, and demagogues may deceive, but I declare to you that there is no remedy for us, and no hope to escape the threatened evils, but in adhering to the Constitution.

Fellow-citizens, pardon me while I say that in presenting my views, I think of no living man, individually, to whom my remarks are to apply. I have come to talk freely to you about the dangers of the country. Little minds ascribe ascribe little objects to those whose views they do not agree with, and he has attained an unenviable reputation whose friends say,"You mean him,"

when I am speaking of treachery and showing the evil consequences of a certain line of policy. I have no personal attacks to
make on an enemy even if I have one. God knows, if I could, with
my own hands, I would gladly place a crown of imperishable
honor on the brow of my most bitter foe, if I could thereby rescue
my country from the perils that environ it! But if I have an
enemy, and have a vindictive spirit, and desired him to become
forever infamous, I could ask no more of him than that he should
support the hellish schemes of those who are now seeking to
subvert the Constitution and destroy our liberty. He is digging a
grave for himself which posterity will never water with a tear.
Let him alone. I have come to discuss the present phase of the
revolution.

We have had a war which raged furiously for four years. It
originated simply in a difference of opinion as to our rights under
the Constitution. This difference existed from the first. It existed
among the framers of the Constitution. It could not be settled by
argument, and an appeal was made to the sword. In was an open,
manly fight. There was nothing secret or ambiguous in the issue.
It was waged by men influenced, in the masses, by patriotic emo-
tions on both sides; and it was not to destroy the Constitution, but
to assert on each side their different views. On our side it was
asserted that the States were separate and independent sov-
ereignties, and that the Constitution was a compact, which each
party was at liberty to dissolve at will, and so we seceded and
declared ourselves out of the Union. On the other hand, it was
contended that we were not out of the Union—notwithstanding
our secession acts; and that the Constitution was not a compact,
but a binding law upon the States resulting from a compact, and
therefore no one of the number could dissolve the connection at
will. Upon this issue we went to war. The war was fought till we
laid down our arms and agreed to what our enemies said—that
we were in the Union.

But there is now another question to settle. It is still within
the range of argument. Its proportions are huge. The issues are
startling. It is not a difference of opinion as to what the Constitution means, and what are our rights under it; but its object is
plainly, unmistakably, to set aside the Constitution and provide
something else. I have never doubted that we were coming to this

issue. In speeches made by me, five, six, eight, and ten years ago, I predicted this, and every page of our history since that time has verified the correctness of the prediction. The people of the North honestly love the Constitution, but the leaders there hate it and intend to destroy it, and the convulsion through which we have passed has thrown the opportunity of making the effort into their hands, and the present military bills, and the one which is not yet promulgated as law, are the means adopted to accomplish their design. These bills are proposed for our acceptance. There is a remarkable feature in these measures, that while force is employed to execute them, they are yet nominally submitted to us for our acceptance or rejection.

I object to the whole scheme, because it is unconstitutional. A distinguished man—pardon me, I ought to say a notorious individual—said to me a few days ago, that I ought not to waste time to prove the unconstitutionality of these measures—a thing which every man, woman, and child in the country knew—and yet he was for accepting! He spoke truthfully. That tottering, gray-haired candidate in Pennsylvania for perpetual infamy, [Thaddeus Stevens (1792–1868)] who is building for himself a monument of malignity that will overtop the pyramids of Egypt, said the Constitution had nothing to do with it. I shall never get done shuddering, and horrors will never cease to rise up in my mind, when I see men taking an oath to support the Constitution, and then legislating to put in force measures which are outside of it. A great many of our own people flippantly say the Constitution is dead. Then your rights and hopes for the future, and all hope for your children are dead. I ask every man, if the Constitution is dead, why are we always, every day, and at every new step, required to take an oath to support it?

Now, I affirm that these military bills are not only contrary to the Constitution, but directly in the face of the amnesty oath you were required to take after the surrender. The government thought proper, in accepting your submission, to take your oath to support the Constitution of the United States and the Union of the States. Why was that oath required if the Constitution was dead?

But it is said the Constitution does not apply to us. Then don't swear to support it.

But it is said again that we are not in the Union. Then why swear to support the Union of these States? What "Union" does that mean? When you took that oath, was it the Union of the Northern States alone that you swore to support? What business have you with that Union? No, it is the Union of all the States known to the Constitution that you have sworn to support.

But they say that oath was prescribed by the President, and that he is not loyal. Then I must answer a fool according to his folly, and a traitor according to his treason. What do they require who passed these bills—this military Juggernaut? They require every man who registers his name to vote, to swear to support the Constitution, and counsel and persuade others to do so—and still it is said the Constitution has nothing to do with it! They say the scheme is outside of the Constitution, and yet, in the process of carrying it out, they require an oath to support the Constitution and to counsel and persuade others to do so! That is more than Mr. Johnson ever required in the oath which he prescribed.

It is my business to support the Constitution, and my duty and pleasure to persuade others to do so. Some of you who favor the acceptance of the military bills take an oath to this effect, and still intend to vote for a convention which you admit to be ordered contrary to the Constitution! How is this? If you have a conscience, I have said enough. If you vote for the convention you are perjured! Oh! I pity the race of colored people who have never been taught what an oath is nor what the Constitution means. They are drawn up by a selfish conclave of traitors to inflict a death-blow upon the life of the republic by swearing them into a falsehood! They are to begin their political life by perjury to accomplish treason! I would not visit the penalty upon them. They are neither legally nor morally responsible, but it is you— educated, designing white men—who thus devote yourselves to the unholy work—who are the guilty parties? You prate about your loyalty! I look you in the eye and denounce you! You are morally and legally perjured traitors! You perjure yourselves and perjure the poor negro to help your treason! You can't escape it! You may boast of it now, while passion is ripe, but the time will come when the very thought will wither your soul and make you hide from the face of mankind.

I shall discharge the obligation of the amnesty oath. It required me to support the Constitution and the emancipation of the negro, and I do. I will not bind my soul to a new slavery, to hell, by violating it. I talk plainly, but I simply want to strike through the incrustation of the hardened conscience, and make men feel and realize their true situation.

I have proved that these military bills violate the Constitution, and that you, in carrying them out, violate it and your amnesty oath and your registry oath. And what is your purpose? It must be a great good you seek to induce you to commit so much crime and folly.

Sometimes men wink at what is, by strict technicalities, wrong in the individual, to accomplish some great good to the public. I do not recognize the correctness of such action; but what do you propose by trampling upon the Constitution and violating your own solemn oaths? Is it to save the State and preserve liberty? This is not the object, but the purpose is as infamous as the measure resorted to to effect it. You first propose to abrogate your State governments by authority of the so-called Congress—a mere conclave of a portion of the members of that body. By whom is this dictated? The principle that whoever forms a government should form it for themselves as well as for others, is a correct one; but the men who propose this for us do not live in any of the ten States to be affected by their legislation. It is not made to suit either black or white, or any other class of our people, but to suit themselves, while they are not affected by it; and if you act upon their proposition, in a manner to suit yourselves, you will not be accepted by them; nay, you violate the Constitution to subvert the government. And by carrying out these measures you disfranchise your own people. Suppose we concede, for argument, that it is right to enfranchise all the negroes; if this be right, by what principle of law or morals do we disfranchise the white people? "Oh, but," you say, "the whites have been rebels." Then they should all be disfranchised, and not a part of them. Besides, the government you are to frame is to be a civil government and last for all time and for peace, when there can be no rebels. I see it stated that General Sickles has advised that the disfranchising feature be repealed or modified, and for the reason that the enfranchised class are not fit to fill the offices. Well, if he has done so, he has acted wisely, and has shown himself capable of appreciating one truth. And it is a great truth—one that will hide a multitude of sins; and it might be well for his fame if this recommendation alone could be remembered of his administration. In the face of the fact that a republican government can rest upon and be perpetuated only by the virtue and intelligence of the people, you propose to exclude the most intelligent from participating in the government forever!

You will by these measures inaugurate a war of races. A people who will abrogate their own government and disfranchise the most intelligent of them at the dictation of those who are not to be affected thereby, and live under the dictation of a foreign power, have no conscience; but if you have a conscience I hope to reach it. By all you hold dear I warn you that by accepting these military bills you inaugurate a measure that will exterminate the African race. Some of you who have come among us are taking the negro by the arm—telling him that you are his friend, and that you gave him his liberty! Ye hypocrites! Ye whited sepulchers!! Ye mean in your hearts to deceive and buy up the negro vote for your own benefit. The negroes know no better; but I would ask them: If these men are faithless to the Constitution of the country, how can they be faithful to you?

Yet these men admit in the very act that they are disregarding the Constitution! They take an oath to support it with the purpose and intent formed beforehand to violate it, and vote for measures contrary to it! They are not fit to be trusted by any animal, dog or man! Such a man would betray his pointer, and such a woman sell her poodle! They are not capable of being the friends of anybody but themselves. I don't pity the whites so much who are to suffer by these measures. "You knew your duty and did it not," and if you are beaten with many stripes we have the authority of Scripture for saying that your punishment is just; but to see the Africans led off by a claptrap which they don't understand, and used because they don't understand it, and thus led to the slaughter by men who are faithless to every principle—under the belief that they are being elevated and exercising God-given rights—is enough to make any man feel sick at heart and experience the deepest pity for the unfortunate race.

This is not the first time that such things have been attempted.

Unfortunately, there have before been both fools and knaves in the world, and some of you, it would seem, will not learn wisdom from the lessons of the past. If the Constitution is dead, we are outside of it, and, pray, what government have we? We have nothing, in that case, but the will of an unlawful conclave, and don't you know this means only anarchy, and then despotism and tyranny? What inducement is held out to you to accept their propositions? You say it is to get back into the Union! And for this you are willing to submit to disfranchisement and the inauguration of a policy that tends to a war of races! all to get back into the Union—just where you are already, and always were!

What do you want to get back into that sort of a Union for? If you are not now in it, what can you expect by getting in such as they present to you? You say it is to get representation in the Union! Is not Kentucky in the Union? Has she any representation? The telegraph informs us that a resolution has been introduced into the so-called Congress making inquiries whether Maryland, Delaware, and Kentucky have State governments or not! Are you so stupid as not to see what all this means? The result will be the substitution of the Radical party for all governments, both State and Federal; and the substitution of Radical will for all law! Take that home with you and digest it. That's where you are going! Kentucky is excluded from representation because it is alleged her representatives were voted for by disloyal men. What is meant by disloyal? Every man who does not support the Radical party will soon be declared disloyal, and every State which does not vote the Radical ticket will be disloyal, and her government illegal. I tell you, unless patriotism shall wake up from the stun which the horrid confusion of war has given it, the Radical party will be our only government, and Radical will our only law.

I look for this revolution to go on. Whoever thinks this war upon the Constitution will stop with the ten States is a madman, or a simpleton to be pitied, or a knave to be despised. I have expected them to take charge of Connecticut because she dared to elect a governor that did not agree with the Radical party; and sure enough Sumner in a late letter strikes that keynote. He says a similar bill for all the States is a short cut to universal suffrage. The so-called Congress immediately on its meeting took charge of Kentucky and excluded her whole delegation with one exception. If they can reject these, they can reject every one who differs with them, and they will do so; and they will receive only those who agree with them. These they will receive. I care not what may have been their sins heretofore; if the very worst Secessionist in all the land will whine around the streets and say he is Radical now, he is as good as the saints in heaven for Radical purposes. They care not for race or color, nor for antecedents; if you now favor Radical schemes you are loyal, and if you oppose them you are disloyal!

But you say you are in favor of going into the Union, because if you do not your property will be confiscated. A gentleman of this city a few days ago said to me that he was in favor of the acceptance of these military bills because he thought it the best we could do. I said to him: "You do not say that for yourself, but for your brick stores!" But, you are not half so wise as you are knavish! You would lose the Constitution and the country to save your brick stores, and thus, by your very course, you will lose your brick stores also! I am ashamed to talk or use arguments about confiscation in time of peace! It is a war power, not known to international law except as a war power, to be used only in time of war, upon an enemy's goods! Confiscation in time of peace is neither more nor less than robbery!

But you say they have all the power and they will exercise it, unless we do as they bid us. And will you, in this case, *abandon your only protection?* It is like going out into the highway and surrendering your purse to the robber to keep him from taking it. . . .

But I will dwell no more on this subject. Confiscation is the law of enemies in war, and in peace it is the law of the robber. If they have the will to rob you, you will never escape by submitting to their power. If you submit, give up the law and substitute the will of the robber; he boldly avows that it is his purpose not to give the black man his rights, but to bring about such measures and so to shape things as to perpetuate the rule of the Radical party! Every man who joins the party, and can satisfy them that he will sincerely help in this work, will be accepted. They will put their arms around your necks and call you brothers. You can make a friend of the devil upon these same terms, and there is but little difference between them. If you please the one you will go to the other, and I am not sure but you will get what you deserve; but I object to your taking the country with you.

But, oh! it is sad to see the Constitution trampled upon and the country destroyed, only to perpetuate their hellish dynasty; and then to see some of our own people join in this unholy work, calling upon us to submit and become the agents of our own dishonor! This is sad, sorrowful, and fills me with shame!

These bills propose at every step to abrogate the Constitution —trample upon the State and its laws—to blot out every hope— to perjure every man who accepts them, with every principle of honor, justice, and safety disregarded, trampled upon, and despised—all to perpetuate the power of their wicked authors. Can this scheme succeed? Will it succeed? That is the question. I feel truly thankful in my heart that I have an answer which lifts my soul amid all the gloom and apprehension of the hour. Some of you may not appreciate it, but to me it is the only oasis in this desert. This scheme will never, never succeed, and I proclaim its ultimate failure to-day in your hearing. I know that some think it will. The air is full of the words of those who proclaim that there is no power to prevent it. Men have before this been weak and foolish, and cowards and traitors have before believed as you talk now, but I have a reason for the faith that is in me, which is absolutely sublime in the strength of its foundations.

First. It will fail because it is not possible to perpetuate a government of force under the forms of a democracy. It may take some time to comprehend this thought, but you will not forget it. That which is now proposed is *force.* It is proposed by men who do not live in this State, and whose agents do not live here; and it is sought to be accomplished by military power, but under the pretense of your sanction—not to please yourselves, but them. There is not an instance in history where a government of force has been perpetuated under the forms of free institutions. It is an impossibility, and can never succeed.

Second. But it is sought to be accomplished by deceit and fraud, which cannot much longer escape detection. The masses of the people of the North love the Constitution, and fought for it and the Union, but the leaders did not fight for it, and do not love it; and they now seek to destroy it under pretense that we must give some further guarantee for our future good behavior than merely supporting the Constitution. As soon as the means by which their deceit and fraud have been covered up are removed, the scheme will be crushed to death by the people. It is a double-shaped monster, like the sentinel at Hell-gate, which can live nowhere except in a political pandemonium.

And what must be the results? I do not say we will come out of all this with free institutions preserved, but this scheme can never succeed. A despotism over the whole country and over all the people, guilty and innocent alike, may ensue. You will fail, but you may bring ruin upon all. Whenever you pull down the temple of liberty, you also will be crushed by the fall. You cannot level or lower us and elevate yourselves. We must either all rise or all go down together. Despotism may come, empires may rise and fall among us, but whether they do or not, we shall not have the reïgn of a Radical party. Understand me: If I say a man cannot live high up in the air, I do not mean he cannot go up in a balloon and remain for a time, or if I say a man cannot live under water, I do not say he cannot go down in a diving bell and remain a while; but the Radicals will as certainly fail to perpetuate their power under this scheme, as that a man will fail who attempts to dwell in the air, or drown who makes his home under water. Such a government would be unnatural—a political monstrosity—and cannot possibly last; but you may destroy the forms as well as the principles of free government, and then you will have a monarchy, an autocracy, an empire, or a despotism, as the case may be.

This very scheme was attempted in Rome by much better men than you Radicals are, and for a much better reason than you give. It is not original with you. You are but plagiarizing traitors at best, and get your scheme from the criminals of long ago. If I did steal, I would try to steal something better and from a more respectable source.

If you will examine, and compare with former times, the productions of such men as Stevens, Phillips, and Sumner, and the lesser followers and second-hand plagiarizers down South, you will find all their miserable jargon about "liberty and equality," the "natural right of man," and "the born right of manhood's suffrage," are borrowed from the men who fomented social and civil wars in Rome, and which have been repeated in every age since, by those who have no statesmanship but the devilish ability of exciting ignorant men to cut each other's throats. . . .

It may be that we of the United States have been so crazy in leaving the Constitution—the only ark of safety—that our Heavenly Father has doomed us to perish, but I am gratified with a hope that it is not so. If not, there is but one method for our rescue, and that is by a prompt restoration of the Constitution. Will it come? Will we escape an agrarian war, with resulting despotism, and save our institutions for our children? I hope we shall. I believe we shall. Though a great effort is being made—a designed effort—to destroy us as Rome was destroyed, I believe the effort will fail. I have great faith in the Anglo-Saxon blood. I derive great encouragement from Anglo-Saxon history. Our liberty was not born in a day. It is not the work of one generation. It is the fruit of a hundred struggles, and its guarantees have been perfecting for eight hundred years. Many have been the efforts to destroy it. . . .

I tell you the American people will not always be deceived. They will rise in defense of their Constitution—and traitors will tremble. They who rallied three million strong to defeat what they considered an armed assault on the Constitution and Union, will not sleep until a few hundred traitors from behind the masked battery of Congressional oaths and deceptive pretensions of loyalty shall utterly batter down the Constitution and Union forever. I warn you, boastful, vindictive Radicals, by the history of your own fathers, by every instinct of manhood, by every right of liberty, by every impulse of justice, that the day is coming when you will feel the power of an outraged and betrayed people. Go on confiscating! Arrest without warrant or probable cause; destroy *habeas corpus;* deny trial by jury; abrogate State governments; defile your own race, and flippantly say the Constitution is dead! On, on, with your work of ruin, ye hell-born rioters in sacred things! but remember for all these things the people will call you to judgment. Ah! what an issue you have made for yourselves. Succeed, and you destroy the Constitution! Fail, and you have covered the land with mourning. Succeed, and you bring ruin on yourselves and all the country! Fail, and you bring infamy upon yourselves and all your deluded followers! Succeed, and you are the perjured assassins of liberty! Fail, and you are defeated, despised traitors forever! Ye who aspire to be Radical governors and judges in Georgia, I paint before you this day your destiny. You are but cowards and knaves, and the time will come when you will call upon the rocks and mountains to fall on you and the darkness to hide you from an outraged people.

Does it do you good to trample on the Constitution—deceive the negroes and ruin the country? It may be sweet now, but I tell you the sulphurous fires of public infamy will never be quenched on your spirits. I pity you from my soul. Would that the time had never come when I had to stand upon Georgia's soil and thus talk to Georgians. A struggle is coming. It may be a long and bloody one, and you who advocate this wicked scheme will perish in it, unless the people now arouse and check its consummation. Let every true, law-loving man rally at once to the standard of the Constitution of his country. Come. Do not abandon your rights. Defend them. Talk for them, and if need be, before God and the country, fight and die for them. Do not talk or think of secession or disunion, but come up to the good old platform of our fathers —the Constitution. Let all, North and South, come and swear before God that we will abide by it in good faith, and oppose everything that violates it. The man who loves the Constitution now, and is willing to live and die for it, is my friend and brother, though he come from the frozen peak of Mt. Washington; and the man who is for trampling upon it is my enemy, and I shall hold him so, though he come from the sunny clime of the orange and the cotton bloom. That is my issue.

Oh how sorry a creature is the man who cannot stand up for the truth, when the country is in danger. There never was such an opportunity as now exists for a man to show of what stuff he is made. . . .

But some one says: "How will you resist it?" I will resist it first by not approving it. If everybody would do that it would be effectually resisted so far as we are concerned. But the so-called Congress has provided a cover for itself in advance, under which to hide from the odium attaching to this scheme. It has provided that you can vote either for or against a convention and again vote for or against whatever constitution it may frame. It is sought to make us responsible for whatever may be the consequences and relieve them. After a while, when you become alarmed at the results, they will say, "We did not do this. We only gave you a chance and you did it."

But if we defeat this, it is said, military rule will continue. Certainly—until wicked men shall be driven from power. But let it be so. General Pope seems to be a gentleman, and I infinitely prefer his rule to the rule of such men as you will get under this scheme. Besides, the new government, if inaugurated, will not be able to live a day without military protection. It is safer to be governed by power than by treachery. . . .

I advise you to register. There is no dishonor in that. It is arming yourself with an important power to be wielded against the nefarious scheme, but don't vote for a convention—don't go for anything whatever which is an assent to the scheme, but be against it at every step. Never go half way with a traitor, nor compromise with treason or robbery. If they hold a convention, vote against ratification—vote against all their measures and men, and indict every one who, under such void authority, invades your rights according to existing State lawᵣ. That's my policy. Fight this scheme all the time. I have no more idea of obeying than John Hampden had of paying ship-money, because I have taken an oath to support the Constitution and I intend to keep it.

This whole scheme is in violation of all the issues of the war —all the promises during its progress—and all the terms of surrender. More than a hundred thousand men abandoned Lee's army because they were assured that if they laid down their arms they would be in the Union again with all their rights as before. I knew the promise was false, and warned you against the seductions of the syren. The people—the soldiers of the United States—were then willing to fulfill the obligation; but the politicians intended to deceive you. Such men as Sumner and Stevens never intended to carry out the pledge of the nation. They would acknowledge the independence of the Confederate States to-day, before they would agree to restore the old Union, even with slavery abolished. I respect the Northern man who honestly fought for the Union, but I despise the traitors who, under the name of the Union, have used the Northern people to destroy the South, and then to destroy the Constitution. The people of the North have been long discovering this deception, but they will be compelled to see it before the traitors can go much further in their work. . . .

My colored friends, will you receive a word of admonition? Of all the people, you will most need the protection of the law. You will most suffer by anarchy and usurpation. Do you believe that the man who is faithless to the Constitution of the country will be faithful to you? If a man will take an oath to support the Constitution and then violate it, can you rely upon his keeping any promise to you? No; I tell you such people are friends to nothing but their own interest. They are betrayers of the Constitution to keep themselves in office; they desire to use you to help them get office, and they will betray you whenever they find it to their interest to do so.

They tell you they are your friends. It is false; they are your very worst enemies. They tell you they set you free. It is false. These vile creatures who come among you and put themselves on a level with you, never went with the army except to steal spoons, jewelry, and gold watches. They are too low to be brave. They are dirty spawn, cast out from decent society, who come down here and seek to use you to further their own base purposes.

They promise you lands, and teach you to hate the Southern people, whom you have known always and who never deceived you. Are you foolish enough to believe you can get another man's land for nothing, and that the white people will give up their land without resistance?

If you get up strife between your race and the white race, do you not know you must perish? You are now ten to one the weaker race. You will grow weaker every day. You can have no safety in the Constitution and no peace except by cultivating relations of kindness with those who are fixed here, who need your services, and who are willing to protect you. . . .

These men intend your extermination. Some of them are writing books in favor of your extermination, and I have myself heard some of them avow that you ought to be exterminated or driven from the country. These are the same people whose fathers found the Indians here. They declared the earth was the Lord's and belonged to his saints, and that they were his saints.

Then they killed and drove off the poor Indian and took his lands. If you do not make and keep friends of the Southern people, your fate is that of the Indians! Woe to your race! You well know your race is not prepared to vote. Why do you care to do what you do not understand? Improve yourselves. Learn to read and to write; be industrious; lay up your means; acquire homes; live in peace with your neighbors; and drive off, as you would a serpent, the miserable, dirty adventurers who come among you, and who, being too low to be received into white society, seek to foment among you hatred for the decent portion of the white race. You can always know a gentleman, whether from the North or South, and all such respect and esteem—for such will not deceive you. Do not desire to vote until you are qualified to vote, and then look for the right to be given, not in a manner that violates the Constitution, but in accordance with it, and through your own State governments. I feel more deeply for you than I do for the white race. White people ought to know better than to disregard the laws and expect any good. But you do not know the laws; you do not understand deceivers.

I am willing, anxious to welcome among us good and true men from the North, who come to help build up our country, and add to its prosperity. I wish they would come on and come in multitudes. They will find us friends. But when I see the low, dingy creatures—hatched from the venomous eggs of treason—coming here as mere adventurers to get offices through negro votes—to ride into power on the deluded negro's shoulders—and creeping into secret leagues with negroes and a few renegade Southern whites, and talking flippantly about disfranchising the wisest and best men of the land, because they know it is the only possible chance for knaves and fools like themselves to get place, I can but feel ashamed that such monsters are to be considered as belonging to the human species. I warn you, my colored friends, if you would be respectable in society, or prosperous in your purse, or decent in your own feelings, to avoid all such people. They will hug you and call you friend, and talk about your friends, but they will pull you down to degradation, to sorrow, to poverty, and to shame. They have white skins but black hearts, and will ruin your characters if you associate with them. They

are creatures born of political accidency and treasonable conspiracy, and are the enemies of all good governments and of all
decent people.

And now, my friends, of all races, of all colors, of all nations,
of all sexes, of all ages—let us resolve to stand by our Constitution, and surrender it to no enemy. This is our country. Let us
resolve that we will never be driven from it, nor ostracised in it.

10

An Agent of the Freedmen's Bureau

John W. DeForest's "Business and Pleasures," 1868

William DeForest (1826–1906), a native of Connecticut, was one of the significant literary figures of Mid-nineteenth-cenury America. He published several books before the outbreak of the Civil War. Following the firing on Fort Sumter, he recruited a company of volunteers and served in campaigns in Louisiana and the Shenandoah Valley. In 1865, he was assigned to the Freedmen's Bureau in Greenville, South Carolina, where he remained until his discharge in 1868. DeForest is best known for his postwar novel, *Miss Ravenel's Conversion from Secession to Loyalty,* published in 1867. The Bureau of Refugees, Freedmen, and Abandoned Lands had been established by Congress in March 1865 to ease the transition of the Negro from slavery to freedom. It provided food, shelter, and clothing for Southerners, both white and Negro, established schools for the freedmen, supervised their labor contracts, and assisted in settling them on confiscated or abandoned lands. The life of the agency was extended and its powers enlarged in the spring of 1866. The Freedmen's Bureau represented the one attempt by Congress to deal directly with matters of social and economic reconstruction. Its agents played a strong role in the protection of the civil rights of Negroes and in the support of the Radical Republican governments in the South. A recent study of the Freedmen's Bureau is George R. Bentley, *A History of the Freedmen's Bureau* (Philadelphia, 1955). DeForest's articles dealing with his experiences in the Freedmen's Bureau are in James H. Croushore and David M. Potter, eds., *A Union Officer in the Reconstruction* (New Haven, 1948). In the following article, note (1) the problems of adjustment of both Negroes and whites; (2) the nature of Negro complaints to the Bureau agent; and (3) the eagerness of the Negroes for transportation.

John William DeForest, "A Bureau Major's Business and Pleasures," *Harper's Magazine,* XXXVII (November 1868), 767–71.

Most of the difficulties between whites and blacks resulted from the inevitable awkwardness of tyros in the mystery of free labor. Many of the planters seemed to be unable to understand that work could be other than a form of slavery, or that it could be accomplished without some prodigious binding and obligating of the hireling to the employer. Contracts which were brought to me for approval contained all sorts of ludicrous provisions. Negroes must be respectful and polite; if they were not respectful and polite they must pay a fine for each offense; they must admit no one on their premises unless by consent of the landowner; they must have a quiet household and not keep too many dogs; they must not go off the plantation without leave. The idea seemed to be that if the laborer were not bound body and soul he would be of no use. With regard to many freedmen I was obliged to admit that this assumption was only too correct and to sympathize with the desire to limit their noxious liberty, at the same time that I knew such limitation to be impossible. When a darkey frolics all night and thus renders himself worthless for the next day's work; when he takes into his cabin a host of lazy relatives who eat him up, or of thievish ones who steal the neighboring pigs and chickens; when he gets high notions of freedom into his head and feels himself bound to answer his employer's directions with an indifferent whistle, what can the latter do? My advice was to pay weekly wages, if possible, and discharge every man as fast as he got through with his usefulness. But this policy was above the general reach of Southern capital and beyond the usual circle of Southern ideas.

One prevalent fallacy was the supposition that the farmer could, of his own authority, impose fines; in other words, that he could withhold all or a part of the laborer's pay if he left the farm before the expiration of his contract. The statement, "You can not take your man's wages for July because he has refused to work for you during August," was quite incomprehensible from the old-fashioned, patriarchal point of view.

"But what am I to do with this fellow, who has left me right in the hoeing season?" demands a wrathful planter.

"You have no remedy except to sue him for damages resulting from a failure of contract."

"Sue him! He ha'n't got nothing to collect on."

"Then don't sue him."

Exit planter, in helpless astonishment over the mystery of the new system, and half inclined to believe that I have been making game of him. I could, of course, have sent for the delinquent and ordered him to return to his work; but had I once begun to attend personally to such cases I should have had business enough to kill off a regiment of Bureau officers; and, moreover, I never forgot that my main duty should consist in educating the entire population around me to settle their difficulties by the civil law; in other words, I considered myself an instrument of reconstruction.

The majority of the complaints brought before me came from Negroes. As would naturally happen to an ignorant race, they were liable to many impositions, and they saw their grievances with big eyes. There was magnitude, too, in their manner of statement; it was something like an indictment of the voluminous olden time—the rigmarole which charged a pig thief with stealing ten boars, ten sows, ten shoats, etc. With pomp of manner and of words, with a rotundity of voice and superfluity of detail which would have delighted Cicero, a Negro would so glorify his little trouble as to give one the impression that humanity had never before suffered the like. Sometimes I was able to cut short these turgid narratives with a few sharp questions; sometimes I found this impossible and had to let them roll on unchecked, like Mississippis. Of course the complaints were immensely various in nature and importance. They might refer to an alleged attempt at assassination or to the discrepancy of a bushel of pea vines in the division of a crop. They might be against brother freedmen, as well as against former slave owners and "Rebs." More than once have I been umpire in in the case of a disputed jackknife or petticoat. Priscilly Jones informed me that her "old man was a-routin' everybody out of the house an' a-breakin' everything"; then Henry Jones bemoaned himself because his wife Priscilly was going to strange places along with Tom Lynch; then Tom Lynch wanted redress and protection because of the disquieting threats of Henry Jones. The next minute Chole Jackson desired justice on Viney Robinson, who had slapped her face and torn her clothes. Everybody, guilty or innocent, ran with his or her griefs to the Bureau officer; and sometimes the Bureau officer, half distracted, longed to subject them all to some huge punishment. Of the complaints against whites the majority were because of the retention of wages or of alleged unfairness in the division of the crops.

If the case brought before me were of little consequence, I

usually persuaded the Negro, if possible, to drop it or to "leave it out" to referees. Without a soldier under my command, and for months together having no garrison within forty miles, I could not execute judgment even if I could see to pronounce it; and, moreover, I had not, speaking with official strictness, any authority to act in matters of property; the provost court having been abolished before I entered upon my jurisdiction. If the complaint were sufficiently serious to demand attention, I had one almost invariable method of procedure: I stated the case in a brief note and addressed it to the magistrate of the "beat" or magisterial precinct in which the Negro resided. Then, charging him to deliver the letter in person and explaining to him what were his actual wrongs and his possibilities of redress, I dismissed him to seek for justice precisely where a white man would have sought it. Civil law was in force by order of the commanding general of the department; and the civil authorities were disposed, as I soon learned, to treat Negroes fairly. Such being the case, all that my clients needed in me was a counselor.

"But the square won't pay no sawt 'tention to me," a Negro would sometimes declare. To which I would reply: "Then come back and let me know it. If he neglects his duty we will report him and have him removed."

Of the fifty or sixty magistrates in my district I had occsion to indicate but one as being unfit for office by reason of political partialities and prejudices of race. New York City would be fortunate if it could have justice dealt out to it as honestly and fairly as it was dealt out by the plain, homespun farmers who filled the squire-archates of Greenville, Pickens, and Anderson.

But the Negro often lacked confidence in the squire; perhaps; too, he was aware that his case would not bear investigation; and so, instead of delivering my letter in person, he often sent it by a messenger. As the magistrate could not act without the presence of the complainant, nothing was done. A week or fortnight later the Negro would reappear at my office, affirming that "dese yere Rebs wouldn't do nothin' for black folks nohow."

"What did the squire say?" I would ask.

"Didn' say nothin'. Jes took the ticket an' read it, an' put it in his pocket."

"Did you see him?"

"No. I was feared he wouldn' do nothin'; so I sont it roun' to him."

"Now then, go to him. If you have a story to tell, go and tell it to him, and swear to it. I shall do nothing for you till you have done that."

And so the process of education went on, working its way mainly by dint of general laws, without much regard to special cases. As this is the method of universal Providence and of the War Department, I felt that I could not be far wrong in adopting it. But even this seemingly simple and easy style of performing duty had its perplexities. Magistrates rode from ten to thirty miles to ask me how they should dispose of this, that, and the other complaint which had been turned over to them for adjudication. Their chief difficulty was to know where the military orders ended and where civil law began; and here I was little less puzzled than they, for we were acting under a hodgepodge of authorities which no man could master. I had files of orders for 1865, and 1866, and 1867; files from the Commissioner, and from the Assistant Commissioner, and from the general commanding the department; the whole making a duodecimo volume of several hundred closely printed pages. To learn these by heart and to discover the exact point where they ceased to cover and annul the state code was a task which would have bothered not only a brevet major but a chief justice. My method of interpretation was to limit the military order as much as might be, and so give all possible freedom of action to the magistrate.

Occasionally my office was the scene of something approaching to the nature of a disturbance. Once I heard an uproar in the outer passage; and then appeared two farmers leading a tall Negro by a long rope which secured his hands, the three closely followed by a small mob of expostulating and threatening Negroes belonging to the village. The white men were tremulous with astonishment and alarm, and at the same time not a little indignant.

"Putty rough talk for black 'uns," said one of them, indicating with a toss of his head the menacing freedmen who now filled my doorway. "Some of 'em may git a knife into 'em if they don't keep their distance."

Meanwhile Edward Cox, a mulatto of convivial habits, and

disposed, like many white men of similar tastes, to take a leading part in public affairs, was vociferously questioning the prisoner: "What you been doing? Have you done anything?"

"Took a pair of trousers," confessed the long, ragged, stupid-looking subject of arrest.

"Were they yours? Did you steal 'em?" persisted Edward. "Oh, you stole 'em, eh? Then I've got nothing to say for you. Come, boys, get out o' the way; clar out now, I tell ye; don't be bothering the Major. When a man steals, I've got nothin' to say for him, no matter how black he is."

Closing the door on the rabble, I heard the statement of the captors. The Negro, it seems, was a stranger in the district, who had called at the house of one of the farmers to beg and had been furnished with a dinner of cold pieces. Immediately after his refreshment he had disappeared in company with a newly washed pair of homespun trousers, which had been hung out to dry. Enraged by the "meanness of the critter," by ten miles of hard riding to overtake him, and by the noisy interference of the Greenville Negroes, the prosecutor was bent upon severe punishment. I took captors and captive to a magistrate's office and left them there. In half an hour I went back and found that, on the intercession of the squire and on the darkey's solemn declaration of penitence, the farmer had not only forgiven him, but had hired him as a laborer.

My worst perplexities arose from cases in which I had to deal with repectable white citizens. Just imagine the North conquered by the South, Confederate officers stationed in every community as agents of the "Copperhead Bureau," and all the Bridgets of the land flowing to them with complaints against their masters and mistresses. Would not the "Copperhead Bureau Agent" find himself very often in a quandary? Would he be able always to satisfy both his clients and his own sense of justice and social propriety?

Mr. John Doe, one of the leading citizens of Greenville, complained to me that he had hired a colored woman named Sarah to work for him and that she had failed to come, to the detriment of his household affairs. I sent a note to Sarah informing her that she must fulfill her contract. An hour later Mrs. Richard Roe, the wife of another leading citizen, then absent at the North, entered my office in her best robes and gave me the soundist scolding that I have had since my boyhood.

"This Sarah lives in my yard," was her story. "I only received her out of charity, as she is sickly and has a small child. I gave her the rent of a cabin on condition that she should do my washing. Then I found that she could not earn her food otherwheres, and I allowed her rations weekly—as a charity. This week she has neglected her washing and is aiming to get off without doing it. I can hire other people easily enough, but I do not wish to be imposed upon. I insist that she shall do that washing. She shall not leave, Sir, until it is done. To make sure of my point I have locked up her things in my cabin, and I have the key in my pocket. I am not going to be deceived and cheated by Negroes."

Then followes a series of sharp scoffs at the interfering disposition of Bureau officers, which my regard for myself forbids me to repeat. What could I do? The imperfect information of Mr. John Doe and the imbecile laziness of this colored Sarah had put me in a ridiculous position. Falling back on the fact that I had been assigned to duty for the benefit of Negroes rather than of whites, and remembering that Sarah was to get wages at her new place, wheras now she was barely earning a subsistence, I shut my eyes to justice and refused to withdraw my order. I attempted to silence Mrs. Roe by remarking that it was a very small affair; but she replied with tart pertinency, "It was not too small, Sir, for you to meddle with it."

So I remained dumb, in all the greatness and meanness of despotic power, and persisted in having my stupid way. With no small satisfaction I learned next day that Mr. John Doe had had his share of humiliation. Meeting him on her way homeward, Mrs. Roe descended from her buggy and gave him a piece of her mind.

"To think of a Southern *gentleman* appealing to these Yankees!" she sneered. "I thought that it was a point of honor among us Southerners to stand by each other and not to turn informers against each other before our conquerors. It may do for niggers and mean whites, Sir; but have Southern gentlemen come to this?"

"Mrs. Roe! Mrs. Roe!" shouted the wounded and inflamed Doe, panting to get in a word in his defense; but the torrent of feminine sarcasm was too much for him, and he was as glad to finish the combat as had been the Bureau officer. When Sarah came to his house he sent her back to Mrs. Roe; then Mrs. Roe, satisfied with so much of victory, sent her back to Mr. Doe; then Sarah lived a fortnight with the Does, did next to nothing, as usual, and was turned away.

Of course there were numberless little disturbances which were not brought up for my official action. Mr. Peter Cauble was a blacksmith, nearly eighty years of age, but still vigorous, who had acquired by industry, economy, and wise investment a fortune of seventy thousand dollars, and had seen it disappear in the grand hocus-pocus of the Confederacy. A rough, high-tempered, but kindhearted and generous nature, he was one of the men to whom the poor and outcast of his district chiefly resorted for help. White or black, good or bad, Peter Cauble gave them food, found them shelter, and went bail for them. Society had pointed out his proper place in it and made him chairman of the Commissioners of the Poor. One misty spring morning Peter Cauble arose at four o'clock, as was his hale custom, and, taking a hoe on his shoulder, went out to work in his garden. He was threading a pathway which led along a little bank, when some unknown person ran against him and, at the same moment, hailed him with the impudent salutation, "How are you, Pete?"

Who it was Peter Cauble could not see for his spectacles were in his pocket, and the morning was still darkness; but he raised his hoe with both hands and brought the staff of it across the stranger's head, rolling him off his feet and down the bank. The prostrated individual then bounced up and ran away.

It was a Negro. For three or four days the adventure made a great noise in the village. The reactionaries declared that this man was on his way home from a Union League meeting, and that there was a widespread conspiracy to address all the respectable whites by their Christian names. The Radical Negroes called Peter Cauble a Reb and talked about confiscating his land. But the two parties chiefly interested in the affair settled it amicably.

"Bill—" said Peter Cauble, on discovering that the man whom he had floored was one of his colored acquaintance, "Bill, I knocked you down the other morning. I think I served you right;

but if you don't think so, we'll go and settle it before the Major; you tell your story, and I'll tell mine; what do you say, Bill?"

"I ha'nt no use for the Major," replied Bill sheepishly. "I'm ready to call it squar. I'd been drinkin' that night and didn' know what I was about. I don't want nuffin to do with the Major."

For nothing were the Negroes more eager than for transportation. They had a passion, not so much for wandering, as for getting together; and every mother's son among them seemed to be in search of his mother; every mother in search of her children. In their eyes the work of emancipation was incomplete until the families which had been dispersed by slavery were reunited. One woman wanted to rejoin her husband in Memphis, and another to be forwarded to hers at Baltimore. The Negroes who had been brought to the up-country during the war by white families were crazy to get back to their native flats of ague and country fever. Highland darkeys who had drifted down to the seashore were sending urgent requests to be "fotched home again." One aunty brought me her daughter, who suffered with fits, and begged me to give them a "ticket" to Anderson so that they might consult a certain famous "fit doctor" there resident. Others desired me to find out where their relatives lived, and send for them.

In short, transportation was a nuisance. I believed in it less than I believed in the distribution of rations and in modes of charity generally. It seemed to me that if the Negroes wanted to travel they should not insist on doing it at the expense of the nation, but should earn money and pay their own fare, like white people. I learned to be discouragingly surly with applicants for transportation papers and to give them out as charily as if the cost came from my own pocket. I claim that in so doing I acted the part of a wise and faithful public servant.

From the class properly known as refugees—that is, Unionists who had been driven from their homes during the war by the Rebels—I had no requests for transportation. Not that they were few in number; the mountains near by Greenville were swarming with them; but they had the Anglo-Saxon faculty for getting about the world unassisted. The mean whites, those same "low-down" creatures who bored me to death for corn and clothing, were equally independent of aid in changing their habitations.

The "high-toned" families which had fled to the up-country from the cannon of Dupont and Gillmore also made shift to return to their houses in Charleston or their plantations on the sea islands, without any noticeable worrying of government officials. The Negroes alone were ravenous after transportation.

I soon found that many of my would-be tourists were chiefly anxious to enjoy that luxury, so dear to the freedman's heart, "going a-visiting." A woman would obtain transportation of me on the plea that she wanted to rejoin a child in Charleston whom she had not seen for ten years and who was suffering for her care; then, having enjoyed a sufficient amount of family gossip in the city, she would apply to the Bureau officer there to save her from starvation by returning her to Greenville. I became wickedly clever in fathoming this deceit and used to ask in a friendly way, "When do you want to come back?"

"Well, Mars'r, I doesn't want to stop mo'n a fo'tnight," would perhaps be the answer.

"Ah! if that is all," I would lecture, "you had better wait till you want to stay for good, or till you have money enough to pay for your own pleasure excursions."

It was necessary, I thought, to convince the Negroes of the fact that the object of the government was not to do them favors, but justice; and of the still greater fact that there is very little to get in this world without work.

Planters who were about to remove to more fertile regions sometimes asked transportation for their Negroes, on the ground that these latter would be benefited by the change of locality and that it could not be effected without government assistance. Of course this seemed rational; and I understood that aid of this sort was freely rendered by some Bureau officers; but I rejected all such applications. Grant one, grant a thousand; and the government would be bankrupt. At last a general order from the Commissioner sanctioned transportation for this purpose; but the planter's application must be approved by the Assistant Commissioner of the state where he resided and by the Assistant Commissioner of the state to which he proposed to emigrate; he must give satisfactory security that he would feed and pay his hands; he must then get the approval of the Commissioner. What with postal and official delays these preliminaries generally consumed at least a month; and as the planting season pressed, this complicated circumlocution was usually abandoned before it was completed, the applicant either giving up his migration or conducting it at his own expense. Whether the result were intended or not, it was a good one. In so vast and fertile a region as the South the industry which can not succeed alone rarely deserves success. Charity is either an absolute necessity or an absolute evil.

Although I received no precise instructions as to visiting the various portions of my district, it was probably presumed by my superiors that I would make occasional tours of inspection, and so attend to local disorders on the spot where they occurred. I did not do this; I made but a single journey of above fifteen miles; I did not absent myself more than a single night from my station, except once when summoned to Charleston. My satrapy, it must be remembered, contained two state districts or counties, and eventually three, with a population of about eighty thousand souls and an area at least two thirds as large as the state of Connecticut. Consider the absurdity of expecting one man to patrol three thousand square miles and make personal visitations to thirty thousand Negroes.

Then I had no assistant to attend to the complainants who constantly presented themselves at my office. They averaged five a day, or a total of something like two thousand during my fifteen months of duty. Moreover, they came from distances of five, ten, twenty, and even thirty miles. I planted myself firmly in Greenville and let my world come to me. Toward the end of my term of service an order was promulgated to the effect that Bureau officers should thereafter "travel more" and that they should regularly visit the important points of their districts, giving previous notice of their tours to the inhabitants. Knowing what labor this signified and how impossible it would be to perform it in any satisfactory manner, I welcomed the decree from the headquarters of the army which mustered all volunteer officers out of the service, and declined an appointment as civilian agent of the Bureau. How far and with what good result my successors performed their tourist labors I should be glad to know.

11

"The Weak Need Protection"

George Fitzhugh on the Freedman and His Future, 1870

George Fitzhugh (1806–1881) had been one of the most prominent defenders of slavery before the Civil War. His books *Sociology for the South* (1854) and *Cannibals All!* (1857) were not only detailed arguments in support of the Southern institution but they were also fierce denunciations of the North's free and competitive society. When the war was over, Fitzhugh acquiesced in the result and became reconciled to emancipation and Negro suffrage. Ironically, he was employed for a time as an agent of the Freedmen's Bureau and for about a year served with a Negro as a justice on the Freedmen's Court. His relations with the Negroes reflected the spirit of paternalism that pervaded his own *ante bellum* publications.

During the postwar years, Fitzhugh wrote extensively for *DeBow's Review* and other magazines. With the triumph of Congressional reconstruction and his departure from the Freedmen's Bureau, his attitude became less philosophical and more critical. In 1869 he published an article in *Lippincott's Magazine* entitled "The Freedman and His Future" in which he argued that education would prove to be a handicap to the Negro. Fitzhugh's statement was challenged in a subsequent article by William R. Hooper. The article that follows was Fitzhugh's answer to Hooper—a rejoinder in which he clarified his position on the role of the freedman. A good biography of Fitzhugh, although devoting small space to his postwar activities, is Harvey Wish, *George Fitzhugh, Propagandist of the Old South* (Baton Rouge, 1943). In the selection that follows, note (1) Fitzhugh's arguments against educating the Negro freedmen; (2) his comments on land monopoly and what he calls "slavery to capital; (3) evidences of Fitzhugh's belief in racial inequality; and (4) his proposals for the protection of the freedmen.

George Fitzhugh, "The Freedman and His Future: A Rejoinder, "*Lippincott's Magazine,* V (February 1870), 191–97.

There is no subject of such vital and world-wide interest as the disposition to be made, consistent with humanity, of the savage or uncivilized races. I shall make no apology, therefore, for requesting you, Mr. Editor, to continue to lend your columns to the discussion of this subject. I congratulate myself that already I have elicited most valuable statistics from Mr. Hooper in his reply, published in your December Number, to my essay on this subject in September. Three years hence, guided by the light of those statistics, we shall certainly be able to dispose of this subject, in one of its phases, understandingly and finally. By that time two hundred thousand negro pupils and their teachers will either be demoralized, or tens of thousands of those pupils will be found successfully competing with the whites as farmers, mechanics, merchants, engineers, physicians, lawyers, clergymen, authors, etc, etc.

I think I have already had ample experience and abundant evidence of the ill effects of attempting to give literary education to negroes—at Hilton Head, before emancipation the very Paradise of the Union, where two years of liberty and literature demoralized the negroes and many of their teachers, wholly arrested the production of Sea Island cotton, and brought on anarchy, illness, insubordination, and starvation; at Washington, where negroes most do congregate, and negro schools, colleges and universities most abound, side by side with squalid poverty, mendicity, famine and hideous, frequent crimes of every hue and dye; at and about Richmond and Petersburg and Norfolk, and at and about every city and village in the South; and last, not least, in the peninsula above Fortress Monroe, where for several years they have occupied all the farms, with all the stock and farming utensils on them, free from rent or hire, with rations and abundance of white teachers thrown in gratis. Here, even here, I was told, two years after the war, that they had not made grain enough to feed themselves for four months of the year. Everywhere at the South, as liberty and literature have gone up with the negroes, agriculture has gone down, and universal crime and famine supervened.

In the conclusion of his reply, Mr. Hooper says that "these (his facts) are an answer to my *assertions.*" I admit his statement of facts, which he sums up by saying that two hundred and fifty-six thousand negro pupils are now attending school (with what result he does not deign to inform us, except that these schools will turn out negro schoolmasters), and that Frederick Douglass, who never was at one of these schools, and is not a negro, is the editor of a newspaper. [Douglass (1817-1895) was the son of a Negro slave and a white father.] Had any practical good ever resulted from the attempts to give literary education to negroes—attempts which have been carried on assiduously for more than four thousand years—first by Egyptians and Arabs, and for the last four hundred years by almost all the white nations of the world—Mr. Hooper would certainly have cited the instances of such success; but, finding none, he endeavors, driven to desperation, to prove that literary education benefits negroes by naïvely informing us that Fred Douglass, who is no negro, edits a paper.

Educate negroes? Surely: educate them from early childhood for all those industrial pursuits for which they are adapted. But don't attempt to make carpenters, or manufacturers, or house-servants, or hostlers, or gardeners of the men, nor seamstresses, nor washerwomen, nor cooks, nor chambermaids of the women. They are too slow, too faithless, too unskillful to succeed in such pursuits when brought in competition with whites. But they are admirably adapted—better adapted than white men —for field-work (in which two-thirds of the white population of the earth are, from dire necessity, engaged), also for working on railroads and canals, for wood-cutting, and for coal and iron mining. Educate them (the full-blooded negroes) for these pursuits, and they will be the most happy, useful and productive population in the world.

From infancy I have lived where the black population exceeded the white by two to one. From long observation and tedious study I think I have learned to comprehend the nature of the savage or uncivilized race. In one material and all-controlling respect it differs wholly from that of the whites. All savages are CONTENTED—all Caucasians DISCONTENTED. Content begets *vis inertia* of mind and body with the savage, and therefore he can never improve, accumulate property, or acquire that dominion over his fellow-beings which results in slavery to capital; which so-called yet miscalled slavery alone begets, sustains and advances civilization.

So long as savage nature continues (and literary education intensifies and increases it, for even among the whites literary men are remarkable for that *insouciance* or improvidence which is the distinguishing characteristic of the savage), so long as negroes are *contented,* they will have no property, no useful arts, no separate ownership of lands, no law, little or no government, and indeed none of the institutions of civilized life. They are by necessity of nature all equals, all paupers, all ignorant, all wasteful, generous, amiable and improvident—all communists and agrarians; yet, properly taken care of and provided for by the whites, and educated to proper industrial pursuits, they become the most valuable part of every population, because the most productive. To teach them to read, write, cipher, etc., and then to throw them, unprotected, into free competition with the selfish, avaricious, designing, cheating white race, is all that their peculiar friends, North and South, propose.

The common laborer, be he black or white, slave or freeman, is the most valuable of all "live stock." We take care of—nay, we love—our blooded horses, our blooded cattle, our blooded hogs. Should we not more love, more take care of, the amiable and generous negro, who is more valuable than they, and is, besides, our fellow-man? The English understand this thing, and during the dearth of employment for cotton operatives occasioned by our late war they provided amply and munificently for those operatives. We must provide for the negroes in infancy, in old age, in sickness and in winter, for Nature unfits them to provide for themselves. By diminishing their wages we can effect this purpose without loss to ourselves—in fact, only compelling them, in this way, to take care of themselves. The negroes are now fast diminishing in numbers, and will slowly die out entirely if we continue to teach them what is useless to them, and neglect to teach them, and compel them to learn, those arts and pursuits for which they are alone fitted.

Human equality, established and enforced by law in despite of Nature, between inferior and superior races, is the most cruel engine of torture that the wit of man could possibly invent. Hear what Mr. Greeley said, twenty years ago, of such equality or free competition even in New York, where there is no inferior race: "Briefly, it seems to me if some malignant spirit had undertaken to contrive a social framework which should subject the poor, the humble, the ignorant to the greatest possible amount and variety of temptations—which should virtually constrain many and irresistibly draw far more to the ways of dissipation and sin—he could hardly, in the light of Christianity and of such civilization as we have, devise anything more admirably adapted to his purpose than the social system under which we now live." Now, every word of this is strictly and accurately true when society is composed of inferior and superior races, but not true as to white society in New York, of which Mr. Greeley is treating.

The immense public and private charities of New York ward off or greatly mitigate the otherwise intolerable evils of free competition, which rages there more fiercely than anywhere else. With all her faults and failings, New York City is one of the most desirable residences for rich and poor in the world, and hence the mighty immigration that is continually pouring into her. New York is not the Devil's work, for New York made Mr. Greeley in fortune, fame and character, and he is a kind-hearted, humane man, a philosopher, a scholar and an ornament to his country—a little wild, however, about negroes and Fourierism. [Charles Fourier (1772-1837), a French utopian socialist, who provided the model for a number of communitarian experiments, including Brook Farm in Massachusetts.]

When mistaken philanthropy has demoralized the negroes by making indifferent scholars of them, and thereby unfitting them for bodily labor —when by educating negro teachers it has diffused the poison of insubordination, of idleness and theft far and wide through the land—when free-love and concubinage have taken the place of lawful marriage, and the negroes are turned over to us Southrons to manage—we will institute a wholly different system. We will encourage the negroes to labor in the fields, give them good wages, comfortable houses, plenty of wholesome food; or, if they will not thus labor, leave them to starve. We Southrons from time immemorial have been kind, humane, generous and tender-hearted.

Let not our Northern friends, then, fear to turn the freedmen over to us. It is our interest to treat them well, and our feelings and sympathies coincide with our interests. We see every day around us the bad effects of improper education of negroes. Those who when slaves were accustomed to field-work are better laborers than ever, and are contented, honest and doing well. Those brought up as house-servants, mechanics, etc., are half their time out of employment, thievish, half starved and discontented. Negro aristocracy in the South is dead, and can never be revived. The pampered menials of *ante-bellum* days have become ragged, starving mendicants and thieves.

Having tried to explain why savages can never become civilized, because they are *contented* and never own separate property in lands, or capital or property of any kind of sufficient amount to make the few property-holders the masters, in effect, of the non-property-holders, I now proceed to show how land monopoly, or the dominion of capital over labor—for all capital proceeds from the land—begets, sustains and advances civilization among all the varieties of the white race. Now, by land monopoly, I mean only separate individual property in lands and houses, such as exists all around us, has ever and everywhere existed with the white race, and which never has and never can exist with the savage races. . . .

Land monopoly, or the ownership of land by the few—such as we see around us—and civilization, seem to have been congenital with the white race; and indeed we cannot conceive how the one could exist without the other. Land monopoly of necessity begets civilization, because those who own lands compel those who own none to fabricate not only the necessaries and comforts, but the luxuries of life for them, the land-owners, for the privilege of living on and drawing a support from their lands. I cannot conceive how civilization could possibly exist where lands were held in common, or where each man held just so much as he could cultivate, and consequently each man cultivated his own lands. If all men had to procure their livelihood by the labor of their own hands, would not all live as plainly as possible, dress in skins and furs, live in caves, support themselves by fishing and hunting as far as possible, and till their lands as little as possible? In such a state of things all the arts that distinguish civilized life would perish, and all men become savages. But the white race, everywhere and at all times, have been *discontented*, provident, rapacious, ambitious, accumulative, selfish, avaricious, competitive and overreaching. In the struggle of life, the war of wits, a few monopolize the lands, and all other capital that grows out of land, directly or indirectly. These few institute what is called "slavery to capital," the greatest of human blessings, because it begets civilization, and renders the earth a hundred times more productive than it can ever be where all lands are held in common, multiplies population a hundredfold, and places the most abject slave of capital, the poorest laborer, in the enjoyment of more comforts and luxuries than were ever dreamed of by savage princes. Never before were there such large accumulations of capital in private hands as in our day; never was the dominion of capital over labor so complete as now, yet capital and labor are most harmoniously employed in increasing each other's profits. The Suez Canal, the Pacific Railroad, and a thousand other recent great works instituted and carried on by great capitalists, have not only given profitable employment to millions of laborers, but have opened up illimitable fields for cultivation, to which overtaxed laborers can at any moment migrate. These capitalists, by furnishing easy and cheap access to markets, are really increasing the productive capacity of the earth five times as fast as population increases. Ours is the golden age (for the white race, at least), for never before could a living be earned with so little labor. And all this is owing to the miscalled "slavery to capital."

In Turkey, where there is little capital, no taxes, and scarce any private or public debt, and consequently no slavery to capital, the whole population is sunk in ignorance, pauperism and indolence. In England, where there is most of private capital and of public and private debt, there is most of wealth and prosperity; and her population, wealth and prosperity only began to increase rapidly after the chartering of her national bank and the funding and increase of her national debt. If Turkey would give her bonds gratis for a hundred millions a year for ten years to come to enterprising private individuals, she would thereby beget capital, set industry to work, reward skill and labor, and beget wealth and high civilization. It is the dominion of capital over labor that begets wealth, invention, improvement, refinement and high civilization.

Negroes and all other savages are incapable of inaugurating even land monopoly, the first step necessary to establish such dominion. Teach negroes to make and accumulate money, and to acquire and administer property, and they at once become civilized, although ignorant of the alphabet.

There was a high civilization and much wealth in Europe and Western Asia long anterior to the invention of letters. Homer, the greatest of authors, knew not a letter in the book. His works conclusively show that the useful and ornamental arts were generally known and successfully practiced long before his time—in fact, immemorially—by the white race. His exquisite description of the fabrication of the shield of Achilles would, if it stood alone, prove that the mechanic arts have gained nothing by the use of letters; whilst his own works go far to sustain the opinion of Plato, that the human mind has been enfeebled by the invention of letters. But Homer's works are not the only evidences of the superiority of the illiterate ancients in the mechanic arts, thousands of architectural remains, older than the invention and use of a phonetic alphabet, show that architecture has declined just as literature has advanced.

But to descend to our own times and to come nearer home, very many Virginia overseers could neither read nor write, yet they managed farms and negroes much more judiciously and profitably than Mr. Jefferson or any other scholar, philosopher or agricultural chemist. Too much learning had not taken away their common sense or run them mad. Many men around us, who can neither read nor write, have made handsome properties as farmers, many such as captains of vessels, and a few even as merchants. Nothing so incapacitates a man for making money as profound and various learning. Literature is a luxury in which the poor cannot afford to indulge. Teach negroes to earn their bread and make money, and when they have done so leave them to learn their alphabet if they be fools enough to do so.

Ce n'est que le premier pas qui coute. [It is only the first step that costs.] The over-sanguine, visionary friends of the ignorant negro, half conscious of this fact, propose to omit the *first step,* which the negro's nature inhibits him, and will ever inhibit him, from taking, and leap at once to the second. To make, to amass and to wield capital is the first step in the road to civilization. A literary education is sure to succeed this step. Reverse the order of nature and teach the negro first to read, and then start him to learn to labor and to make money by hand-work, and he will find that his school education unfits him to compete with those who have been working with their hands all the while he was at school. He will find his wants increased, and his ability to supply them diminished. He will be thrown upon the world a miserable, discontented, aspiring, idle, help less, hopeless thief and vagrant. This picture is not overdrawn. We see around us, every day and every hour, the pauperism and wretchedness that false education entails on negroes; and with them all education is false that attempts to teach them other than the coarsest, commonest and hardest labor. Employed at such labor alone, they will prove them selves our most useful, valuable and productive citizens.

I have seen the circus-horse Champion dance. He danced most infa mously, but without doubt his education had cost him ten thousand lashes. Negroes sometimes learn to read about as well as Champion danced, for their organs of speech are as unfitted for reading as the horse's legs for dancing. Yet to acquire a little reading they probably suffer "more pangs and fears than wars or women have." The cruelty of a circus education does not exceed the cruelty of the successful literary education of negroes. And *cui bono?* [For whose advantage?]

Should Mr. Hooper answer this article, I hope he will try to sustain his "assertion," that savage nature may be expelled and eradicated from negroes by education, so that they shall differ from whites only in their skins and their hair, and be morally and intellectually just what the whites are, by proofs beginning with the building of the first Pyramids, and extending to the present hour; just as I have tried by proofs, thus beginning, continuing and ending, to show that the black man is and ever has been, and ever will be, from the necessity of his God-given nature, an irreclaimable savage. To tell us that two hundred and fifty-six thou sand are going to schools, without showing that they have been improved by schooling, is almost to admit that literature is useless to negroes. To tell us that a bright mulatto, Fred Douglass, edits a paper, is as good as an admission that full-blooded negroes are too stupid to make any use of literary attainments. Since Mr. Hooper has stepped forward as the cham pion of negro literary education, the public will expect and require of him to sustain his "assertion" and theory by proofs as numerous as those which I have adduced to sustain what he calls my "assertions." I take no offence at the term. I know that I am habitually dogmatical. I believe Mr. Hooper to be a fair, candid man, and a well-informed and courteous adversary. The questions at issue between us are the most vital and momentous ever submitted to the arbitrament of public opinion. Their solution involves the fate of all the savage races, for civilized nations are everywhere pressing upon the uncivilized or savage races. They will all be exterminated, unless they can be rendered useful as I propose, or educated into white men in all save color and hair, as Mr. Hooper proposes.

When I say that all laboring men without property are the *slaves* of capital, and that *slavery* to capital (beginning with land monopoly) is the sole parent of civilization, I use the terms "slaves" and "slavery" metaphorically for want of better, for there is no word in the English language that exactly expresses the relation of labor and capital. So, when we say one State has enslaved another, we speak of political slavery, and this term is used metaphorically. Thus Russia has politically enslaved Poland, although she has liberated the masses of her people from the vilest servitude. No honest man is ashamed of being poor and of working for his living, but no one likes to be called a slave. The laboring poor are freemen, heavily taxed or exploited by capitalists, yet more than compensated for such exploitation by the invaluable blessings which capital bestows. I entirely approve of the association and combinations of workingmen to keep up the rate of wages. Capitalists, like other men, would be sure to abuse unlimited power. The war between Capital and Labor is evidence of a healthy state of society. When it ceases, despotism, ignorance and pauperism will supervene. . . .

NOTE.—Since the above was written, an editorial of the New York *Commercial Advertiser* has been seen by me, criticising my article on "Land Monopoly" which appeared in the September Number of this Magazine. The editor charges me with inconsistency in my doctrines before and since the war on the subject of slavery and of negroes. I shall not raise an issue on this subject, because in defending and vindicating my consistency I might have to use arguments and cite facts offensive to the North, and because to write about myself would be obtrusive egotism. I accept the situation. I am entirely reconciled to negro suffrage and negro legal and political equality: social relations will regulate themselves, and capital and skill will regulate industrial relations. We of the South wish to be friends with the North. We are trying to conciliate her, and to attract immigration, skill and capital from the North. Nothing do we despise and contemn so much as the silly, old-fogy Marplots who are trying to keep alive ill-feeling between the North and South by prating continually about sectional superiority or inferiority, sectional peculiarities and sectional prejudices. Such writing is bad enough in Northern men: when indulged in by Southern men, since we are the weaker section, it betrays equal folly, vindictiveness, bad taste and bad policy. For my part, from the bottom of my heart I adopt the President's motto, "Let there be peace."

The editor does not dispute my first proposition, to wit: That (as he properly quotes it) "the monopoly of property or capital by the few is the parent of civilization." Nor does he explicitly deny my second, and far more vital and practical, proposition, to wit: "That the uncivilized races are incapable of such monopoly, and hence can never have self-sustaining civilization." I add, that "a very few (freedmen) will acquire property," etc. The editor, with the most innocent naïveté and simplicity, remarks on this: "If any, why not a majority?" I answer: Many of the freedmen are mulattoes and quadroons, and some of them may acquire property in considerable amounts and manage it judiciously by virtue of their white blood.

I ask the editor, If Chang and Eng* be united by a ligament of flesh, why may not all children be so united? Why are not Chang and Eng's children so united? Why are there so few albinos? And why are their children black? Are not Chang and Eng and all albinos monstrosities—abnormal, sporadic, anomalous human beings? And are not negroes who make fortunes equally rare, anomalous and sporadic? Is it not therefore true that the uncivilized races cannot institute slavery to capital, and therefore cannot be civilized?

Does not the editor know that the freedmen, who in great numbers were furnished with the best lands, and with stock and farming utensils, and rations and clothes and teachers, seven years ago, are to-day much poorer than when slaves? Yes, he knows it, and knows that none of the savage races are civilizable, because none of them ever did, or ever can, hold separate, individual, private property in lands, or amass and wield sufficient amounts of capital to give the few dominion over and command of the labor of the many?

We live in the midst of an awful crisis in human affairs. I believe that the whites are about to exterminate the savage races by assuming that they are capable of civilization, giving them equal legal and political rights, and then throwing them unprotected into free competition with those whites. The weak need protection, and not so-called liberty and equality. I would arrest the Caucasian race in its mad, cruel and exterminating career. I would give special protection by legal regulations to the inferior races, and to do so would, as far as experience proved it to be necessary, limit and restrict their rights and liberties. It is impossible to give to any class special protection without subjecting it to special disabilities. . . .

*Editor's NOTE. Chang and Eng [Bunker] were Siamese Twins born near Bangkok of Chinese parents. Taken to Europe, they were widely shown as curiosities. P. T. Barnum, the noted American showman, saw them in New York, acquired their contract, and exhibited them as the original Siamese Twins at his New York American Museum. They prospered, became American citizens, bought a Southern plantation which they cultivated with slaves, and married two sisters of the neighborhood. The four produced a total of twenty-one children, none of them Siamese Twins. They lost their slaves and their wealth during the Civil War, recouped their fortunes in show business after the war, and returned to their North Carolina holdings to farm. They died the same day in 1874.

12

The Liberal Republican Revolt

Carl Schurz, "Why Anti-Grant and Pro-Greeley," 1872

In 1868 Ulysses S. Grant was easily elected to the Presidency over his Democratic opponent, New York's wartime governor Horatio Seymour, but whereas Grant's margin in the electoral college was one-sided and impressive, his popular vote revealed a growing opposition to Republican power. Before his administration was two years old, opposition to Grant developed within the Republican party itself. Manifesting itself at first on the state level, the growing dissatisfaction soon resulted in a serious rift in the party. The so-called Liberal Republicans attracted to their ranks such party leaders as Lyman Trumbull, Charles Sumner, Carl Schurz, and Charles Francis Adams and secured significant support among the nation's newspapers. Determined either to prevent Grant's renomination in 1872 or to form a new party, these critics were particularly disturbed by the course of radical reconstruction in the South and by the corruption that had come to characterize the Grant administration. In a convention in Cincinnati on May 1, 1872, the Liberal Republicans nominated Horace Greeley to oppose Grant for the presidency, a mistake, as many of them soon discovered. In their platform, they demanded the immediate removal of all political disabilities on Southern whites and declared that local self-government, rather than the power of the national government, was a more effective safeguard for the protection of individual rights—a demand, in effect, that the Southern state governments be returned to Southern white control. Of equal importance to the Liberal Republicans was their effort to push civil service reform as the solution to the scandals and corruption of the Grant regime. Carl Schurz (1829–1906), a refugee of the German revolution of 1848–49, came to the United States in 1852, where he soon espoused the antislavery cause and became a prominent figure in the Republican party. In 1868, he delivered the keynote address at the convention that nominated Grant and shortly afterward was elected to the United States Senate from Missouri. In the Senate, Schurz became an early critic of the Grant administration and a pioneer in the movement for civil service reform. In 1872, he was one of the leaders of the Liberal Republican revolt. The following speech was delivered during the Presidential campaign, on July 22, 1872, in St. Louis. For a biography of Schurz, see Claude M. Fuess, *Carl Schurz, Reformer(1829–1906),* (New York,1932); and for a brief study of the Liberal Republican revolt, see Earle D. Ross, *The Liberal Republican Movement* (New York, 1919). In the following speech, note (1) Schurz' criticism of radical reconstruction policies; (2) his attitude toward Grant and his charges against the Grant administration; and (3) his proposals for change.

Frederic Bancroft, ed., *The Speeches, Correspondence and Political Papers of Carl Schurz* (6 vols., New York: G. P. Putnam's Sons, 1913), II, 392–443.

WHEN I was honored with a seat in the Senate of the United States, I expected to support the Administration which then came into power. The tasks it was called to perform were of unusual importance. The civil war was over. Its logical results, the abolition of slavery and the organization of free-labor society in the South, were just being reduced to political form and embedded in the Constitution of the Republic. It remained to fortify those results by reconciling to them the minds of the Southern people, so that their development could be securely left to the working of local self-government instead of the rule of force. To this end, a wise and generous policy, appealing to the best instincts of human nature, was required to assuage the passions and animosities the war had left behind it, and to make those who had been overcome in the conflict of arms, as much as possible satisfied with the new order of things. During a great period of public danger the Constitutional restrictions of power had not infrequently yielded to commanding necessity; the law had been overrun by the exigencies of the moment, and the people had become accustomed to a government of force. It was necessary to restore the integrity of Constitutional government and make the laws respected by the governing party as well as those who were governed. Great abuses had crept into public service, aggravated by the irregular practices of warlike times. The public interest imperatively demanded a thorough reform. The people were loaded down with enormous burdens, and while willing to bear all for their country, they looked for reasonable relief by a sound financial policy.

While these problems were uncommonly perplexing, the incoming Administration was favored with extraordinary opportunities. The ruling party had wielded almost undisputed power. It had a great history behind it from which it might have drawn a noble inspiration for new efforts aiming at something higher than selfish advantage. It had conquered under a banner of peace. There was an abundance of character and talent in its ranks to fit it for the work of reform. The newly elected President had the confidence of the country in advance. The masses of the people were well disposed. The greatness of the task to be performed, as well as of the possibilities presented, could scarcely fail to excite the noblest ambition. A success great enough to be the envy of the world was within reach. It did not require very great men to see and appreciate such opportunities, but it required what I might call the genius of smallness to lose them all.

More than three years of the Administration are now behind as a part of the history of the Republic. And what has become of our hopes? A disappointment which makes further hope appear like mockery.This Administration, which commenced its career under such happy auspices, has in so alarming a degree developed some of the very worst tendencies of our political life, that its continuance in authority appears as a danger and menace to our free institutions. In no period of our history, perhaps, has the selfishness of power and the grasping greed of party stood more insidiously, stubbornly and conspicuously in the way of manifest duty.

Let us take a survey of the field and trust to the evidence of our senses. The first great object of our policy should have been to renationalize the South; to revive among the Southern people feelings calculated to attach their hearts again to the fortunes of this Union; for, let us not indulge in the delusion that the holding together by force of its component parts is a basis upon which a republic can safely rest or long endure. It requires that bond which binds together the hearts of the people and not their bodies only. And to create that bond was for us the highest object of statesmanship. . . . In order to revive patriotic feeling and National attachment in the South, we had to convince the people that we were their friends and not only their conquerors, that we had their welfare at heart, and not only our advantage. Only when we made them believe in the purity and unselfishness of our intentions could we hope to regain their affection.

Let us see what was done by the Administration and the ruling party. The great social revolution grown up out of the war had resulted by logical necessity in the enfranchisement of the colored people. Only by the exercise of political rights can the free laborer maintain his independence. But the colored voters, untutored and inexperienced, fell under the leadership of unscrupulous adventurers. I do not say that this could have been entirely prevented. It was one of the usual consequences of great social revulsions. But its effect might well have been limited in time and extent by a wise policy. As it was, a system of robbery and ruinous misgovernment ensued which has hardly a parallel in history. Most of those States were, with incredible rapidity, burdened with enormous debts without any equivalent. Scores of millions disappeared as by magic, in the capacious darkness of private pockets. Impoverished as those States were by the war, they were now stripped naked. The public expenses became absurdly extravagant, the taxes unbearable. Under such loads industry was discouraged and flagged; enterprise sank down with hopeless despair; production diminished; and incredible as it may seem, while the rest of the country was prosperously progressing, the value of property in many of those States appeared in the census of 1870, after five years of peace, far below the figures exhibited by the census of 1860. Such have been the effects of so-called carpet-bag government in the South.

Who was responsible for this? Those governments were, and are at this moment carried on in the name and under the auspices of the Republican party. It was through them that the Southern people felt the touch of the ruling power. It was in them that they saw its spirit working. Was that impression wrong? Consider impartially what reasons they had for it. While the most reckless and rapacious of political bloodsuckers were thus plundering those communities, a system of political disabilities was maintained which excluded a large number of the intelligent property-holding men from eligibility to office, and thus from active participation in the administration of public affairs; a large number of those who had the greatest stake in good government were thus told that it was no business of theirs. While in this way, on the one side, the work of the plunderers was facilitated, it was not wonderful that on the other the summons —you shall love this Government! did not meet with an enthusiastic response. The removal of political disabilities, although its good effect could not have been doubted, was studiously put off until it could no longer be denied . . . and when amnesty was granted, it was done with such useless restrictions and with such a grudging grace as to make it appear that those who gave it would much rather have withheld it. . . .

Look over the legislation of Congress touching the late insurrectionary States. Study it attentively,—the bayonet law, the Ku-Klux law, as they now present themselves in retrospective view. The ends that legislation was to reach were apparently good. Grave and most reprehensible disorders had occurred in the South. Voters had been terrorized in the exercise of their rights. Innocent and inoffensive persons had been cruelly persecuted, oppressed, maltreated, killed by organized bands of marauders. The laws I spoke of were ostensibly intended to protect the rights of citizens and to repress such disorder. Well-meaning persons, to whom, even when opposing the passage of those laws, I always gave credit for good intentions, were drawn into their support by their generous sympathies for those whom they considered in peril. But what was the character of those laws, what their effect and what the great aim of some of the master-spirits who designed them? Not only did they, in protecting the rights of some, break down the bulwarks of the citizen against arbitrary authority, and by transgressing all Constitutional limitations of power, endanger the rights of all; not only did they awaken in the breasts of many, however well disposed, the grave apprehension that a government or a ruling party assuming so much would stop at nothing, but such measures served directly to sustain in power the very adventurers who by their revolting system of plunder were violently keeping alive the spirit of disorder which that legislation was to repress. Some of the very worst of that thieving fraternity have been constantly hanging around Congress bawling and pressing for the extremest measures, with no other view but that every such act would be likely to give them a new lease of power and extended freedom to steal. How much they care about the protection of the rights of citizens and the lives of innocent persons, I do not know, but I am certain that they value such laws especially as a political machinery to control ballot-boxes and as receiving an extension of their plundering license. How well those laws serve that purpose you will learn by study-

ing the history of the South during the last few years. I have been
informed that at this very moment in a certain part of North
Carolina over five hundred indictments, found in some way under that legislation, are held by the United States authorities *in
terrorem* over the heads of so many voters and their friends, to
make them vote and exert their influence at the impending State
election as the managers of the Grant party direct.

It is thus that the ruling party makes itself felt in those States;
it is in this light that the majesty of the National Government
appears to those people, not as a friend to lift them up from their
prostration, to guide them out of their errors with a generous
hand and to make them look up to the National flag as a symbol
of justice and fairness equal to all; not that—but as the ally and
the abettor of the robbers who suck their blood, as the mainstay
of a system which drains their resources, blasts their hopes,
emasculates their energies, mocks their enterprise and con-
demns them to utter poverty, distress and ruin.

You, honest Republicans, whose ears have been assiduously
filled with horrible Ku-Klux stories, and whose minds are un-
versed in the mysteries of party management, you may look with
surprise at this dark picture. You understand that the affection
of those people cannot be successfully invited by the cry, "You
must love us if it takes your last penny." You ask, how is it
possible that so wicked a game should be carried on by the leaders of a party wont to boast of its great principles. It would be
impossible had not that party fallen under the control of a
selfishness so unscrupulous as to put party success above the best
principles it ever possessed.

You must know that "carpet-baggerdom" is exceedingly faithful to the party, except, perhaps when its leading spirits, quar-
relling over the spoils, fall out among themselves. It lives upon
party fidelity and it preaches it as its political gospel. It relies
upon the virtue of party fidelity to cover a multitude of sins. It
sends its representatives to Congress strong enough in number to
make up majorities. They are the staunchest and most zealous
supporters of the Administration for value received. They are
the household troops, always ready to march forward and back-
ward, and to wheel to the right and to the left as the Administration managers direct. There are exceptions as there are white

crows, but they are few. Whatever legislative scheme the Administration may set up, by whatever means of partisan tyranny in caucus or in Congress the opposition of independent men is to be put down, those household troops can be counted on. They faithfully aid the Administration in governing the country, in governing you. For that they receive their patronage, and by that patronage the Administration aids and sustains them in their States. They distribute it among their retainers who are equally faithful. Thus they organize their home forces through whom they rule the party at home. These forces are at their service and through them at the service of the Administration. Thus their system furnishes votes in Congress, delegations to National Conventions boiling over with enthusiasm for the renomination of the President, and it is expected to furnish electoral votes to continue him in power. I suspect, however, it will not furnish enough. In the meantime carpet-bag government, upheld by the patronage of the Government, and by the countenance of the ruling party, lustily plies its trade and fills its pockets; and you, honest Republicans, wonder why the late rebels will not become loyal enough to vote the Republican ticket.

But to me this seems certain: as long as party ascendancy is maintained by such means, as long as party selfishness stands in the way of honest government, as long as the National power appears as the ally and abettor of corruption and robbery in the South, that hearty reconciliation, that universal restoration of cordial feeling which this country stands much in need of, and which every patriotic citizen must desire with the whole ardor of his soul, cannot and will not come. As long as a system prevails which sacrifices the welfare of a part of the people on the altar of party advantage, we shall be met with distrust and alarm, for it is not from such sources that affection springs. I should be the last man to excite such distrust, and I may say without boasting, that I have done my share to remove it. And, having done this, I may throw the resposibility for the failure upon those who love the possession of power more than the accomplishment of the high objects for which that power should have been exerted. I charge the Administration and those who control the Republican party that by their partisan selfishness they have shown themselves utterly unfit to encourage and develop the good impulses slumbering in the Southern people, and thus to solve the great problem of National reconciliation. I assert that thus they have disappointed the hopes and forfeited the confidence of the American people, and that the power they wield has become barren of good, and fruitful of danger in their hands.

The partisan selfishness which sacrificed the great opportunity of renationalizing the South, has shown its evil tendency no less glaringly upon another field. The people looked to this Administration for a thorough reform of the abuses which had crept into the public service. Corrupt and unworthy officers had to make way for better men. Public servants had to be made aware that the interests of the people should be the highest object of their action; that to the Republic they owed their undivided devotion and their best efforts, and that they had no right to claim any advantage from their offices beyond the strict allowance of the law. Honor and duty should be their watchword. It was expected of the President that he would inspire all with his example.

The first period of the Administration when the Government was so conspicuously employed to make provision for relatives and personal favorites, which we cannot think of without shame and humiliation, we should be glad to forget, remembering only the many good appointments that were made, had the sequel been better than the beginning, but the disgrace of a nepotism more scandalous than anything the history of this Republic knows of— a nepotism which taught every public servant that in the opinion of the Chief Magistrate they might without impropriety exhaust their official opportunities to make themselves and their kinsfolk comfortable, was followed by practices more directly touching the character and integrity of our institutions. I will not speak here of the cases of embezzlement, defalcation, fraud and downright thieving which occurred under this administration, and the number and magnitude of which as they accumulated startled the tax-paying people. . . .

And yet bad as this may all be, it is by no means the worst feature of the case. Bad as that policy may have been which, throwing aside those moral agencies apt to bring forth a fruitful cooperation of the best elements in the South, and to reunite the country in National feeling, delivered the Southern people over to their plunderers and tormentors; bad as the frauds and abuses may have been which disgraced our public service; bad as the management of the patronage may have been which in the highest place set a demoralizing example of selfishness, strove to corrupt legislation and transformed the whole service into a vast political agency; bad as the contempt of law and the violations of the Constitution may have been, which have grown into a most dangerous habit under this Administration—far worse, of infinitely more alarming import is the circumstance that the Republican party, the party once so noble in its impulses and so fearless in its actions has been so completely subjugated by the Administration and its political managers, as not only to lose its ability to rise up against such misdeeds and abuses, but even the spirit to discriminate between right and wrong and to call things by their right names. Whatever wrongs and abuses may exist they can be corrected as long as we have the courage to seek the truth and to recognize it. But a political party which fails to recognize abuses as such has lost the moral ability to correct them. Its very ascendancy will thenceforward stand in the way of true reform. . . .

General Grant came into office under circumstances of extraordinary promise. He had, as General-in-Chief, directed the closing operations of the war. His success had centered upon him the gratitude and esteem of the loyal people, and in granting to the defeated foe a generous capitulation, he had, in a high degree, won even their respect and confidence. There was scarcely a man in the Nation to whose voice they would have more willingly listened, when admonishing them to submit to the inevitable, to accomodate themselves in good faith to the legitimate results of the war, to respect the rights of their neighbors, however humble, and to develop for the common good the opportunities presented by the new order of things—such admonitions being accompanied by work and acts of conciliation and goodwill. No man could have done more to revive their best and most patriotic impulses, to quiet their apprehensions, and assure their minds as to the safety of their rights as citizens, to make them feel that they were not to be the step-children of the Republic, to inspire them with new interest in its fortunes, thus neutralizing their heartburnings and animosities, giving the peace of measurable contentment to their country, and restoring the long-lost cordiality of feeling between the different parts of the Union. . . .

Truly, since the organization of the Government no man had more power for good; no President, save Washington himself, was elected under more flattering auguries, and there is probably not one whose performances stand in more glaring contrast to his opportunities.

There is nothing so apt to dazzle the eyes of the multitude as military glory. Even the most discerning minds cannot easily resist its charms. We are fond of believing that a man who has successfully commanded an army must be able to govern a nation. But that universality of talent is but rarely met with. I venture to say that it is not in this instance. This is not a harsh judgment, for General Grant has his failings in common with some of the greatest captains in history. His career as President warrants the conclusion that he has never been able fully to appreciate the difference between military command and the complex duties and resposibilities of civil administration. I doubt whether it has ever become clear to his mind what the Presidency means in our system of government. . . .

I will not wrong President Grant. He is by no means a monster of iniquity. He is simply a man who makes use of his high official position to suit his own convenience regardless of other interests. He does not sit in his closet a designing usurper, gloomily pondering how he may subvert the free institutions of the Republic. Neither does he ponder how he may preserve them. He does not ponder at all. . . . He does not mean to break down the authority of the laws; he simply wants them not to hamper him in his doings. He does not mean systematically to outrage the public sense of decency by nepotism and low associations, to corrupt the service and to degrade our political life. He only wants to make his relatives and favorites comfortable, to associate with men who are congenial to him and to take the best care of his interests he can. He is not incapable of occasionally doing a good thing. He prefers a good appointment to a bad one, other things being equal. He undoubtedly desires that affairs should go well, his own welfare included. The cry for civil service reform growing popular, he came very near being a civil service reformer. He started probably with good intentions, and would perhaps have carried them out had he not found it to be his interest to control the political machine in the old way for his re-election. Then the absolute command of the civil service machinery appeared to him much more useful than civil service reform. He would probably have consented to let the Ku-Klux law drop by its own limitation, but considering his interest in the pending campaign he did not blush to urge his friends in Congress to continue in his hands the most alarming power to suspend the writ of habeas corpus while his own re-election is pending. He does not mean to be a despot, but he wants to have his will.

Such is the character of his personal government. . . . It is absolutely barren of ideas and originality, bare of striking achievements, void of noble sentiments and inspiring example. It is simply dull and heavy, stupid and stubborn in its selfishness. . . .

And now, finally, I approach a subject which is, if possible, of still higher importance to us all. Seven years have elapsed since the close of the civil war. No thinking man can have watched the progress of things in the South without having gathered instructive experience. It must have become clear to all of us that the development of the new order of society there cannot be secured wholly by an extraneous pressure, which would involve a change in the nature of our institutions, but must ultimately be left to the workings of local self-government.

Two things are now settled and evident: First, that the equality of rights, irrespective of race or color, the enfranchisement of the emancipated class which sprung as a local necessity from the great revolution, and which stands embodied in the Constitution of the Republic, is an irreversible fact. Every sane man recognizes that. There are certainly but few individuals in the South who close their eyes against it. The other thing is, that the rule of unprincipled and rapacious leaders at the head of the colored population has resulted in a government of corruption and plunder, and gives no promise of improvement. I will not throw the blame upon the colored people, who entered the political field without experience and a just understanding of their true interests, and more than once I publicly expressed the opinion that much of the mischief might have been averted had the Southern whites at the start, instead of leaving the field to unscrupulous adventurers, won for themselves the confidence of the colored people by assuring them in good faith the security of their new rights. However that may be, the result is known. In some States the carpet-bag governments have already broken down, and in others they cannot much longer endure. They have made it inevitable that in most, if not all of them, the control of local affairs should presently fall into the hands of those classes which, to a great extent, stood against us during the civil war. It cannot be avoided, unless you adopt a system of interference which will subvert the most essential principles of our government. To those classes, then, will in a great measure the task be confided of developing the new order of things. It must be our dearest wish, as it is our highest interest, that this task be well performed. And we should assiduously bring to bear upon them all the moral influences within our reach to make them do it well.

Are they ready to receive such influences in the right spirit? Southern society has been gradually undergoing a change. The old political leaders who brought on secession, and now stick to their old creeds, are dropping by the wayside. The young element which has gone through the practical school of war is coming to the front. They know that something has happened. They know that this decision cannot be overthrown again, and that it would be foolish to squander their time in trying. They know that they have lost efforts behind them, and that they have a life before them which can be made useful. They are leaving in the rear their old leaders who are still groping among the ruins of the past, and they begin to stand upon their own feet. They are inclined to march forward and to develop the opportunities of the new order of things. They are capable of a new, honorable and patriotic ambition, for they feel that this is after all their country, and that their fortunes are bound up in the fortunes of this our common Republic. They want to be recognized as American citizens again in the fullness of an American citizen's rights. This is the young South which is lifting its head. . . .

Will the people of the North coldly tell them: "We will have nothing to do with you; we care for partisan power and not for your friendship and well-doing!" Are there dissatisfied Liberals who will tell them: "Well, we would have taken you by the hand had the Cincinnati Convention nominated this or that man; but now you will have to submit for another four years, and we may then, perhaps, be in a condition to do something for you."

Fellow-citizens of the North, is it possible that at a moment when the joy of National reconciliation, a reconciliation on the ground of all you fought for, may illumine the whole Republic if you but will it—is it possible that you should think of things small and paltry by the side of so great a consummation? Is it not clear to you, that that reconciliation you will find the best, nay the only safe guarantee for future peace and harmonious progress, and that we can never hope successfully to solve the other great problems pressing upon us, until this one is disposed of? Have you considered what the consequences will be, if you throw those who approach you with warm hearts and patriotic intentions back into a sullen despondency, a despondency which must spring from the belief that whatever evidence they may give of good will, it will be rejected? . . .

As for me, I have faith in the spirit and good sense of the American people. They feel instinctively that they have arrived at a turning point; that they have to elect between that torpid submission to narrow-minded party rule which, like dry-rot, deadens the body-politic—and free, fresh and stimulating contests of opinion which will embrace the whole people once more with a healthy, progressive influence. It is the choice between stagnation and movement. I trust that the revolution which has begun will neither go back nor stop. Let those who want to serve the cause of free government throw themselves resolutely into the waves with the courageous confidence that the genius of the American Republic will lead to a happy issue.

13

"Society Turned Bottom-Side Up"

James S. Pike on the Prostrate State of South Carolina, 1874

The organization of new state governments in the South under the auspices of the Reconstruction Acts began in 1868. These Radical Republican governments were controlled to a very large extent by carpetbaggers, scalawags, and newly enfranchised Negroes. They were strenuously opposed and severely criticized by conservative white Southerners, and as time went on, this criticism spread to Northerners as well. The participation of inexperienced Negroes in the governmental process, the frequent examples of graft and corruption and the ineptitude of the political leaders produced a stereotype in the popular mind that proved difficult to erase in later years.

Among the most caustic Northern critics of the radical governments was James Shepherd Pike (1811–1882). Pike, a veteran newspaperman who had served as Washington correspondent of Greeley's *New York Tribune* during the 1850's, was a staunch antislavery man and an ardent Republican. During the war, he was United States Minister to the Netherlands, returning in 1866 to resume his newspaper work. In 1874, Pike published his famous account of South Carolina's radical state government in action. His work was more emotional than scholarly but represents an attitude toward the Negro and the South that was becoming all too pervasive in the North. Like many Northern antislavery men, Pike held a strong antipathy toward the Negro. For a sound appraisal of Pike, see Robert F. Durden, *James Shepherd Pike: Republicanism and the American Negro, 1850–1882* (Durham, 1957). In the selection that follows, note (1) Pike's assessment of "Negro rule" in South Carolina; (2) his comments on compulsory education for Negroes as a solution to the problem; and (3) the nature and tone of the rhetoric used.

James S. Pike, *The Prostrate State: South Carolina Under Negro Government* (New York: D. Appleton and Company, 1874), 9–21, 58–65.

Columbia, the capital of South Carolina, is charmingly situated in the heart of the upland country, near the geographical centre of the State. It has broad, open streets, regularly laid out, and fine, shady residences in and about the town. The opportunity for rides and drives can hardly be surpassed. There are good animals and good turnouts [carriages] to be seen on the streets at all times; and now, in midwinter, the weather invites to such displays. It seems there was a little real winter here at Christmas and New Year's, when the whole country suffered such an excess of sudden cold. There was even skating and sleighing for a week. But now there is no frost, and the recollection of it is dispelled by the genial spring weather that prevails.

Yesterday, about 4 P.M., the assembled wisdom of the State, whose achievements are illustrated on that theatre, issued forth from the State-House. About three-quarters of the crowd belonged to the African race. They were of every hue, from the light octoroon to the deep black. They were such a looking body of men as might pour out of a market-house or a court-house at random in any Southern State. Every negro type and physiognomy was here to be seen, from the genteel serving-man to the rough-hewn customer from the rice or cotton field. Their dress was as varied as their countenances. There was the second-hand black frock-coat of infirm gentility, glossy and threadbare. There was the stove-pipe hat of many ironings and departed styles. There was also to be seen a total disregard of the proprieties of costume in the coarse and dirty garments of the field; the stub-jackets and slouch hats of soiling labor. In some instances, rough woolen comforters embraced the neck and hid the absence of linen. Heavy brogans, and short, torn trousers, it was impossible to hide. The dusky tide flowed out into the littered and barren grounds, and, issuing through the coarse wooden fence of the inclosure, melted away into the street beyond. These were the legislators of South Carolina.

In conspicuous bas-relief over the door of exit, on the panels of the stately edifice, the marble visages of George McDuffie and Robert Y. Hayne overlooked the scene. Could they veritably witness it from their dread abode? What then? "I tremble," wrote Jefferson, when depicting the character of Southern slavery, "I tremble when I reflect that God is just." But did any of that old band of Southern Revolutionary patriots who wrestled in their souls with the curse of slavery ever contemplate such a descent into barbarism as this spectacle implied and typified? "My God, look at this!" was the unbidden ejaculation of a low-country planter, clad in homespun, as he leaned over the rail inside the House, gazing excitedly upon the body in session. "This is the first time I have been here. I thought I knew what we were doing when we consented to emancipation. I knew the negro, and I predicted much that has happened, but I never thought it would come to this. Let me go."

Here, then, is the outcome, the ripe, perfected fruit of the boasted civilization of the South, after two hundred years of experience. A white community, that had gradually risen from small beginnings, till it grew into wealth, culture, and refinement, and became accomplished in all the arts of civilization; that successfully asserted its resistance to a foreign tyranny by deeds of conspicuous valor, which achieved liberty and independence through the fire and tempest of civil war, and illustrated itself in the councils of the nation by orators and statesmen worthy of any age or nation—such a community is then reduced to this. It lies prostrate in the dust, ruled over by this strange conglomerate, gathered from the ranks of its own servile population. It is the spectacle of a society suddenly turned bottom-side up. The wealth, the intelligence, the culture, the wisdom of the State, have broken through the crust of that social volcano on which they were contentedly reposing, and have sunk out of sight, consumed by the subterranean fires they had with such temerity braved and defied.

In the place of this old aristocratic society stands the rude form of the most ignorant democracy that mankind ever saw, invested with the functions of government. It is the dregs of the population habilitated in the robes of their intelligent predecessors, and asserting over them the rule of ignorance and corruption, through the inexorable machinery of a majority of numbers. It is barbarism overwhelming civilization by physical force. It is the slave rioting in the halls of his master, and putting that master under his feet. And, though it is done without malice and without vengeance, it is nevertheless none the less completely and absolutely done. Let us approach nearer and take a closer view. We will enter the House of Representatives. Here sit one hundred and twenty-four members. Of these, twenty-three are white men, representing the remains of the old civilization.

These are good-looking, substantial citizens. They are men of weight and standing in the communities they represent. They are all from the hill country. The frosts of sixty and seventy winters whiten the heads of some among them. There they sit, grim and silent. They feel themselves to be but loose stones, thrown in to partially obstruct a current they are powerless to resist. They say little and do little as the days go by. They simply watch the rising tide, and mark the progressive steps of the inundation. They hold their places reluctantly. They feel themselves to be in some sort martyrs, bound stoically to suffer in behalf of that still great element in the State whose prostrate fortunes are becoming the sport of an unpitying Fate. Grouped in a corner of the commodious and well-furnished chamber, they stolidly survey the noisy riot that goes on in the great black Left and Centre, where the business and debates of the House are conducted, and where sit the strange and extraordinary guides of the fortunes of a once proud and haughty State. In this crucial trial of his pride, his manhood, his prejudices, his spirit, it must be said of the Southern Bourbon of the Legislature that he comports himself with a dignity, a reserve, and a decorum, that command admiration. He feels that the iron hand of Destiny is upon him. He is gloomy, disconsolate, hopeless. The gray heads of this generation openly profess that they look for no relief. They see no way of escape. The recovery of influence, of position, of control in the State, is felt by them to be impossible. They accept their position with a stoicism that promises no reward here or hereafter. They are the types of a conquered race. They staked all and lost all. Their lives remain, their property and their children do not. War, emancipation, and grinding taxation, have consumed them. Their struggle now is against complete confiscation. They endure, and wait for the night.

This dense negro crowd they confront do the debating, the squabbling, the law-making, and create all the clamor and disorder of the body. These twenty-three white men are but the observers, the enforced auditors of the dull and clumsy imitation of a deliberative body, whose appearance in their present capacity is at once a wonder and a shame to modern civilization.

Deducting the twenty-three members referred to, who comprise the entire strength of the opposition, we find one hundred and one remaining. Of this one hundred and one, ninety-four are colored, and seven are their white allies. Thus the blacks outnumber the whole body of whites in the House more than three to one. On the mere basis of numbers in the State the injustice of this disproportion is manifest, since the black population is relatively four to three of the whites. A just rectification of the disproportion, on the basis of population merely, would give fifty-four whites to seventy black members. And the line of race very nearly marks the line of hostile politics. As things stand, the body is almost literally a Black Parliament, and it is the only one on the face of the earth which is the representative of a white constituency and the professed exponent of an advanced type of modern civilization. But the reader will find almost any portraiture inadequate to give a vivid idea of the body, and enable him to comprehend the complete metamorphosis of the South Carolina Legislature, without observing its details. The Speaker is black, the Clerk is black, the door-keepers are black, the little pages are black, the chairman of the Ways and Means is black, and the chaplain is coal-black. At some of the desks sit colored men whose types it would be hard to find outside of Congo; whose costume, visages, attitudes, and expression, only befit the forecastle of a buccaneer. It must be remembered, also, that these men, with not more than half a dozen exceptions, have been themselves slaves, and that their ancestors were slaves for generations. . . .

One of the things that first strike a casual observer in this negro assembly is the fluency of debate, if the endless chatter that goes on there can be dignified with this term. The leading topics of discussion are all well understood by the members, as they are of a practical character, and appeal directly to the personal interests of every legislator, as well as to those of his constituents. When an appropriation bill is up to raise money to catch and punish the Ku-klux, they know exactly what it means. They feel it in their bones. So, too, with educational measures. The free school comes right home to them; then the business of arming and drilling the black militia. They are eager on this point. Sambo can talk on these topics and those of a kindred character, and their endless ramifications, day in and day out.

There is no end to his gush and babble. The intellectual level is that of a bevy of fresh converts at a negro camp-meeting. Of course this kind of talk can be extended indefinitely. It is the doggerel of debate, and not beyond the reach of the lowest parts. Then the negro is imitative in the extreme. He can copy like a parrot or a monkey, and he is always ready for a trial of his skill. He believes he can do anything, and never loses a chance to try, and is just as ready to be laughed at for his failure as applauded for his success. He is more vivacious than the white, and being more volatile and good-natured, he is correspondingly more irrepressible. His misuse of language in his imitations is at times ludicrous beyond measure. He notoriously loves a joke or an anecdote, and will burst into a broad guffaw on the smallest provocation. He breaks out into an incoherent harangue on the floor just as easily, and being without practice, discipline, or experience, . . . he will go on repeating himself, dancing as it were to the music of his own voice, forever. He will speak half a dozen times on one question, and every time say the same things without knowing it. . . .

But the old stagers admit that the colored brethren have a wonderful aptness at legislative proceedings. They are "quick as lightning" at detecting points of order, and they certainly make incessant and extraordinary use of their knowledge. No one is allowed to talk five minutes without interruption, and one interruption is the signal for another and another, until the original speaker is smothered under an avalanche of them. Forty questions of privilege will be raised in a day. At times, nothing goes on but alternating questions of order and of privilege. The inefficient colored friend who sits in the Speaker's chair cannot suppress this extraordinary element of the debate. Some of the blackest members exhibit a pertinacity of intrusion in raising these points of order and questions of privilege that few white men can equal. Their struggles to get the floor, their bellowings and physical contortions, baffle description. The Speaker's hammer plays a perpetual tattoo all to no purpose. The talking and the interruptions from all quarters go on with the utmost license. Every one esteems himself as good as his neighbor, and puts in his oar, apparently as often for love of riot and confusion as for any thing else. It is easy to imagine what are his ideas of propriety and dignity among a crowd of his own color, and these are illustrated without reserve. The Speaker orders a member whom he has discovered to be particularly unruly to take his seat. The member obeys, and with same motion that he sits down, throws his feet on to his desk, hiding himself from the Speaker by the soles of his boots. In an instant he appears again on the floor. After a few experiences of this sort, the Speaker threatens, in a laugh, to call "the gemman" to order. This is considered a capital joke, and a guffaw follows. The laugh goes round, and then the peanuts are cracked and munched faster than ever; one hand being employed in fortifying the inner man with this nutriment of universal use, while the other enforces the views of the orator. This laughing propensity of the sable crowd is a great cause of disorder. They laugh as hens cackle—one begins and all follow.

But underneath all this shocking burlesque upon legislative proceedings, we must not forget that there is something very real to this uncouth and untutored multitude. It is not all sham, nor all burlesque. They have a genuine interest and a genuine earnestness in the business of the assembly which we are bound to recognize and respect, unless we would be accounted shallow critics. They have an earnest purpose, born of a conviction that their position and condition are not fully assured, which lends a sort of dignity to their proceedings. The barbarous, animated jargon in which they so often indulge is on occasion seen to be so transparently sincere and weighty in their own minds that sympathy supplants disgust. The whole thing is a wonderful novelty to them as well as to observers. Seven years ago these men were raising corn and cotton under the whip of the overseer. To-day they are raising points of order and questions of privilege. They find they can raise one as well as the other. They prefer the latter. It is easier, and better paid. Then, it is the evidence of an accomplished result. It means escape and defense from old oppressors. It means liberty. It means the destruction of prison-walls only too real to them. It is the sunshine of their lives. It is their day of jubilee. It is their long-promised vision of the Lord God Almighty. . . .

The rule of South Carolina should not be dignified with the name of government. It is the installation of a huge system of brigandage. The men who have had it in control, and who now have it in control, are the picked villains of the community. They are the highwaymen of the State. They are professional legislative robbers. They are men who have studied and practised the art of legalized theft. They are in no sense different from, or better than, the men who fill the prisons and penitentiaries of the world. They are, in fact, of precisely that class, only more daring and audacious. They pick your pockets by law. They rob the poor and the rich alike, by law. They confiscate your estate by law. They do none of these things even under the tyrant's plea of the public good or the public necessity. They do all simply to enrich themselves personally. The sole, base object is, to gorge the individual with public plunder. Having done it, they turn around and buy immunity for their acts by sharing their gains with the ignorant, pauperized, besotted crowd who have chosen them to the stations they fill, and which enable them thus to rob and plunder. . . .

Does anybody suppose that such a condition of things as exists to-day in South Carolina is to last? Such a supposition is to ignore the history and the character of mankind. Suppose the men, or a large portion of the white men, of South Carolina who have gone through the War of the Rebellion are cowed and demoralized by its results; how is it with the individuals of the rising generation who are fast taking their places? Is not the hot blood of the South in their veins? They have the ardor of youth. They have the stimulus of young ambition; they have the pride of ancestry; they have the inherited valor of successive generations. Have they no part to play in the future? We may rest assured that no depressing circumstances of the present are going to destroy or repress the natural development that comes of race and of blood. Opportunity alone is wanting; and that, we know, is always found by the bold and aspiring. . . .

Those who suppose that any thing short of a good government in the State of South Carolina, and, we may add, of any other State similarly situated in the South, is going to long stand, or be tolerated, may well take heed, if their judgments are ever to find expression in action. . . . Where there is actual injustice, or radical wrong in the government, it breeds resistance. That wrong may be even in part sentimental. It is none the less real for that. The present government of South Carolina is not only corrupt and oppressive, it is insulting. It denies the exercise of the rights of white communities, because they are white. The city of Charleston is an example . . . The black government of the State denies it the right to superintend its own voting; or to count its own votes. . . .

The question is often asked if education is not the remedy for the blackness of darkness that prevails in South Carolina. Yes, indeed, if that were possible. Make it compulsory then. But what is education? Is it the glib recitation of the alphabet, or the multiplication-table? Is it the knowledge of reading and writing? This is all that compulsory education can give, in its most successful forms. But here is a race to be educated in the very elements of manhood. They have to be taught positively and negatively. The education they require is the formation of a race the opposite of the existing race. They have to be taught not to lie, not to steal, not to be unchaste. To educate them properly is to revolutionize their whole moral nature. The groundwork of that education which will make them fit rulers of a republic will not even have been laid when they shall be taught reading and writing. It is the reading negroes of the South Carolina Legislature who lead in its most infamous venalities and corruptions. This sort of education merely lends a cutting edge to their moral obtuseness. Education, to be what it ought to be with the existing race of negroes in the South, means to undo the habits and practices and modes of thought and want of thought engendered by centuries of slavery. It means the moral enlightenment and regeneration of a whole people debauched and imbruted for ages. Such is the gigantic task demanded of an education suited to existing circumstances.

We do not mean to say that all this is necessary to entitle the colored man to the privileges of citizenship, but only mean it as a reply to the glib suggestion of compulsory education as a ready remedy for the existing disorders and crimes that disgrace republican government and menace its future. Neither is it any answer to say that other people are ignorant, and superstitious, and degraded. When the ignorant and superstitious and degraded subjects of other nationalities have shown themselves capable of governing the better classes of society, it will be time to plead their example and their qualifications for the functions of rulers.

But they are the classes who have never yet in history exercised the functions of government. And thus the fact that they exist from age to age, and that their presence does not destroy governments, proves nothing. They have lived as pupils in the State, and not as its masters, as they now live in South Carolina. Let us not be misunderstood. We are not talking about denying rights of citizenship. We are denouncing governments of ignorance and vice, and demanding a remedy.

Again, there is no parallel to be drawn between the exceptional venality of Northern Legislatures and the corruptions of South Carolina government. They do not spring from the same causes. The former can be promptly remedied by exposure and by an appeal to the intelligence and virtue of the constituency; in the other case there is no such tribunal to appeal to. It is a moral morass in which there is neither standing nor holding ground.

14

"Let All Men Enjoy Equal Liberty and Equal Rights"

A Southern Negro on the Civil Rights Bill, 1874

For years after the passage of the Reconstruction Acts, some Republican leaders saw the necessity for new and wider civil rights legislation in order to protect Negroes from the discrimination that was everywhere appearing. Charles Sumner especially fought hard for a new Civil Rights Act that would eliminate segregation in the schools and outlaw all other forms of discrimination to which Negroes were subjected. Summer died in 1874, but in his last years Congress debated such a bill. In 1875 it passed, but according to one authority, more as a memorial to Sumner than as protection for Negroes. The Civil Rights Act of 1875 was the first attempt of the United States government to deal directly with the problem of segregation. By its terms Negroes were to be accorded equal treatment in accommodations, inns, public conveyances, and theaters. No mention was made in the act, however, of segregation in the schools, Sumner's primary concern. Among those who argued for the new bill was Richard Harvey Cain (1825–1887), a Negro Congressman from the Charleston district of South Carolina. Cain, born of free parents in Virginia, had spent most of his life in the North, where he entered the ministry and eventually became an elder in the African Methodist Episcopal Church. After serving in Ohio, Iowa, and Brooklyn, he was transferred to South Carolina in 1865. A member of South Carolina's constitutional convention in 1868, he served two years in the state senate (the legislature so bitterly condemned by Pike) before his election to Congress in 1872. The following speech was delivered in the House of Representatives on January 10, 1874. Note (1) Representative Cain's answer to his colleague's charge that the civil rights legislation would enforce social rights; (2) evidence he cited to show that blacks and whites did not enjoy equality of treatment; (3) arguemnts used to defend equality of treatment in schools, colleges, and public accomodations; (4) how he used participation in the war to support his views; and (5) elements of his appeal giving it the character of eloquence.

Congressional Record (43rd Congress, 1st Session), 565–67 (Jan. 10, 1874).

Mr. SPEAKER, I feel called upon more particularly by the remarks of the gentleman from North Carolina [Mr. VANCE] on civil rights to express my views. For a number of days this question has been discussed, and various have been the opinions expressed as to whether or not the pending bill should be passed in its present form or whether it should be modified to meet the objections entertained by a number of gentlemen whose duty it will be to give their votes for or against its passage. It has been assumed that to pass this bill in its present form Congress would manifest a tendency to override the Constitution of the country and violate the rights of the States.

Whether it be true or false is yet to be seen. I take it so far as the constitutional question is concerned, if the colored people under the law, under the amendments to the Constitution, have become invested with all the rights of citizenship, then they carry with them all rights and immunities accruing to and belonging to a citizen of the United States. If four, or nearly five, million people have been lifted from the thralldom of slavery and made free; if the Government by its amendments to the Constitution has guaranteed to them all rights and immunities, as to other citizens, they must necessarily therefore carry along with them all the privileges enjoyed by all other citizens of the Republic.

Sir, the gentleman from North Carolina [Mr. VANCE] who spoke on the question stated some objections, to which I desire to address a few words of reply. He said it would enforce social rights, and therefore would be detrimental to the interests of both the whites and the blacks of the country. My conception of the effect of this bill, if it be passed into a law, will be simply to place the colored men of this country upon the same footing with every other citizen under the law, and will not at all enforce social relationship with any other class of persons in the country whatsoever. It is merely a matter of law. What we desire is that our civil rights shall be guaranteed by law as they are guaranteed to every other class of persons; and when that is done all other things will come in as a necessary sequence, the enforcement of the rights following the enactment of the law.

Sir, social equality is a right which every man, every woman,

and every class of persons have within their own control. They
have a right to form their own acquaintances, to establish their
own social relationships. Its establishment and regulation is not
within the province of legislation. No laws enacted by legislators
can compel social equality. Now, what is it we desire? What we
desire is this: inasmuch as we have been raised to the dignity, to
the honor, to the position of our manhood, we ask that the laws
of this country should guarantee all the rights and immunities
belonging to that proud position, to be enforced all over this
broad land.

Sir, the gentleman states that in the State of North Carolina
the colored people enjoy all their rights as far as the highways
are concerned; that in the hotels, and in the railroad cars, and in
the various public places of resort, they have all the rights and
all the immunities accorded to any other class of citizens of the
United States. Now, it may not have come under his observation,
but it has under mine, that such really is not the case; and the
reason why I know and feel it more than he does is because my
face is painted black and his is painted white. We who have the
color—I may say the objectionable color—know and feel all this.
A few days ago, in passing from South Carolina to this city, I
entered a place of public resort where hungry men are fed, but
I did not dare—I could not without trouble—sit down to the table.
I could not sit down at Wilmington or at Weldon without entering
into a contest, which I did not desire to do. My colleague, the
gentleman who so eloquently spoke on this subject the other day,
[Mr. ELLIOTT,] a few months ago entered a restaurant at Wilmington and sat down to be served, and while there a gentleman
stepped up to him and said, "You cannot eat here." All the other
gentlemen upon the railroad as passengers were eating there; he
had only twenty minutes, and was compelled to leave the restaurant or have a fight for it. He showed fight, however, and got his
dinner; but he has never been back there since. Coming here last
week I felt we did not desire to draw revolvers and present the
bold front of warriors, and therefore we ordered our dinners to
be brought into the cars, but even there we found the existence
of this feeling; for although we had paid a dollar apiece for our
meals, to be brought by the servants into the cars, still there was
objection on the part of the railroad people to our eating our

meals in the cars, because they said we were putting on airs. They refused us in the restaurant, and then did not desire that we should eat our meals in the cars, although we paid for them. Yet this was in the noble State of North Carolina.

Mr. Speaker, the colored men of the South do not want the adoption of any force measure. No; they do not want anything by force. All they ask is that you will give them, by statutory enactment under the fundamental law, the right to enjoy precisely the same privileges accorded to every other class of citizens.

The gentleman, moreover, has told us that if we pass this civil-rights bill we will thereby rob the colored men of the South of the friendship of the whites. Now, I am at a loss to see how the friendship of our white friends can be lost to us by simply saying we should be permitted to enjoy the rights enjoyed by other citizens. I have a higher opinion of the friendship of the southern men than to suppose any such thing. I know them too well. I know their friendship will not be lost by the passage of this bill. For eight years I have been in South Carolina, and I have found this to be the fact, that the higher class, comprising gentlemen of learning and refinement, are less opposed to this measure than are those who do not occupy so high a position a position in the social scale.

Sir, I think that there will be no difficulty. But I do think this, that there will be more trouble if we do not have those rights. I regard it important, therefore, that we should make the law so strong that no man can infringe those rights.

But, says the gentleman from North Carolina, some ambitious colored man will, when this law is passed, enter a hotel or railroad car, and thus create a disturbance. If it be his right, then there is no vaulting ambition in his enjoying that right. And if he can pay for his seat in a first-class car or his room in a hotel, I see no objection to his enjoying it. But the gentleman says more. He cited on the school question, the evidence of South Carolina, and says the South Carolina University has been destroyed by virtue of bringing into contact the white students with the the colored. I think not. It is true that a small number of students left the institution, but the institution still remains. The buildings are there as erect as ever; the faculty are there as attentive to their duties as ever they were; the students are coming in as they did before. It is true, sir, that there is a mixture of students now; that there are colored and white students of law and medicine sitting side by side; it is true, sir, that the prejudice of some of the professors was so strong that it drove them out of the institution; but the philanthropy and good sense of others were such that they remained; and thus we have still the institution going on, and because some students have left, it cannot be reasonably argued that the usefulness of the institution has been destroyed. The University of South Carolina has not been destroyed.

But the gentleman says more. The colored man cannot stand, he says, where this antagonism exists, and he deprecates the idea of antagonizing the races. The gentleman says there is no antagonism on his part. I think there is no antagonism so far as the country is concerned. So far as my observation extends, it goes to prove this: that there is a general acceptance upon the part of the larger and better class of the whites of the South of the situation, and that they regard the education and the development of the colored people as essential to their welfare, and the peace, happiness, and prosperity of the whole country. Many of them, including the best minds of the South, are earnestly engaged in seeking to make this great system of education permanent in all the States. I do not believe, therefore, that it is possible there can be such an antagonism. Why, sir, in Massachusetts there is no such antagonism. There the colored and the white children go to school side by side. In Rhode Island there is not that antagonism. There they are educated side by side in the high schools. In New York, in the highest schools, are to be found, of late, colored men and colored women. Even old democratic New York does not refuse to give the colored people their rights, and there is no antagonism. A few days ago, when in New York, I made it my business to find out what was the position of matters there in this repect. I ascertained that there are, I think, seven colored ladies in the highest school in New York, and I believe they stand No. 1 in their class, side by side with members of the best and most refined families of the citizens of New York, and without any objection to their presence.

I cannot understand how is is that our southern friends, or a certain class of them, always bring back this old ghost of prejudice and of antagonism. There was a time, not very far distant in the past, when this antagonism was not recognized, when a feeling of fraternization between the white and the colored races existed, that made them kindred to to each other. But since our emancipation, since liberty has come, and only since—only since we have stood up clothed in our manhood, only since we have proceeded to take hold and help advance the civilization of this nation—it is only since then that this bugbear is brought up against us again. Sir, the progress of the age demands that the colored man of this country shall be lifted by law into the enjoyment of every right, and that every appliance which is accorded to the German, to the Irishman, to the Englishman, and every foreigner, shall be given to him; and I shall give some reasons why I demand this in the name of justice.

For two hundred years the colored men of this nation have assisted in building up its commercial interests. There are in this country nearly five millions of us, and for a space of two hundred and forty-seven years we have been hewers of wood and drawers of water; but we have been with you in promoting all the interests of the country. My distinguished colleague, who defended the civil rights of our race the other day on this floor, set this forth so clearly that I need not dwell upon it at this time.

I propose to state just this: that we have been identified with the interests of this country from its very foundation. The cotton crop of this country has been raised and its rice-fields have been tilled by the hands of our race. All along as the march of progress, as the march of commerce, as the development of your resources has been widening and expanding and spreading, as your vessels have gone on every sea, with the stars and stripes waving over them, and carried your commerce everywhere, the black man's labor has gone to enrich your country and to augment the grandeur of your nationality. This was done in the time of slavery. And if, for the space of time I have noted, we have been hewers of wood and drawers of water; if we have made your cotton-fields blossom as the rose; if we have made your rice-fields wave with luxuriant harvests; if we have made your corn-fields rejoice; if we have sweated and toiled to build up the prosperity of the whole country by the productions of our labor, I submit, now that the war has made a change, now that we are free—I submit to the nation whether it is not fair and right that we should come in and enjoy to the fullest extent our freedom and liberty.

A word now as to the question of education. Sir, I know that, indeed, some of our republican friends are even a little weak on the school clause of this bill; but, sir, the education of the race, the education of the nation, is paramount to all other considerations. I regard it important therfore, that the colored people should take place in the educational march of this nation, and I would suggest that there should be no discrimination. It is against discrimination in this particular that we complain.

Sir, if you look over the reports of superintendents of schools in the several States, you will find, I think, evidences sufficient to warrant Congress in passing the civil-rights bill as it now stands. The report of the commissioner of education of California shows that, under the operation of law and of prejudice, the colored children of that State are practically excluded from schooling. Here is a case where a large class of children are growing up in our midst in a state of ignorance and semi-barbarism. Take the report of the superintendent of education of Indiana, and you will find that while efforts have been made in someplaces to educate the colored children, yet the prejudice is so great that it debars the colored children from enjoying all the rights which they ought to enjoy under the law. In Illinois, too, the superintendent of education makes this statement: that, while the law guarantees education to every child, yet such are the operations among the school trustees that they almost ignore, in some places, the education of colored children.

All we ask is that you, the legislators of the nation, shall pass a law so strong and so powerful that no one shall be able to elude it and destroy our rights under the Constitution and laws of our country. That is all we ask.

But, Mr. Speaker, the gentleman from North Carolina [Mr. VANCE] asks that the colored man shall place himself in an attitude to receive his rights. I ask, what attitude can we assume? We have tilled your soil, and during the rude shock of war, until our hour came, we were docile during that long, dark night, waiting patiently the coming day. In the Southern States during that war our men and women stood behind their masters; they tilled the soil, and there were no insurrections in all the broad lands of the South; the wives and daughters of the slaveholders were as sacred then as they were before; and the history of the war does not record a single event, a single instance, in which the colored people were unfaithful, even in slavery; nor does the history of the war record the fact that on the other side, on the side of the Union, there were any colored men who were not willing at all times to give their lives for their country. Sir, upon both sides we waited patiently. I was a student at Wilberforce University, in Ohio, when the tocsin of war was sounded, when Fort Sumter was fired upon, and I shall never forget the thrill that ran through my soul when I thought of the coming consequences of that shot. There were one hundred and fifteen of us, students at that university, who, anxious to vindicate the stars and stripes, made up a company, and offered our services to the governor of Ohio; and, sir, we were told that this was a white man's war and that the negro had nothing to do with it. Sir, we returned—docile, patient, waiting, casting our eyes to the heavens whence help always comes. We knew that there would come a period in the history of this nation when our strong black arms would be needed. We waited patiently; we waited until Massachusetts, through her noble governor, sounded the alarm, and we hastened then to hear the summons and obey it.

Sir, as I before remarked, we were peaceful on both sides. When the call was made on the side of the Union we were ready; when the call was made for us to obey orders on the other side, in the confederacy, we humbly performed our tasks, and waited patiently. But, sir, the time came when we were called for; and, I ask, who can say that when that call was made, the colored men did not respond as readily and as rapidly as did any other class of your citizens? Sir, I need not speak of the history of this bloody war. It will carry down to coming generations the valor of our soldiers on the battle-field. Fort Wagner will stand forever as a monument of that valor, and until Vicksburgh shall be wiped from the galaxy of battles in the great contest for human liberty that valor will be recognized.

And for what, Mr. Speaker and gentlemen, was the great war made? The gentleman from North Carolina [Mr. VANCE] announced before he sat down, in answer to an interrogatory by a gentleman on this side of the House, that they went into the war conscientiously before God. So be it. Then we simply come and plead conscientiously before God that these are our rights, and we want them. We plead conscientiously before God, believing that these are our rights by inheritance, and by the inexorable decree of Almighty God.

We believe in the Declaration of Independence, that all men are born free and equal, and are endowed by their Creator with certain inalienable rights, among which are life, liberty, and the pursuit of happiness. And we further believe that to secure those rights governments are instituted. And we further believe that when governments cease to subserve those ends the people should change them.

I have been astonished at the course which gentlemen on the other side have taken in discussing this bill. They plant themselves right behind the Constitution, and declare that the rights of the State ought not to be invaded. Now, if you will take the history of the war of the rebellion, as published by the Clerk of this House, you will see that in 1860 the whole country, each side, was earnest in seeking to make such amendments to the Constitution as would forever secure slavery and keep the Union together under the circumstances. The resolutions passed, and the sentiments expressed in speeches at that time, if examined by gentlemen, will be found to bear out all that I have indicated. It was felt in 1860 that anything that would keep the "wayward sisters" from going astray was desirable. They were then ready and willing to make any amendments.

And now, when the civil rights of our race are hanging upon the issue, they on the other side are not willing to concede to us such amendents as will guarantee them; indeed, they seek to impair the force of existing amendments to the Constitution of the United States, which would carry out the purpose.

I think it is proper and just that the civil-rights bill should be passed. Some think it would be better to modify it, to strike out the school clause, or to so modify it that some of the State constitutions should not be infringed. I regard it essential to us and the people of this country that we should be secured in this if in nothing else. I cannot regard that our rights will be secured until the jury-box and the school-room, those great palladiums of our liberty, shall have been opened to us. Then we will be willing to take our chances with other men.

We do not want any discriminations to be made. If discriminations are made in regard to schools, then there will be accomplished just what we are fighting against. If you say that the schools in the State of Georgia, for instance, shall be allowed to discriminate against colored people, then you will have discriminations made against us. We do not want any discriminations. I do not ask any legislation for the colored people of this country that is not applied to the white people. All that we ask is equal laws, equal legislation, and equal rights throughout the length and breadth of this land.

The gentleman from North Carolina [Mr. VANCE] also says that the colored men should not come here begging at the doors of Congress for their rights. I agree with him. I want to say that we do not come here begging for our rights. We come here clothed in the garb of American citizenship. We come demanding our rights in the name of justice. We come, with no arrogance on our part, asking that this great nation, which laid the foundations of civilization and progress more deeply and more securely than any other nation on the face of the earth, guarantee us protection from outrage. We come here, five millions of people—more than composed this whole nation when it had its great tea-party in Boston Harbor, and demanded its rights at the point of the bayonet—asking that unjust discriminations against us be forbidden. We come here in the name of justice, equity, and law, in the name of our children, in the name of our country, petitioning for our rights.

Our rights will yet be accorded to us, I believe, from the feeling that has been exhibited on this floor of the growing sentiment of the country. Rapid as the weaver's shuttle, swift as the lightning's flash, such progress is being made that our rights will be accorded to us ere long. I believe the nation is perfectly willing to accord this measure of justice, if only those who represent the people here would say the word. Let it be proclaimed that henceforth all the children of this land shall be free; that the stars and stripes, waving over all, shall secure to every one equal rights, and the nation will say "amen."

Let the civil-rights bill be passed this day, and five million black men, women, and children, all over the land, will begin a new song of rejoicing, and the thirty-five millions of noble-hearted Anglo-Saxons will join in the shout of joy. Thus will the great mission be fulfilled of giving to all the people equal rights.

Inasmuch as we have toiled with you in building up this nation; inasmuch as we have suffered side by side with you in the war; inasmuch as we have together passed through affliction and pestilence, let there be now a fulfillment of the subline thought of our fathers—let all men enjoy equal liberty and equal rights.

In this hour, when you are about to put the cap-stone on the mighty structure of government, I ask you to grant us this measure, because it is right. Grant this, and we shall go home with our hearts filled with gladness. I want to "shake hands over the bloody chasm." The gentleman from North Carolina has said he desires to have forever buried the memory of the recent war. I agree with him. Representing a South Carolina constituency, I desire to bury forever the tomahawk. I have voted in this House with a free heart to declare universal amnesty. Inasmuch as general amnesty has been proclaimed, I would hardly have expected there would be any objection on this floor to the civil-rights bill, giving to all men the equal rights of citizens. There should be no more contest. Amnesty and civil rights should go together. Gentlemen on the other side will admit that we have been faithful; and now, when we propose to bury the hatchet, let us shake hands upon this measure of justice; and if heretofore we have been enemies, let us be friends now and forever.

Our wives and our children have high hopes and aspirations; their longings for manhood and womanhood are equal to those of any other race. The same sentiment of patriotism and of gratitude, the same spirit of national pride that animates the hearts of other citizens, animates theirs. In the name of the dead soldiers of our race, whose bodies lie at Petersburg and on other battle-fields of the South; in the name of the widows and orphans they have left behind; in the name of the widows of the confederate soldiers who fell upon the same fields, I conjure you let this righteous act be done. I appeal to you in the name of God and humanity to give us our rights, for we ask nothing more. [Loud applause.]

15

Force, Fraud, and Intimidation

"The Mississippi Plan," 1875

By gradual steps, radical reconstruction rule was brought to an end in the Southern states, replaced by white-dominated conservative governments. The granting of amnesty to white Southerners, the weariness of the North with reconstruction problems, the rise of new issues to distract the people, and the employment in the South of terroristic activities all contributed to the fall of the radical state governments. Typical of the means adopted by Southerners to rid themselves of Northern and Negro influence was the program adopted by Mississippians in the election year of 1875. Democrats in Mississippi simply resolved to win the election, regardless of the kind of tactics that might prove necessary. Armed bands roamed the state, terrorizing whites and Negroes alike, provoking riots and breaking up Republican political meetings. A large number of people were killed in the process. Intimidation of voters on election day was widespread. When the votes were counted, the radical regime had been overturned and the state returned to conservative, white Democratic rule. The success of what became known as the "Mississippi Plan" seemed to justify its employment. Other states took the cue and copied the methods of the Mississippians. Although the Governor appealed to the Federal government for help and protection, no assistance was forthcoming, further reflection of the growing apathy of the national government toward the problems of reconstruction. Congress later investigated the election, but other than the issue of a report from which the following extract is taken nothing came of it. For a good discussion of the election campaign, see Vernon L. Wharton, *The Negro in Mississippi, 1865–1880* (Chapel Hill, 1947). In the following selection, note (1) the nature of the allegations concerning political conditions in Mississippi; (2) the findings of the committee respecting these allegations; (3) what specific conclusions the committee reached; (4) the committee's assessment of the situation; and (5) proposed remedies.

Mississippi in 1875: Report of the Select Committee to Inquire into the Mississippi Election of 1875. . . , Senate Reports, No. 527 (44th Congress, 1st Session), III, ix–xxxix.

THE SPECIAL committee appointed under a resolution of the Senate adopted on the 31st of March last, and instructed to inquire how far the rights of the people of Mississippi, guaranteed by the Constitution of the United States, and secured especially by the fifteenth amendment, were violated by force, fraud, or intimidation at the election held in that State on the 2d of November, 1875, respectfully submit to the Senate the testimony taken, with the conclusions of the committee thereon.

The testimony will fully support the allegation that force, fraud, and intimidation were used generally and successfully in the political canvass of 1875.

But before proceeding to a detailed statement of the facts and conclusions sustained and warranted by the proof, the committee think it proper to refer to the suggestions and excuses offered in justification of the outrages committed.

It has been alleged that Governor Ames was an unfit person to hold the office to which he was elected in the year 1873; but, on the contrary, the committee find from the evidence, as well as from general report in Mississippi, that Governor Ames was not only not amenable to any just charge affecting his personal integrity, his character as a public officer, or his ability for the duties of chief magistrate of that State, but that his fitness in all these particulars was sustained by the testimony of those who were not in accord with him politically. . . .

The evidence submitted tends strongly to show, what cannot be denied, that there were many persons in office in the State of Mississippi, especially in elective offices, in the several counties, who were either incapable or dishonest; and there were a few of the same character connected with the State government. The conduct of these persons, however, was not approved by the governor nor by the masses of the republican party.

Complaints and charges against a class of persons called "carpet-baggers" are frequent in the depositions of witnesses opposed to the republican party in the State. It is to be admitted that a small number of the immigrants from other States misused the confidence of the black people, secured office, and betrayed the trusts confided to them. But the number of such persons, compared to the whole number of immigrants, was very small; and it is but just to say that the great majority are intelligent, upright, and brave men from the North who are entirely incorruptible, and who, in peril of their lives, are now struggling against serious odds to maintain their political opinions and to secure a just administration of the Government.

It is alleged that during the last six or eight years the expenses of the State have been unnecessarily increased, and that heavy taxes have been imposed for which no adequate return has been received by the people. Comparisons are made between the rate of taxation previous to the war and since the year 1870, and the conclusion is drawn that large sums of money are extorted from the people, and wasted, or, through negligence and extravagance, misapplied.

It is undoubtedly true that taxes are higher in the State of Mississippi than they were previous to 1860; but the rate of increase is far less than in some of the Northern States, where no serious complaints are made against the administration of public affairs.

It is to be observed, also, that previous to the war taxes were not levied for the support of schools in Mississippi; indeed, there was no system of public instruction; and that since the war school-houses have been erected in all parts of the State for the education of the children of both races, and large sums of money have been expended annually for the maintenance of schools, including schools for training teachers.

It is also true that previous to the war the taxes were imposed upon slaves and upon business, while since the war the taxes have been laid chiefly upon personal property and upon land. . . .

It is also alleged in justification of the acts of intimidation, and of the crimes committed during the canvass and at the election, that Governor Ames had organized, or attempted to organize, a force, termed the negro militia. . . .

Some of the officers selected by him were native-born white citizens who had served in the late war on the side of the confederates, and he solicited and accepted recruits from the white as well as from the black population.

This effort on the part of the governor, it is now claimed, was the occasion seized by the democrats for organizing and arming themselves, ostensibly to resist the black militia; but, in fact, . . . it became the means by which the colored inhabitants and the white republicans of the State were overawed, intimidated, and deprived of their rights as citizens.

These organizations were the instruments also by which numerous murders were committed upon persons who were then active, or who had been active, in the republican party. . . .

The outrages perpetrated by the white people in the canvass and on the day of election find no justification whatever in the acts or the policy of Governor Ames concerning the State militia.

The effort on his part to organize the militia for the preservation of the public peace seems to the committee to have been not only lawful but proper, and the course of the democrats in organizing and arming themselves to resist the governor in his efforts to preserve the public peace was unlawful, and the proceedings should have been suppressed by the State authorities if possible; and, in case of failure on their part, by the Government of the United States. . . .

Nor do these outrages find any excuse in the statement made repeatedly by witnesses, that the negroes were organizing or threatened or contemplated organizing themselves into military bands for the destruction of the white race. The evidence shows conclusively that there were not only no such organizations, but that the negroes were not armed generally; that those who had arms were furnished with inferior and second-hand weapons, and that their leaders, both religious and political, had discountenanced a resort to force. Many rumors were current among the whites that the negroes were arming and massing in large bodies, but in all cases these rumors had no basis.

In a sentence, it may be asserted that all the statements made that there was any justifiable cause for the recent proceedings in Mississippi are without foundation.

On the other hand, it is to be said, speaking generally, that a controlling part, and, as we think, a majority, of the white democratic voters of the State were engaged in a systematic effort to carry the election, and this with a purpose to resort to all means within their power, including on the part of some of them the murder of prominent persons in the republican party, both black and white. . . .

(1.) The committee find that the young men of the State, especially those who reached manhood during the war, or who have arrived at that condition since the war, constitute the nucleus and the main force of the dangerous element.

As far as the testimony taken by the committee throws any light upon the subject, it tends, however, to establish the fact that the democratic organizations, both in the counties and in the State, encouraged the young men in their course, accepted the political advantages of their conduct, and are in a large degree responsible for the criminal results.

(2.) There was a general disposition on the part of white employers to compel the laborers to vote the democratic ticket. This disposition was made manifest by newspaper articles, by the resolutions of conventions, and by the declarations of landowners, planters, and farmers to the workmen whom they employed, and by the incorporation in contracts of a provision that they should be void in case the negroes voted the republican ticket.

(3.) Democratic clubs were organized in all parts of the State, and the able-bodied members were also organized generally into military companies and furnished with the best arms that could be procured in the country. The fact of their existence was no secret, although persons not in sympathy with the movement were excluded from membership. Indeed their object was more fully attained by public declarations of their organization in connection with the intention, everywhere expressed, that it was their purpose to carry the election at all hazards.

In many places these organizations possessed one or more pieces of artillery. These pieces of artillery were carried over the counties and discharged upon the roads in the neighborhood of republican meetings, and at meetings held by the democrats. For many weeks before the election members of this military organization traversed the various counties, menacing the voters and discharging their guns by night as well as by day. . . .

(4.) It appears from the testimony that, for some time previous to the election, it was impossible, in a large number of the counties, to hold republican meetings. In the republican counties of Warren, Hinds, Lowndes, Monroe, Copiah, and Holmes meetings of the republicans were disturbed or broken up, and all attempts to engage in public discussion were abandoned by the republicans many weeks before the election.

(5.) The riots at Vicksburgh on the 5th of July, and at Clinton on the 4th of September, were the results of a special purpose on the part of the democrats to break up the meetings of the republicans, to destroy the leaders, and to inaugurate an era of terror, not only in those counties, but throughout the State, which would deter republicans, and particularly the negroes, from organizing or attending meetings, and especially deter them from the free exercise of the right to vote on the day of the election. The results sought for were in a large degree attained.

(6.) Following the riot at Clinton, the country for the next two days was scoured by detachments from these democratic military organizations over a circuit of many miles, and a large number of unoffending persons were killed. The number has never been ascertained correctly, but it may be estimated fairly as between thirty and fifty. . . .

(7.) The committee find, especially from the testimony of Captain Montgomery, supported by numerous facts stated by other witnesses, that the military organization extended to most of the counties in the State where the republicans were in the majority; that it embraced a proportion not much less than one-half of all the white voters, and that in the respective counties the men could be summoned by signals given by firing cannons or anvils; and that probably in less than a week the entire force of the State could be brought out under arms.

(8.) The committee find that in several of the counties the republican leaders were so overawed and intimidated, both white and black, that they were compelled to withdraw from the canvass those who had been nominated, and to substitute others who were named by the democratic leaders, and that finally they were compelled to vote for the ticket so nominated, under threats that their lives would be taken if they did not do it. This was noticeably the case in Warren County, where the democratic nomination of one Flanigan for sheriff was ratified at the republican county convention, held in Vicksburgh, the members acting under threats that if it were not done they should not leave the building alive. Similar proceedings occurred in other counties.

(9.) The committee find that the candidates, in some instances, were compelled, by persecution or through fear of bodily harm, to withdraw their names from the ticket and even to unite themselves ostensibly with the democratic party. J. W. Caradine, a colored candidate of Clay County, was compelled to withdraw his name from the republican ticket and to make speeches in behalf of the democratic candidates and policy. . . .

(10.) The committee find that on the day of the election, at several voting places, armed men assembled, sometimes not organized and in other cases organized; that they controlled the elections, intimidated republican voters, and, in fine, deprived them of the opportunity to vote the republican ticket. . . .

(12.) The committee find in several cases, where intimidation and force did not result in securing a democratic victory, that fraud was resorted to in conducting the election and in counting the votes. In Amite County, the legally-appointed inspectors of election, to whom in Mississippi the duty is assigned of receiving and counting the ballots, were compelled by intimidation to resign on the morning of election, in order to secure a fraudulent return. . . .

(13.) The evidence shows that the civil authorities have been unable to prevent the outrages set forth in this report, or to punish the offenders. This is true not only of the courts of the State, but also of the district court of the United States, as appears from the report of the grand jury made at the term held in June last, when the evidence of the offenses committed at the November election and during the canvass was laid before that body. . . .

(14.) The committee find that outrages of the nature set forth in this report were perpetrated in the counties of Alcorn, Amite, Chickasaw, Claiborne, Clay, Copiah, De Soto, Grenada, Hinds, Holmes, Kemper, Lee, Lowndes, Madison, Marshall, Monroe, Noxubee, Rankin, Scott, Warren, Washington, and Yazoo, and that the democratic victory in the State was due to the outrages so perpetrated.

(15.) The committee find that if in the counties named there had been a free election, republican candidates would have been chosen, and the character of the legislature so changed that there would have been 66 republicans to 50 democrats in the house, and 26 republicans to 11 democrats in the senate; and that consequently the present legislature of Mississippi is not a legal body, and that its acts are not entitled to recognition by the political department of the Government of the United States, although the President may, in his discretion, recognize it as a government *de facto* for the preservation of the public peace.

(16.) Your committee find that the resignation of Governor Ames was effected by a body of men calling themselves the legislature of the State of Mississippi, by measures unauthorized by law, and that he is of right the governor of that State.

(17.) The evidence shows, further, that the State of Mississippi is at present under the control of political organizations composed largely of armed men whose common purpose is to deprive the negroes of the free exercise of the right of suffrage and to establish and maintain the supremacy of the white-line democracy, in violation alike of the constitution of their own State and of the Constitution of the United States.

The events which the committee were called to investigate by the order of the Senate constitute one of the darkest chapters in American history. Mississippi was a leading State in the war of the rebellion, and an early and persistent advocate of those fatal political heresies in which the rebellion had its origin. To her, in as large a degree as to any other State, may be charged justly the direful evils of the war; and when the war was ended the white inhabitants resisted those measures of equality which were essential to local and general peace and prosperity. They refused to accept the negro as their equal politically, and for ten years they have seized every fresh opportunity for a fresh denial of his rights. At last they have regained supremacy in the State by acts of violence, fraud, and murder, fraught with more than all the horrors of open war, without its honor, dignity, generosity, or justice.

By them the negro is not regarded as a citizen, and whenever he finds a friend and ally in his efforts to advance himself in political knowledge or intellectual culture, that friend and ally, whether a native of the State or an immigrant from the North, is treated as a public enemy. The evil consequences of this policy touch and paralyze every branch of industry and the movements of business in every channel.

Mississippi, with its fertile soil, immense natural resources, and favorable commercial position, is in fact more completely excluded from the influence of the civilization and capital of the more wealthy and advanced States of the Union than are the distant coasts of China and Japan. Men who possess capital are anxious to escape from a State in which freedom of opinion is not tolerated, where active participation in public affairs is punished often with social ostracism, always with business losses, and not infrequently, as the record shows, with exile and the abandonment of property, through fear of death.

Consequently, lands depreciate in value, the rewards of labor become more and more uncertain, taxes more and more burdensome, the evils of general disorder are multiplied and intensified, and by an inevitable rule of social and public life, the evils themselves, reacting, increase the spirit of disorder. Unless this tendency can be arrested, every successive chapter in the annals of that State will be darker and bloodier than the preceding one.

This tendency cannot be arrested by the unaided efforts of the peaceful, patriotic, and law-abiding citizens. There is a small body of native white persons, who, with heroic courage, are maintaining the principles of justice and equality. There is also a small body of men from the North, who, with equal courage, are endeavoring to save the State from anarchy and degradation. If left to themselves, the negroes would co-operate with these two classes.

But arrayed against them all are a majority of the white people, who possess the larger part of the property; who uniformly command leisure, whether, individually, they possess property or not; who look with contempt upon the black race, and with hatred upon the white men who are their political allies; who are habituated to the use of arms in war and in peace; who in former times were accustomed to the exclusive enjoyment of political power, and who now consider themselves degraded by the elevation of the negro to the rank of equality in political affairs.

They have secured power by fraud and force, and, if left to themselves they will by fraud and force retain it. Indeed, the memory of the bloody events of the campaign of 1875, with the knowledge that their opponents can command, on the instant, the presence of organized bodies of armed men at every voting-place, will deter the republican party from any general effort to regain the power wrested from them. These disorders exist also in the neighboring States, and the spirit and ideas which give rise to the disorders are even more general.

The power of the National Government will be invoked, and honor and duty will alike require its exercise. The nation cannot witness with indifference the dominion of lawlessness and anarchy in a State, with their incident evils and a knowledge of the inevitable consequences. It owes a duty to the citizens of the United States residing in Mississippi, and this duty it must perform. It has guaranteed to the State of Mississippi a republican form of government, and this guarantee must be made good.

The measures necessary and possible in an exigency are three:

1. Laws may be passed by Congress for the protection of the rights of citizens in the respective States.

2. States in anarchy, or wherein the affairs are controlled by bodies of armed men, should be denied representation in Congress.

3. The constitutional guarantee of a republican form of government to every State will require the United States, if these disorders increase or even continue, and all milder measures shall prove ineffectual, to remand the State to a territorial condition, and through a system of public education and kindred means of improvement change the ideas of the inhabitants and reconstruct the government upon a republican basis.

16

The South in 1875

Charles Nordhoff's Travels Through the Cotton States

In 1875, Charles Nordhoff (1830–1901), Washington correspondent for the *New York Herald,* traveled extensively through the Southern cotton states in order to observe at first hand the operation of reconstruction policies and programs as well as to inform himself and others of the conditions then existing in the South. The trip had been suggested by James Gordon Bennett, editor of the *Herald,* and Nordhoff's observations were first printed in the columns of that newspaper. Nordhoff had been a journalist for most of his career. In 1857 he was appointed an editor by Harper and Brothers, and in 1861 assumed the position of managing editor of the *New York Evening Post.* He remained with the *Post* throughout the war. In 1874 he went to work for Bennett and the *Herald* as Washington correspondent and continued to serve in the national capital until his retirement in 1890. Nordhoff's newspaper reports of his Southern journey were collected and published in book form in 1876. Although Nordhoff was a lifelong Republican, his view of Southern conditions and of the workings of reconstruction reflect a rare impartiality. For this reason, his account ranks among the best. For another description of the Southern states, but at an earlier period, see Robert Somers, *The Southern States Since the War, 1870–71* (London, 1871). The following summary of Nordhoff's conclusions is taken from the first part of his book. Note (1) his reasons for wishing to make an on-the-spot examination of the "Cotton States"; (2) what he discovered about such topics as a war of revenge, hostility to the Federal Union, and re-enslavement of the blacks; (3) his estimate of Southern Republican governments; (4) what he thought concerning the political status and role of Southern blacks; (5) what he thought might be done to reduce the tensions between the two races; (6) his judgment of President Johnson's reconstruction policy; (7) what he found respecting the economic and social status of the blacks; and (8) what developments he observed justifying a hopeful future for the Southern states.

Charles Nordhoff, *The Cotton States in the Spring and Summer of 1875* (New York: D. Appleton and Company, 1876), pp. 9–25.

IT WAS my fortune to spend the winter of 1874–'75 in Washington, in almost daily attendance upon the debates of Congress, and in more or less intimate friendly relations with many of its leading members, of both parties. The Southern question was, during the whole of the three months' session, that which attracted most attention, and was in public and private most earnestly discussed. The Louisiana affair, the Vicksburg riot, the Alabama question, the Arkansas muddle, were all the topics of continual excited conversation in and out of Congress. I was extremely desirous to find a basis of fact on which to found a trustworthy opinion of the condition of the South; but was constantly confused by statements apparently partisan, and, at any rate, unsatisfactory. The leaders of both parties in Congress were, for the most part, no more accurately informed than I; and debate and legislation on Southern affairs during the whole winter were mainly based either upon a general notion that we still live under a Constitution, or upon narrow views of party expediency or necessity. The Democrats for the most part dealt in incoherent and ineffective generalities about violated liberties. Of the Republicans, one faction steadily pressed coercive measures but weakly, because they had no certain knowledge of the condition of affairs on which they spoke and were asked to legislate. Thus the Habeas Corpus and Force Bill and the Arkansas Message were defeated with great difficulty; the Civil Rights Bill was passed, only to become a dead letter in the South, and a source of annoyance to its supporters in the next Presidential canvass; and the report of the first New Orleans committee, though based on evidence not afterwards controverted, was received with so much doubt that a second committee was thought necessary—to investigate the first.

Under these circumstances I accepted gladly an offer from Mr. Bennett to make for him an exploration of the principal Southern States, and see for myself what I had vainly tried to discover by questioning others. My journey began early in March, and ended in July. I visited successively Arkansas, Louisiana, Mississippi, Alabama, North Carolina, and Georgia; and the results of my observations were printed in letters to the *New York Herald.* These letters, with some additions and corrections, form the larger part of the present volume. They became, on their publication in the *Herald,* the subject of a contentious discussion in the journals of both parties, North and South, and, I must confess, had not the good fortune to please partisans anywhere. It was probably inevitable that they should offend those whose preconceived views or whose interests they did not advance, for I sought only for facts, and did not care what side they favored; but it has been a great satisfaction to me to receive many private letters from Southern men, both Republicans and Democrats, acknowledging the correctness of my statements, and the general justice of my views and conclusions.

Though my letters consisted almost entirely of statements of fact, I found, from first to last, opinions and conclusions imputed to me, by partisan writers, which I did not and do not entertain. It was but natural, perhaps, that each side should accept such facts as served its purposes, and draw inferences from them which were not my own. But I do not wish to be misunderstood, and propose, therefore, to prefix to the record of my observations my own deductions. And to make clear my point of view, it is proper to say that I am a Republican, and have never voted any other Federal ticket than the Republican; I have been opposed to slavery as long as I have had an opinion on any subject except sugar-candy and tops; and I am a thorough believer in the capacity of the people to rule themselves, even if they are very ignorant, better than any body else can rule them.

The following, then, are the conclusions I draw from my observations in the Cotton States:

1. There is not, in any of the States of which I speak, any desire for a new war; any hostility to the Union; any even remote wish to re-enslave the blacks; any hope or expectation of repealing any constitutional amendment, or in any way curtailing the rights of the blacks as citizens. The former slave-holders understand perfectly that the blacks can not be re-enslaved. "They have been free, and they would drive us out of the country if they thought we were about to re-enslave them. They are a quiet and peaceable people, except when they are exasperated; but then they are terrible. A black mob is a ruthless and savage thing," said a Southern man to me; and another remarked, "If ever you, in the North, want to re-enslave the negroes, you must give us

three months' notice, so that we may all move out, with our wives and children. They were a source of constant anxiety to us when we held them in slavery. To attempt to re-enslave them would be only to invite them to murder us, and lay the country waste."

In Mississippi alone did I find politicians silly enough to talk about the Caucasian race, and the natural incapacity of the negro for self-government; and even there the best Republicans told me that these noisy Democratic demagogues were but a small, though aggressive and not unpowerful, minority; and even in Mississippi, a strong Republican, a Federal law officer, an honest and faithful man, assured me that the northern half of the State, which, with the exception of the region lying about Vicksburg, is the most prone to occasional violence and disorder, was, when I was there, to his personal knowledge, as peaceful and orderly as any part of New York or Ohio.

Even the extreme excitement of a political canvass in Mississippi this fall, in which the Democrats are trying to rid themselves of the justly hateful rule of a corrupt faction, has led to but few disturbances; and we are not to forget that this State is a frontier country, in which every body goes armed; and that it has for its governor a man who has neglected all the usual means of preserving the peace, or preventing disturbances. With a governor alive to his duty to the State, there would, I believe, have been none. Nor is it just to lay the whole blame of all that has happened on the whites. In the South the negro is not always a lamb. He is sometimes the aggressor.

2. That the Southern whites should rejoice over their defeat, now, is impossible. That their grandchildren will, I hope and believe. What we have a right to require is, that they shall accept the situation; and that they do. What they have a right to ask of us is, that we shall give them a fair chance under the new order of things; and that we have so far too greatly failed to do. What the Southern Republican too often requires is that the Southern Democrat should humiliate himself, and make penitent confession that slavery was a sin, that secession was wrong, and that the war was an inexcusable crime. Is it fair or just to demand this? Slavery is now seen, all over the South, to have been a huge economical blunder, and a proposition to re-establish it would not get fifty thousand votes in the whole South. That seems to me

an extremely important point gained. As to the moral question, it belongs to the clergy, and has no place in our present politics.

3. The Southern Republicans seem to me unfair and unreasonable in another way. They complain constantly that the Southern whites still admire and are faithful to their own leaders; and that they like to talk about the bravery of the South during the war, and about the great qualities of their leading men. There seems to me something childish, and even cowardly, in this complaint. The Southern man who fought and believed in it, would be a despicable being if he should now turn around and blacken the characters of his generals and political leaders, or if he should not think with pride of the feats of arms and of endurance of his side; or if, having been plundered by Republicans since the war, he should fling up his hat for that party. I say this as a Republican, and believe the mass of Northern Republicans think just as I do.

4. Moreover, it is a fact that the men of brains, of influence, of intelligence, in the South, did, almost to a man, consent to secession, and take an active part in the war against the Union. It was, I believe, and most of them now believe, a great blunder on their part; but they have paid a heavy penalty for their mistake, for most of them were wealthy, and are now poor. It is not fair in us to demand that they shall be reviled and put down by their own people; nor, I believe, do Northern Republicans want that. A few days ago I received a letter from a Mississippi Republican, who related to me, with indignation, that at a Democratic meeting no cheers were so loud as those which followed a mention of Mr. Jefferson Davis's name. Now, I do not admire Mr. Davis; I think him the weakest and the least respectable of the Southern leaders; and I happen to know that he is not highly thought of in many parts of the South, where his peculiar qualities are well understood, and were felt during the war. But I could not help but agree with a Southern Democrat who said to me, "I don't like Jeff Davis; but he was our leader, and we should be mean creatures, if, when he is spoken against, we did not stand up for him."

5. As to ostracism of Northern men, it stands thus: In all the States I have seen, the Republican reconstructors did shamefully rob the people. In several of them they continue to do so. Now,

all the Republicans in the South are not dishonest; but whoever, in a State like Louisiana or Mississippi now, and Arkansas, Alabama, and others formerly, acts with the Republicans, actually lends his support and countenance to corrupt men. Is it strange that, if he is ever so honest himself, he is disliked for his political course? Did not Republicans in New York bitterly criticise and "ostracize" Mr. Tilden, Mr. O'Conor, Mr. Hewitt, and others, who chose to adhere to and act with the Democratic party, while that was controlled by the Tweed Ring? And do not the New York Republicans make it a reproach to this day, to such Democrats, that they thus did? But the cases are precisely parallel. It "costs something to be an honest Republican in the South," precisely as it cost something to be an honest Democrat in New York before the Tammany Ring was smashed.

6. As to "intimidation," it is a serious mistake to imagine this exclusively a Democratic proceeding in the South. It has been practiced in the last three years quite as much, and even more rigorously, by the Republicans. The Federal United States marshal in Louisiana has used cavalry to intimidate Democrats. Similarly, Federal officers confess they did in Alabama and elsewhere. The negroes are the most savage intimidators of all. In many localities which I visited, it was as much as a negro's life was worth to vote the Democratic ticket; and even to refuse to obey the caucus of his party caused him to be denounced as "BOLTER," and to be forsaken by his friends, and even by his wife or sweetheart. That there has also been Democratic intimidation is undeniable; but it does not belong to the Southern Republicans to complain of it. In North Carolina, a leading and intelligent negro told me that he and others of his race were opposed to the Civil-rights Bill, but they did not dare to let their opposition be known, because, as he said, they would at once have been denounced among their people, and would have lost all influence with them. In Wilmington, a young negro lawyer was mobbed by his people, because he ventured to oppose corrupt candidates for office. This was told me by a colored man.

7. There are no wrongs now in the South which the interference of the Federal Government under the Enforcement acts can reach. This interference is purely and only mischievous. It has disabled and demoralized the Republican State governments,

whose members, sure that they would be maintained by the Federal arm everywhere, abandoned their duties, and took to stealing and maladministration. It has seriously injured the negro, by making him irresponsible to the opinion of his neighbors, and submitting him, in his ignorance, to the mischievous and corrupt rule of black and white demagogues. As a result, it has fostered ill-feeling between the races, from which in the end it is inevitable that the negro must be the greatest sufferer.

8. Those States which have been under Republican control have been shamelessly mismanaged, and are now deeply, and some of them hopelessly, in debt, and with very heavy State and county taxes. Such are Arkansas, Louisiana, Mississippi (this in county and local indebtedness), Alabama, and North Carolina.

9. On the other hand, Georgia, which has been since 1871 ruled by Democrats, has but a trifling State debt, scarcely any county debts, good credit, and low taxation.

10. It is a remarkable fact that, according to the best evidence I could collect on the subject, the negroes in Democratic Georgia own far more real estate, and pay taxes on more property, than in any one of the States which have been under Republican rule, like Arkansas or Louisiana.

11. Wherever one of these States has fallen under the control of Democrats, this has been followed by important financial reforms; economy of administration; and, as in Arkansas and Alabama, by the restoration of peace and good-will.

12. In Louisiana and Mississippi, which remain under Republican control, there is a continuance of barefaced corruption, and of efforts, made by a class of unscrupulous demagogues, to set the races in hostility against each other.

13. The misconduct of the Republican rulers in all these States has driven out of their party the great mass of the white people, the property-owners, tax-payers, and persons of intelligence and honesty. At first a considerable proportion of these were ranged on the Republican side. Now, in all the States I have mentioned, except in North Carolina, the Republican party consists almost exclusively of the negroes and the Federal office-holders, with, in Louisiana and Mississippi, the Republican State and county officers also.

14. Thus has been perpetuated what is called the "color-line"

in politics, the Democratic party being composed of the great
mass of the whites, including almost the entire body of those who
own property, pay taxes, or have intelligence; while the Republican party is composed almost altogether of the negroes, who are,
as a body, illiterate, without property, and easily misled by appeals to their fears, and to their gratitude to "General Grant,"
who is to them the embodiment of the Federal power.

15. This division of political parties on the race or color-line
has been a great calamity to the Southern States.

It had its origin in the refusal of the Southern whites, after the
war, to recognize the equal political rights of the blacks; and
their attempts, in State legislatures, to pass laws hostile to them.
This folly has been bitterly regretted by the wiser men in the
South. A Mississippian said to me, "It was a great blunder. We
could have better afforded to educate and train the colored people, and fit them for the duties of citizenship, than to have had
them alienated from us." He was right; it was a great, though
probably an inevitable, blunder. It flung the negro into the hands
of the so-called Republicans in the Southern States, and these, by
adroitly appealing to his fears and to his gratitude to the Federal
Government, and by encouraging his desire for official power
and spoils, have maintained the color-line in politics, and by its
means kept themselves in power.

It is an indisputable fact that there can be no permanent and
beneficial settlement of political questions in any Southern State
until the color-line is broken. While the white vote, or the greater
part of it, is massed on one side, and the black vote, or the greater
part of it, on the other, as is still the case in Louisiana, Mississippi, Alabama, and Georgia, it is impossible to get settled good
government; for the political issues will, of necessity, be false,
and will have no relation to any real question of administration,
but only to questions of race.

The great mass of the Southern colored voters are illiterate;
they are easily impressed by exhibitions of power; they are
readily alarmed about their safety; and, like all ignorant masses,
they are very apt to follow a leader. The Republican leader has
always had the United States Government to back him. Packard,
chairman of the Republican State Executive Committee of Louisiana, has, as United States marshal, the absolute command of

Federal troops in Louisiana. Spencer, United States Senator from Alabama, and Republican leader in that State, runs up to Louisville, and secures for the asking several companies of infantry and cavalry, to be stationed in Alabama, at a time when, as the United States marshal testifies, there was no need at all for troops; and Perrin, one of Spencer's underlings, at the same time deputy-marshal, supervisor of election, candidate for the Legislature, and distributor of Government bacon, shoots a hole through his own hat, and then orders Federal troops to hunt for imaginary Ku-klux. Governor Ames, as is publicly charged, refuses to stir to prevent a riot at Vicksburg; but after the riot, after forty or fifty blacks have been killed, and when the negroes are demoralized and feel utterly helpless, sends for Federal troops, which come at his command, and re-assure the blacks. Such manifestations of power strike the imagination of the negroes, as they would any ignorant population, and they follow very readily and blindly its possessor. Some colored witnesses in Alabama being asked why they all voted against Sheats, a Republican, for Congress, replied, "because Perrin told them to;" being asked if they would have voted the Democratic ticket if Perrin had told them to, they answered, unhesitatingly, "Yes." But Perrin, as United States deputy-marshal, commanded Federal troops, and gave away Federal bacon.

The leaders whom they thus follow do not instruct them in political duties. They do not discuss political questions before them. They appeal only and continually to the negro's fears and to his sense of obligation to the Federal power. In Alabama they were told that the bacon was sent by General Grant, and its receipt made it their duty to vote the "straight Republican ticket." In some parts of Southern Louisiana the negroes are still summoned from the field to political meetings, "by order of General Butler." I know of a case where a candidate for a county office circulated a printed "general order" commanding all colored men to vote for him, and signed "U.S. Grant, President;" and he received the solid colored vote.

One of the most intelligent and excellent men I met in Louisiana told me that in 1872 he had made a thorough canvass of the part of the State in which he lives, addressing himself entirely to the colored people, by whom he is liked and trusted, and trying to explain to them the necessity for honest local government, and their interest in the matter. "But," said he, "I presently became aware that I was followed by a Republican, an illiterate and low-lived man, whom no colored man would have trusted with five dollars, but who overturned all my arguments by whispering, 'Don't believe what he tells you; they only want to put you back into slavery.' "

So pertinaciously has this base insinuation been used among the blacks, that when last fall the Democrats carried Alabama, I know of two instances in which colored men came into the nearest town to ask white Democrats, in whose honor and kindness they trusted, whether they would be allowed to choose their own masters, and whether they would be separated from their wives and children.

16. The Federal office-holders are largely to blame for the continuance of this evil. They are a very numerous class in every Southern State; and have far greater influence than their fellows in Northern States, especially over the blacks, who have been taught to regard them as their guardians, and political guides and leaders. They are too often, and in the majority of cases indeed, *but by no means in all,* men of low character, Republicans by trade, and of no influence except among the negroes, to whom the lowest Federal officer, even a deputy-marshal's deputy, is a very powerful being, armed with the whole strength of the Federal Government. Georgia has nearly, if not quite, three thousand men in the employ of the Federal Government in various capacities; and most of the States I have visited have an equal number. In such States as Louisiana these men "organize" the negro vote; and they do it as the only means to preserve their places. A Democratic Federal Administration would oust them; therefore they command and persuade the negroes, by all possible inducements, to vote the Republican ticket. The Federal Administration appears to me culpable in this matter, because it has not only permitted its officers in the South to take an active and partisan part in politics, but has apparently encouraged them in doing so. The United States Marshal of Louisiana, for instance, having the command at will of Federal troops, has been chairman of the Republican State Central Committee. The mere fact that he holds these two positions is a dangerous abuse, espe-

cially in a State where a great part of the voters are ignorant, and easily misled.

17. The color-line is maintained mostly by Republican politicians, but they are helped by a part of the Democratic politicians, who see their advantage in having the white vote massed upon their side.

18. Human nature being what it is, no one can be surprised that the Republican leaders who found it easy to mass the colored vote, who found also the Federal power flung into their hands, and themselves its ministers, who by these means alone have been able to maintain themselves in power, regardless entirely of the use they made of this power—that under these conditions they should become and remain both weak and corrupt.

The mass of ignorant men by whose votes they have been kept in power paid no taxes, and were not, therefore, directly affected by the public plundering; and the plunder has been so great, and the number of white men engaged in it so small, that these were always able to divide with the more ambitious colored leaders, who, on their part, have been, as was inevitable, easily corrupted. Nor have the colored men been slow to learn the trickery and baser parts of political management. They were ignorant and poor, and saw power and wealth in their reach; and they did what poor and ignorant white men, having the same temptations set before them, have done the world over, and notably in the city of New York.

While the black vote is massed against the white, there is a continual irritation between the races; and this mainly because the white man, who is the property-owner, sees the black, who in most of these States seldom owns real estate, used by a few designing whites, to lay taxes, to make laws, to carry on the government, regardless of the wishes and rights of the great body of intelligent and substantial citizens.

I know many Southern counties in which the colored men pay in all less than one thousand dollars of the annual taxes, and yet are in so great a majority that their votes, massed by unscrupulous demagogues of both colors, constantly waste and misapply the taxes of the county.

Inevitably in such cases there must be a feeling of hostility by the whites toward the blacks, and it is an evidence of the good nature of the mass of whites that, in the main, they conduct themselves toward the blacks kindly and justly. They concentrate their dislike upon the men who have misled and now misuse the black vote, and this I can not call unjust. It is commonly said, "The negroes are not to blame; they do not know any better."

On the other hand, as the feeling is intense, it is often undiscriminating, and includes the just with the unjust among the Republicans. Hence what is called "ostracism" will last just as long as the color-line is maintained, and as long as Republicans maintain themselves in power by the help of the black vote, and by Federal influence. That this feeling of dislike and suspicion toward Northern men often goes to an unjust and unreasonable extent is very true, and it is not easy for a Northern man to hear with patience stories showing its manifestations.

There are scattered over the States I have visited a number of highly honorable and cultivated Northern families, who have lived there for years. Where, as is often the case, these are Republicans, they are, to a large extent, isolated socially, and this is not pleasant for them. But they seldom complain; and not a few have told me that they did not wonder that Republicans should be held in disfavor in their States, considering how badly corrupt Republican leaders have acted in the South.

19. The evil influence of the mass of Federal office-holders in most of these States is an important, but with us in the North unsuspected, element in protracting ill-feeling and preventing a political settlement. They have very great influence; they are the party leaders. if they do not show themselves zealous Republicans, they are removed; and they are interested in keeping men of brains and influence out of their party. Unfortunately, they have been allowed to control; and the Federal Administration has rejected the assistance in the management of these States of the only men whose help would have been important and effective; namely, the natural leaders of the Southern people.

20. Tradition lives longer among the Southern whites than with us. How else can one account for the fact that you hear everywhere of Whigs, and that the real division of political parties in those States which I have seen is between Whigs and Democrats?

In Louisiana the Whig prejudice and dislike against Democrats is so strong that the party leaders found it necessary to adopt the name Conservative. In Arkansas the Whig leaders are quietly seeking out their followers. In Alabama, when you hear of an independent candidate, he is most likely to have been an old Whig. In Mississippi, even, there are Whigs, but they have as yet no ground to stand on.

Whenever Federal interference in the local affairs of these States ceases, the color-line will be broken, and the population will divide into Whigs and Democrats. The leaders of the present white party will, as a matter of course, strive to prevent this in such States as Louisiana, Arkansas, Georgia, and Alabama; but their efforts will be in vain. There are traditional animosities and differences, and these were not destroyed by the war.

The Southern Whig was usually a Conservative, and opposed to secession; less, I imagine, because he liked the Union, than because he disliked the Democratic leaders who urged secession, and whom he believed to be incapable and often dishonest. The result of the war has not raised the Democratic secession leaders in the esteem of the old Whigs, but for the present they act with the Democrats, under the pressure of Federal interference and to defeat the Republican leaders.

But there are many signs to show that whenever politics in the States I have seen resume their natural condition, the Whigs will rally, and, with the help of such part of the colored vote as they can win over to their side, will try to secure the control of those States. The Whig feeling is especially strong in Louisiana, and there is little doubt that that State, and probably some others, could easily have been made permanently Republican, had the Republican leaders who came to the top there in 1868 been wise and honest men, and had they given the people good government and the means of industrial prosperity.

21. Thus there are in all the States I speak of naturally two parties among the whites. The leaders of one of these could have been induced by the Federal authorities in Washington, with proper efforts and at the proper time, to take a part in the reconstruction; and they could have perfected this important work. Of course, it would have been necessary to take their advice as to the Southern policy; and to give them the selection of Federal offi-

cers in their States. To give them influence in their section they should have been called to prominent places under the Government; but they would, I believe, have insured a peaceable and harmonious settlement. They have, unfortunately, been proscribed in Washington for their share in the war, and thus forced into opposition; and are to-day, often against their wishes, united to the Democratic party. This has been the gravest error of the Republican Administration. Its true policy would have been to trust, and to put in places of authority and responsibility, the most eminent of the Southern public men; to take their advice as to the details of a Southern policy, insisting only that peace and equal justice should be rigidly established in those States. With such a policy there would have been to-day a respectable and powerful Republican party in every Southern State; and, what is of greater importance, a harmonious settlement of all questions.

22. The blunder of the Federal Republican rulers has been that they have not taken care to keep themselves informed of the rapidly changing condition of public sentiment, and the political and industrial condition of the Southern States. They were, in fact, physicians who were treating a patient who, in 1868, was in a highly feverish and dangerous state. They prescribed for him a remedy which, if severe, was yet effective; but it seems never to have occurred to them that under their treatment the patient's condition would change; that a convalescent needed different remedies; that what was necessary in 1868 might be extremely injurious in 1872–'74. They have had no faith in their own remedies.

23. There was, in those Southern States which I have visited, for some years after the war and up to the year 1868, or in some cases 1870, much disorder, and a condition of lawlessness toward the blacks—a disposition, greatest in the more distant and obscure regions—to trample them underfoot, to deny their equal rights, and to injure or kill them on slight or no provocations. The tremendous change in the social arrangements of the Southern States required time as well as laws and force to be accepted. The Southern whites had suffered a defeat which was sore to bear, and on top of this they saw their slaves—their most valuable and cherished property—taken away and made free, and not only free, but their political equals. One needs to go into the far South

to know what this really meant, and what deep resentment and irritation it inevitably bred.

At the same time came the attempt of President Johnson to re-arrange the Southern States in a manner which the wisest and best Democrats I have met in the South have declared to me was unwise and productive of disorder.

I believe Mr. Johnson meant well and patriotically; but my observations have convinced me that he was in error, at least in the time and manner of asserting his policy. He aroused the hopes and desires of the worst class in the Southern States, and disabled the large number of moderate and conservative citizens, who ought to have ruled during the reconstruction of society there, and who, unfortunately, were pushed aside. The result was violence and disorder, not general, as has been charged so often, but still very serious, and not to be endured; and this lasted until time and the punishment of criminals by Federal power under the Enforcement acts brought people to their senses.

I believe that there was, during some years, a necessity for the interference of the Federal power to repress disorders and crimes which would otherwise have spread, and inflicted, perhaps, irretrievable blows on society itself. But, after all, I am persuaded time was the great and real healer of disorders, as well as differences. We of the North do not always remember that even in the farthest South there were large property interests, important industries, many elements of civilization which can not bear long-continued disorders; and, moreover, that the men of the South are Americans, like ourselves, having, by nature or long training a love of order and permanence, and certain, therefore, to reconstitute society upon the new basis prescribed to them, and to do it by their own efforts, so soon as they were made to feel that the new order of things was inevitable.

That there were, during some years after the war, shocking crimes in the States I have visited, no man can deny; but a grave wrong is done when those days are now brought up and those deeds recited to describe the South of to-day.

24. There was, after 1868, in all the States I have seen, great misgovernment, as I have said, mostly by men who called them-

selves Republicans, but who were for the greater part adventurers, camp-followers, soldiers of fortune, not a few who had been
Democrats and "Copperheads" during the war, or Secessionists,
and engaged in the rebellion—some Northern men, but also
many native Southerners.

This misgovernment has been various. Its most marked or
prominent features were the unscrupulous greed and pecuniary
corruption of the rulers and their subordinates, who, in a multitude of cases, notably in Arkansas and Louisiana, were no better
than common robbers.

25. But public robbery was, after all, not the worst crime of the
men who arose in the name of the Republican party to govern
these Southern States. The gravest offense of these "Republican"
State governments was their total neglect of the first duty of
rulers, to maintain the peace and execute justice. They did not
enforce the laws; they corrupted the judiciary; they played unscrupulously upon the ignorant fears of the blacks and upon their
new-born cupidity; they used remorselessly the vilest tools for
the vilest purposes; they encouraged disorder, so that they might
the more effectually appeal to the Federal power and to the
Northern people for help to maintain them in the places they so
grossly and shamelessly abused. . . .

26. The injury done to a community by the total failure of its
rulers to maintain order, repress crime, and execute justice, is
more seriously felt in Louisiana than in any other of the States
of which I am speaking. It is a wonder to me that society has not
entirely gone to pieces in that State; and I became persuaded that
its white population possesses uncommonly high qualities when
I saw that, in spite of an incredible misgovernment, which encouraged every vice and crime, which shamelessly corrupted the
very fountains and sources of justice, and made the rulers a
terror to the peaceably inclined—in spite of this, order and peace
have been gradually restored and are now maintained, and this
by the efforts of the people chiefly.

No thoughtful man can see Louisiana as I saw it last spring
without gaining a high respect for its white people. The State is
to-day as fit for self-government as Ohio or New York. The attitude of the races there toward each other is essentially kindly,
and only the continuous efforts of black and white demagogues

of the basest kind keep them apart politically. The majority of
the white people of the State are well disposed, anxious for an
upright government, ready to help honest and wise rulers, if they
could only get them, to maintain peace and order. I sincerely
believe that whenever they are relieved from Federal oppression
—and in their case it is the worst kind of oppression—they will
set up a government essentially honest and just, and will deal
fairly and justly with the colored citizens.

27. What those States which I have visited most need, for some
years to come, is a vigorous and alert State government; a governor extremely vigilant in repressing and punishing crime, and
possessing the energy and courage to use to the utmost his power
"to maintain peace." Governor Garland, of Arkansas, set an excellent example in this respect, when, last spring, he caused a
couple of miscreants who had shot at a man in pure wantonness,
to be pursued not only through the State, but into the lower part
of Louisiana, where they were finally captured and brought in
irons to Little Rock to be tried. The governor openly declared that
he would catch and punish these fellows, if it cost the whole
contingent fund of the State. Unfortunately, Republican governors, like Ames in Mississippi and Kellogg in Louisiana, do not
use the power in their hands, but tolerate crimes, or if these
affect their partisans, make haste to call on the Federal Government for help.

28. The Southern white population differs from ours in one or
two important respects. In the States I have seen there is a more
marked distinction between the wealthy and the poor than is
commonly found in the North. The numerous class of poor white
farmers are a kind of people unknown among us. Settled upon a
thin and infertile soil; long and constantly neglected before the
war; living still in a backwoods country, and in true backwoods
style, without schools, with few churches, and given to rude
sports and a rude agriculture, they are a peculiar people. They
have more good qualities than their wealthier neighbors, the
planters, always allow them; but they are ignorant, easily preju-
diced, and they have, since the war, lived in a dread of having
social equality with the negro imposed upon them. This fear has
bred hatred of the blacks, which has often, in former years, found
expression in brutal acts to which, I believe, in the majority of

cases, they were instigated by bad men of a class above them.

A mischievous class is found in a number of young men in the remoter parts of these States, who follow no regular occupation, but prey upon the community, white as well as black. They are gamblers and political bummers; they drink whisky and swagger in bar-rooms, armed with revolvers and knives; and it was, during some years after the war closed, their habit, when they needed excitement, to "shoot a nigger."

These are mainly the descendants of the overseer and negro-trader class in the South, and naturally despise honest labor, and take readily to brute force. They have sometimes sufficient education to make a political harangue; and they are a curse to the community. . . .

As this is really a criminal class, it will continue to commit crimes; but they will not be political crimes, nor will they be beyond the power of a reasonably energetic State government, encouraging and demanding the help of the decent people, to punish and repress. As these young bloods have sometimes influential connections, and as they are known to be ready with the pistol, they may, here and there, overawe a local jury; and if their crime is given a political aspect by the action of Federal officers, they may even temporarily win the sympathies of unthinking people. But a vigilant and energetic governor will have no difficulty in mastering the situation, even in the most lawless parts of Mississippi. He need not call on the United States. There is nowhere such a combination as a determined governor can not put down, nor anywhere crime which he can not punish. In the last resort a governor may declare martial law in a county, and if he is wise he will take that occasion to hang up a few disorderly wretches. He will make votes for the next election by doing so, for lawlessness is not general; the mass of the people wish for peace and order. . . .

29. No thoughtful man can examine the history of the last ten years in the South, as he may hear it on the spot and from both parties, without being convinced that it was absolutely necessary to the security of the blacks, and the permanent peace of the Southern communities, to give the negro, ignorant, poor, and helpless as he was, every political right and privilege which any other citizen enjoys. That he should vote and that he should be

capable of holding office was necessary, I am persuaded, to make him personally secure, and, what is of more importance to convert him from a *freedman* into a *free man.*

That he has not always conducted himself well in the exercise of his political rights is perfectly and lamentably true; but this is less his fault than that of the bad white men who introduced him to political life. But, on the other hand, the vote has given him what nothing else could give—a substantive existence; it has made him a part of the State. Wherever, as in Arkansas, the political settlement nears completion, and the color-line is broken, his political equality will help—slowly, but certainly—to make him a respectable person. I will add that in this view many Southern Democrats concur. "If the North had not given the negroes suffrage, it would have had to hold our States under an exclusively military government for ten years," said such a man to me.

30. General manhood suffrage is undoubtedly a danger to a community where, as in these States, the entire body of ignorance and poverty has been massed by adroit politicians upon one side. The attempt to continue for even four years longer such a state of things as has been by Federal force maintained in Louisiana would either cause a necessary and entirely justifiable revolt there, or totally destroy society.

There are scores of parishes and counties where the colored voters are to the white as four, six, and even ten to one; where, therefore, ignorant men, without property, and with no self-restraint or sense of honor in pecuniary trusts, would continue to rule absolutely; to levy taxes which others must pay; to elect judges and fiduciary officers out of their own number; to be the tools of the least scrupulous and the most greedy wretches in the community. There are scores of parishes and counties in Louisiana, Alabama, and Mississippi, where the voice of the people is not the voice of God, but the voice of the worst thief in the community.

But the moment the color-line is broken, the conditions of the problem are essentially changed. Brains and honesty have once more a chance to come to the top. The negro, whose vote will be important to both parties, will find security in that fact. No politician will be so silly as to encroach upon his rights, or allow his opponents to do so; and the black man appears to me to have a sense of respectability which will prevent him, unencouraged by demagogues, from trying to force himself into positions for which he is unfit. He will have his fair chance, and he has no right to more.

31. Whenever the Federal interference in all its shapes ceases, it will be found, I believe, that the negroes will not at first cast a full vote; and, as this will, perhaps, be charged to intimidation, it is useful to explain the real reason.

It was everywhere asserted to me by the Republicans that without white men to "organize" the colored vote—which means to mass it, to excite it, to gather the voters at barbecues, to carry them up with a hurra to the polls, to make "bolting" terrible, to appeal to the fears of the ignorant and the cupidity of the shrewd: without all this the negro will not vote. This was the universal testimony of all Republicans I met in the South, good and bad.

Now the "organizers" of the colored vote are almost altogether the petty Federal office-holders. These have little else to do, and they give themselves to the work. In Alabama, for instance, in 1874, the Republican State Executive Committee was allowed to nominate the United States deputy-marshals for the whole State. Many of these persons were candidates for the Legislature or for local offices; many candidates were also Federal supervisors of election. They appealed to the negro clothed in the majesty of Federal office; they spoke in the name of General Grant; a deputy-marshal could summon troops, and could summarily arrest white men. He was a very great man to a negro. Indeed, a United States deputy-marshal is a very great man to a Southern white man, for he has really extraordinary powers; and in the South nobody nowadays thinks for a moment of resisting "the Government." "We may fight among ourselves," said a Mississippian to me; "but if the whole of my town were engaged in a riot, to produce peace you need not even bring in a squad of Federal troops. You need only stuff the clothes of a Federal sergeant with straw, and bring that effigy into the market-place, and in five minutes you would have absolute quiet." And he did not exaggerate.

Well, take away these petty Federal "organizers," and the negro, left face to face with the white man, no longer marched up in column to the central poll of the county, but voting in his proper precinct, argued with hearing both sides for the first time; knowing by experience, as he will presently, that the Democrat is not a monster, and that a Democratic victory does not mean his re-enslavement, will lose much of his interest in elections. "They won't vote unless they have white organizers," is the universal testimony of the Republican leaders wherever I have been.

Of course, as soon as parties are re-arranged on a sound and natural basis, the negro vote will re-appear; for the leaders of each party, the Whig or Republican and the Democrat, will do their utmost to get his vote, and therein will be the absolute security of the black man. I believe, however, that for many years to come, until a new generation arrives at manhood perhaps, and, at any rate, until the black man becomes generally an independent farmer, he will be largely influenced in his political affiliations by the white. He will vote as his employer, or the planter from whom he rents land, or the white man he most trusts, and with whom, perhaps, he deposits his savings, tells him is best for his own interest. He will, perhaps, in the cities, sell his registration certificate, as in Montgomery in May last. But, at any rate, he will vote or not, as he pleases. And it is far better for him that he should act under such influences than that his vote should be massed against the property and intelligence of the white people to achieve the purposes of unscrupulous demagogues.

32. It struck me as probable and natural that some constitutional modification of the suffrage should come about in such States as Louisiana and Mississippi. An education qualification, applied equally to white and black, seemed to me evident. But the reply was, that it is impossible. These States have a considerable population of poor and illiterate whites, who would resist to the uttermost—now, at least—any limitation which would affect them. "It is more probable that we shall make the State Senate represent property, leaving the House open to every body," said a Louisiana Republican to me; but even that would only make a dead-lock, and is a poor expedient to evade a difficulty. The real

cure, I imagine, lies—after the breaking of the color-line—in general and even compulsory education. But there is room for wide statesmanship in many of the Southern States.

In Georgia there is a law under which a ·citizen can not vote unless he has paid his taxes for the year previous. It applies to white and black alike; but it has resulted in disfranchising a large part of the negro population, who have not yet become accustomed to paying even a poll-tax. It seems to me a perfectly just law, and it is likely to be adopted in other Southern States. It ought to be in force everywhere. If a man evades a poll-tax, he is not fit to vote. . . .

33. The negro, in the main, is industrious. Free labor is an undoubted success in the South. In Georgia he owns already nearly four hundred thousand acres of farming real estate, besides city property. The negro works; he raises cotton and corn, sugar and rice, and it is infinitely to his credit that he continues to do so, and, according to the universal testimony, works more steadfastly and effectively this year than ever before since 1865, in spite of the political hurly-burly in which he has lived for the last ten years.

Nor ought we of the North to forget that a part of the credit of the negroes' industry to-day is due to the Southern planters, who have who have been wise enough to adapt themselves to the tremendous change in their labor system, and honest enough not to discourage the ignorant free laborer by wronging him of his earnings or by driving unjust bargains with him.

The system of planting on shares, which prevails in most of the cotton region I have seen, appears to me admirable in every respect. It tends to make the laborer independent and self-heipful, by throwing him on his own resources. He gets the reward of his own skill and industry, and has the greatest motive to impel him to steadfast labor and to self-denial.

I have satisfied myself, too, that the black man gets, wherever I have been, a fair share of the crop he makes. If anywhere he suffers wrong, it is at the hands of poor farmers, who cultivate a thin soil, and are themselves poor and generally ignorant. It is a curious evidence of the real security of the negro, even in the rudest parts of the South, that some thousands of them have emigrated from Alabama and Georgia into the Yazoo Bottom in

Mississippi, and into the cotton regions of Arkansas and Louisiana—parts of the South where, if we might believe the general reports which have been spread through the North, no negro's rights and life are safe.

34. The black laborer earns enough, but he does not save his money. In the heart of the cotton country, a negro depending on his own labor alone, with the help of his wife in the picking season, may live and have from seventy-five to one hundred and twenty-five dollars clear money in hand at the close of the season. If he has several half-grown boys able to help him in the field, he may support his family during the year, and have from one hundred and seventy-five to two hundred dollars clear money at the year's end. Few laborers as ignorant as the average plantation negro can do as well anywhere in the world.

Of course he lives poorly; but he thrives on corn-meal and bacon, and has few doctor's bills to pay. Unfortunately, as yet, he commonly spends his money like a sailor or a miner, or any other improvident white man. Very few lay by their earnings; yet the deposits in the Freedmen's Bank showed how very considerable were the savings of the few; and I am sorry to say that the criminal mismanagement of this trust has struck a serious blow in the South, for it has given a fresh impetus to the spendthrift habits of the blacks. Moreover, in Democratic Georgia, where alone I was able to get official statistics, the negroes pay tax this year on over seven millions of property, of which nearly four hundred thousand acres are real estate.

They have as yet far less desire to own farms than I hoped to find. They are, like almost all rude people, fond of owning an acre or a house lot; and in Southern towns and cities it is common to find them such owners. But, except in Georgia, a comparatively small number, as yet, are freeholders in the best sense of the word. This, however, will come with time. They have been free but ten years, and in that time have been unsettled by the stress of politics, and have scarcely known, until within the last two years, whether their freedom was a substantial fact, or only a pleasant dream. Moreover, they have, very naturally, enjoyed the spending of their own money, and have had to acquire mules, farm implements, household goods, not to speak of very ancient and shabby buggies, sham jewelry, and gewgaws of all kinds.

In the cities and villages it is a pleasant, and indeed a touching, sight to see the little colored children going to Sunday-school, bright, clean, neatly dressed, frank and fearless, with no trace of the slavery which was the lot of their parents. I think no humane man could see this sight unmoved, remembering, as he must, how short is the time since slavery came to an end.

35. The character of the Southern negro is essentially kindly and good. He is not naturally quarrelsome, and his vices are mostly those which he retains from slavery. For instance, it is the almost universal complaint of the planters that they can not keep stock, either cattle or hogs. It is the bad custom in the South to turn such animals into the woods to shift more or less for themselves, and here they fall a prey to the colored men, who kill and eat them. They have not yet learned to respect property rights so loosely asserted. But this will come with time. Nor are the planter's chickens safe. In fact, petty theft is a common vice of the plantation negro. He learned it as a slave, and has not yet unlearned it.

He spends some of his money for whisky, too; but he is not an habitual drunkard, and is usually good-natured in his cups. Men and women, and even children, smoke, and in some regions they "dip" snuff.

It is an easily contented and happy population, and I do not doubt the judgment of those planters who assured me that they possessed the best laboring force in the world. Nor let any one persuade you that it is dying out. Wherever one travels he sees multitudes of fat, chubby, comical-looking pickaninnies—the country is full of them, and their shining black faces and wondering, staring eyes are the commonest sight in the South.

36. They are anxious to send their children to school, and the colored schools are more abundant in those States which I have seen than I expected to find them. I think it may be said that the colored people, so far, have got their fair share of schools and school money. In such places as New Orleans, Mobile, Selma, and Montgomery, the colored schools are excellently managed and liberally provided for. By general consent of both colors, there are no mixed schools; nor would it be wise to force this anywhere.

It must be remembered that few of the Southern States had public schools before the war. The whites are unaccustomed to them; and enlightened and influential Democrats, as in Georgia,

have difficulty in obtaining appropriations for schools sufficient
to place these on a sound basis. The poorer whites are still in
doubt about the usefulness of a thorough public-school system.
But wherever I have been the blacks have a fair share of school
privileges. Democratic Georgia gives as much every year for the
support of a colored university as for the old State University;
and in places like Mobile, where the schools are under Democratic control, I was surprised at the excellence of the colored
schools, and the liberal manner in which they were maintained
by the Democratic trustees.

37. The negroes have developed quite a genius for the lower
political arts. They have among them not a few shrewd and cal-
culating demagogues, who know as well how to "run the machine," to form a ring, and to excite the voters to their duty, as
any New York City politician. Office is of course a great tempta-
tion to men used to field-work at small wages; and the moderate
pay even of a juryman, with its accompanying idleness, seems
very delightful to them. They have long ago discovered their
numerical strength in many parts of the South, and do not hesitate to say in some places that, as they cast the votes, they ought
to have the offices. At least a dozen times I came upon this saying
in different places; and there are signs which show that if the
present political divisions could continue, the black leaders
would, in counties where the blacks predominate, in two or three
years crowd all the white men out the the Republican party; or,
at least, all who aspired to office. But they would not attempt this
unless they felt assured of the protection of the Federal power;
when they lose that reliance, every body, of both parties, says
they will lose the power of cohesive action.

It is not strange that, on the whole, the blacks, under such
white leadership as they have had, should have badly misused
their political power. They were both poor and ignorant; they had
no characters to lose by misconduct, for it is the misfortune of
slavery that a slave is a being without reputation; and it will
require a generation or two to establish in them, as in the ignorant part of our foreign-born population, that quality which we
call character. In their political relations among each other, they
are as intolerant and as unscrupulous as ignorant men suddenly
possessed of political rights are sure to be. The caucus rules with
a singular tyranny among them. The slightest assertion of politi-

cal independence is resented. The restive negro's name is sent through the county or district, with "BOLTER" affixed to it; and this fixes upon him the stigma of treason. The church, his friends, the young women if he is unmarried, all avoid him; and he is effectually under a ban of excommunication.

38. Unfortunately, the North and South do not know each other. Few Northern Congressmen have visited the South; and those who did too often fell into the hands of partisans, and obtained, whether Republicans or Democrats, only partisan impressions. Party feeling runs high in the South, and nothing is easier than to get a thoroughly one-sided view, for each side has a share of truth on which to build up its statements. An advocate, on either side, could easily make up a very effective case. In Washington the Southern Republican's statement was received, partly because he was a Republican, and generally a Northern man or a negro; partly because he appealed, not to reason or statesmanship, but to the sympathies of his listeners; and often because he was a very adroit demagogue, who knew how to make his points. In the South I was often horrified by tales of brutal murder or intolerance; but if, when my indignation was at its height, I thought to ask, "When did this take place?" the answer was almost always, "In 1865," or "1868," or "1869." It is a common trick of the outrage-monger in the South thus to recite to his Northern visitor tales of some years ago as representing correctly the present condition of Southern society; and this has constantly been done by Southern Republicans in Washington.

39. I come last to speak of the future of the Southern States: I was deeply impressed with the natural wealth, mostly undeveloped, of the States I saw. The South contains the greatest body of rich but unreclaimed soil on this continent. Louisiana seems to me to have elements of wealth as great as California. Georgia has a great future as a manufacturing State, and will, I believe, within a few years tempt millions of Northern and European capital into her borders to engage in manufactures. Alabama now exports iron to Europe—in small quantities, to be sure —and her coal-fields and iron ores will make her the rival of Pennsylvania at no distant date. Mississippi and Arkansas have immense undeveloped tracts of rich cotton lands. North Carolina

has mineral as well as agricultural wealth, which ought to secure her a remarkable future.

40. Almost everywhere, except in Louisiana, Mississippi, and perhaps Arkansas, I noticed an increase of the towns. I saw many new buildings, and others going up; and observant Southern men remarked upon this to me also. Wherever the people have been even moderately prosperous, these improvements begin to make a show. . . .

41. I noticed, also, at many points a tendency to a more varied agriculture; to smaller farms; to the cultivation of fruits and vegetables for distant markets; and in these ways much remains to be done, which, when done, will very greatly increase the wealth of the Southern States. Already in all the Cotton States planters begin to raise corn sufficient for their home supply—an extremely important matter in a region where in winter the roads are bad, and where it is literally true, as an Alabamian said, that "it would pay a planter better to raise corn at home, at a dollar a bushel, than to have it given to him eight or ten miles away."

No one who has seen the States of which I speak can doubt that they have before them a remarkable future. Nothing but long-continued political disturbances can prevent them from making very rapid strides in wealth. Their climate fits them for a greater variety of products than any of our Northern States. . . .

Meantime it is a fact that, if the planters are poor, they owe but little money. Planting has come to a cash basis; and a good crop is good for the land-owner and the laborer, and not mainly for the factor. There is no doubt that there has been much suffering in the South since the war among a class of people who formerly scarcely knew what even prudent economy meant. The emancipation of the slaves destroyed at a blow, for the slave-owners, the greater part of the accumulated capital of these States. The labor is still there. The community will presently be wealthier than ever. But in the redistribution of this wealth the former wealthy class is reduced to moderate means. It is by no means a public calamity; but it makes many individuals gloomy and hopeless, and is one cause of the general depression.

42. Finally, these States have made a new experience in taxation. Aside from the plundering of the Republican rulers, there

is a natural and inevitable increase in taxation, growing out of
the fact that the former slaves are now citizens, who are taught
in schools, tried in courts of justice, confined in State and other
prisons, supported in asylums, and in many other ways are, as all
citizens are, a source of public expense. This is too often forgotten by Southern men when they complain of high taxes. Formerly a negro thief received thirty-nine lashes from the
overseer, and there an end; now a constable catches him and a
prison holds him for trial, a grand jury indicts him, a petit jury
hears evidence for and against him, a judge sentences him if he
is guilty, and thereupon a penitentiary receives him just as it
does his white brother-in-law; or, if this happened in Alabama
under the Republican rule, his father hired him of the State at
twenty cents a day, and let him loaf about the cabin until his
term expired, or he became a candidate for another term. The
misfortune is, that the Federal interference has held these States
under Republican rule against the will of the intelligent part of
their citizens, and has prevented these from learning by experience what are the real difficulties and necessities of government
under the new order of things. In Alabama, last spring, for instance, the Democrats, who are in power, began to discover that
"the price of government has gone up," and that they could not
very greatly lower the State taxes, against which, among other
things, they had long grumbled. In a State like Louisiana or Arkansas, of course merely to stop the stealing will at once and
enormously relieve the community, and a good deal can be
effected by economy in government in Alabama as well. But the
people will discover that they can not get back to the old extremely low taxes.

These are my conclusions concerning those Southern States
which I have seen. If they are unfavorable to the Republican rule
there, I am sorry for it. No men ever had a greater opportunity
to serve their fellow-men and their nation than the Republicans
who undertook the work of reconstruction in the South; and they
could not have desired greater power than was given them. Had
they used their power as statesmen, or even only as honest and
unselfish citizens, not only would the States I speak of to-day
have been prosperous, and their people of both races contented

and happy, but there would now have been, in every one of them, a substantial and powerful Republican party. Nor are the Northern Republican leaders without blame in this matter. These chose for their allies in the South men like Spencer in Alabama, Ames in Mississippi, Kellogg and Packard in Louisiana, Dorsey and Brooks in Arkansas, not to speak of hundreds of subordinate instruments, corrupt, weak, or self-seeking. They suffered the most shameless public plundering to go on in those States without inquiry. They confided the Federal power and patronage to men, many of whom would to-day be in State-prisons if they had their dues. And they have, as the result of their carelessness, seen State after State fall into the hands of the Democrats, and, in a large part of the Union, the name of Republican made odious to all honest and intelligent men; while they have crushed to the earth a considerable number of honest Republicans in the South, who, naturally, found no favor in the eyes of such men as Spencer and Ames.

17

"Hereafter There Is To Be No South"

The Nation and the End of Reconstruction 1877

The Presidential election of 1876 brought the era of reconstruction rapidly to a close. As part of the agreement following a discussion of the election's disputed aspects, President Rutherford B. Hayes ordered the final removal of Federal troops from South Carolina and Louisiana. With the removal of this important prop to reconstruction policy, the last two radical state governments in the South fell to the upsurgence of conservative Democratic power. Reconstruction was over and few in the North welcomed its termination more typically than the magazine *The Nation*. Although the tasks of reconstruction were in some ways unfinished and in other ways only imperfectly accomplished, the American people received this last government action in the South with optimism and relief. At last, they could now turn to "legitimate politics" and the "unsolved problems of modern life" without the annoying distraction of Southern problems and turmoil. The South, the magazine's editor believed, had now been integrated into American life and would soon cease to exist as a section. And what of the Negro? His future would be bound up with that of the white man and no longer require separate consideration. For a discussion of the waning interest in reconstruction, see Paul H. Buck, *The Road to Reunion, 1865–1890* (Boston, 1937) and for the "end" of reconstruction, see two books by C. Vann Woodward, *Reunion and Reaction: The Compromise of 1877 and the End of Reconstruction* (Boston, 1951) and *Origins of the New South, 1877–1913* (Baton Rouge, 1951). In the following article, note (1) what evidence *The Nation* advanced to support its optimism concerning Southern problems; (2) why the editor thought that "hereafter there is to be no South;" (3) what role he thought the Negroes would henceforth play in the life of the country and his reasons for so thinking; and (4) how this editorial compares with *The Nation's* October 26, 1865, editorial (reproduced as Document 2, on p. 34 of this volume).

[Rowland Connor], "The Political South Hereafter," *The Nation*, XXIV (Apr. 5, 1877), 202–03.

THE DISSOLUTION of the last sham government at the South—an event which we have a right to believe cannot now be long delayed—will place the Southern States, as regards the rest of the nation, in a position which they have not before occupied for almost a generation. Heretofore, in the discussion of nearly all national questions, the most embarrassing and vexatious element at any time to be considered, and frequently an overwhelmingly important one, was "the South." This term designated a number of contiguous States, bound together by mutual interest in the maintenance of a social system which was understood to be inimical to the feelings, at least, if not to the welfare, of the inhabitants of all other States; and "the South" was always, therefore, a more definite term than "the East" or "the North." Slavery dominated every other interest, and held the Southern States together in political unity. The phrase "the solid South" was a legitimate one before, during, and even after the war, and only recently has it become a political bugbear. But the threefold cord which bound the Southern States together—the defence and perpetuation of slavery, the struggle for the establishment of an independent confederacy, and the trials of reconstruction—no longer exists, and nothing has taken or can take its place. For a time, perhaps, traditions of the dead "institution," war memories, and the possession of a race of freedmen may together do something toward perpetuating a united South, but the union will surely be mostly in appearance, and any little reality which it may possess will speedily give way before opposing and stronger forces.

We believe the proposition to be almost self-evident, indeed, that hereafter there is to be no South; none, that is, in a distinctively political sense. The negro will disappear from the field of national politics. Henceforth the nation, as a nation, will have nothing more to do with him. He will undoubtedly play a part, perhaps an important one, in the development of the national civilization. The philanthropist will have still a great deal to do both with him and for him, and the sociological student will find him, curiously placed as he is in contact and competition with other races, an unfailing source of interest; but as a "ward" of the nation he can no longer be singled out for especial guardianship or peculiar treatment in preference to Irish laborers or Swedish immigrants. There is something distasteful, undeniably, in the idea of one who has played so important a part in our past political history making his final exit in the company of the Carpet-baggers; but for this unfortunate coincidence the negro is not to be blamed.

The disappearance of the factitious interest which made the South politically a unit will permit the rapid development of several natural and obvious disintegrating forces which, indeed, have been already in operation for some time, but the results of which have been obscured by the overshadowing interloper which has just been disposed of. Climate, soil, natural productions, diversity of pursuit, and varieties of race will certainly disintegrate politically the States of the South as well as the States of the North. The "sunny" South, of course, was a fiction, an agreeable convention only, for in the matter of climate the South presents variations comparable at least with any to be found in the North. St.

Louis, St. Augustine, and New Orleans, for instance, are as diverse in climate as are any three cities which might be selected in the Northern States. The pecuniary ties, moreover, which unite some Southern States to the North are already stronger than any which bind them to their former political associates. Missouri, for instance, in its commercial relations and sympathies is a Northern State, as, in a modified sense, are Maryland and Delaware; and Florida apparently is set apart already as the winter home of wealthy and invalided Northern men, whose influence upon the tone of its politics begins to be perceptible notwithstanding the hubbub of its recent performances in counting electoral votes. Again, it is evident that the cotton, rice, tobacco, and cane-producing districts of the South will attract very different classes of people, and beget very different manners and opinions from those inevitably associated with mining and manufacturing communities. Thus, South Carolina will soon differ from Missouri even more than Vermont does from Pennsylvania or Minnesota from Massachusetts. Political disintegration at the South may show itself most plainly at first in connection with the discussion of economic questions. There is to-day throughout all the Southern States, probably, a traditional inclination towards free-trade, although the leaning is not a very decided one, and the change from this to an opposing attitude is a process which may be witnessed soon in several of them. Is it not possible, at least, that the cotton and rice States may increase their present leaning towards free-trade, while Louisiana, Virginia, and Kentucky demand protection against Cuban sugar and tobacco? Or, on the other hand, may not South Carolina yearn for Government aid in the establishment of manufactories, and New Orleans sigh for free-trade in Mississippi products? Will the present great poverty of the Southern States, again, incline them to give ear to the jingle of "silver" theories, and make "greenback" delusions easy of belief, or will the memory of their own once plentiful "scrip" be a sufficient protection against indulgence in financial heresies? And will the South look with longing eyes upon visions of canals and railroads until it heedlessly begins the cry for internal improvements at Government expense, or will it be warned by the ghosts of Crédit Mobilier and Northern Pacific? It is evident, we believe, without lengthening the list of these enumerations or suggestions, that the Southern States may soon be as divided upon the subjects of tariff, currency, *laissez-faire* or paternity in government, etc., as we have been and still are at the North, and if New Hampshire and North Carolina should happen to join hands in defence of some political theory in opposition (say) to Louisiana and New York, "the South" would soon become as vague an expression, from a political point of view, as "the West" is now.

The future of the freedman will be bound up undoubtedly with that of the white man, and does not now require separate consideration. Great numbers of negroes will certainly remain upon the cotton-fields, rice-swamps, and cane and tobacco plantations, and, being employed as field-hands, their political opinions for a long time to come will inevitably reflect those of their employers. Others will learn to work in factories or become mechanics and small farmers, and, generally, all over the South for a long time, negroes will fill the places now filled at the North by Irish, German, and Chinese laborers. The political influence of the freedman, considered as distinct from that of the white man, will be almost imperceptible. His ultimate influence upon our civilization, as determined by the relative fecundity of the two races, and their action and reaction upon one another as the negro becomes better educated and more independent, is a subject which can be discussed more profitably a generation hence.

Generally speaking, while the political breaking up of the South will do away with a powerful barrier to national advancement, and will bring each State into closer sympathy with the national Government, nevertheless we hardly expect to receive any immediate and valuable aid from the South toward the solution of our present executive, judicial, and legislative problems. In this, however, we may happily be mistaken. It is true that the South has long been more "provincial" than the North, that it is far from possessing similar educational advantages, that it is now almost barren of literary productions or literary and scientific men, and that these facts would seem to indicate a natural soil for the germination and growth of all kinds of crude and coarse theories of society and government; but, on the other hand, it is not easy to imagine the South developing theories more crude than some now cherished in Indiana and Pennsylvania, and which find shelter even in New York and Massachusetts. We are inclined to believe, also, that the average man of the South is a more pliant and enthusiastic follower of his chosen leader than the average man of the North, and the Gordons, Hills, Lamars, and Hamptons may be depended upon to exert a widespread and, in the main, healthful influence. We cannot forget that it was the well-digested plan of a Southern Gordon with regard to the collection of revenue to which a Northern Morton could give no friendly reception and could make no better reply than a taunt and a sneer. But the important point to be remembered here is the fact that *all* political contributions of the South, of whatever character, will hereafter go towards the upbuilding of a national as distinguished from a "sectional" unity. For the first time in our history we are entitled to assert that there is no danger of national dissolution. Heretofore our chief attention haas been given to the saving of national life, and only incidentally have we been able to consider its character or to decide upon the best methods of perfecting it. We can now devote ourselves to legitimate politics—that is, to studies of governmental science—with a fair prospect of being able to throw some light upon many of the unsolved problems of modern life.